James Mack Henry Frederick

National Party Platforms of the United States

Presidential candidates, electoral and popular votes

James Mack Henry Frederick

National Party Platforms of the United States
Presidential candidates, electoral and popular votes

ISBN/EAN: 9783337403058

Printed in Europe, USA, Canada, Australia, Japan

Cover: Foto ©Suzi / pixelio.de

More available books at **www.hansebooks.com**

NATIONAL

PARTY PLATFORMS

OF THE UNITED STATES
PRESIDENTIAL CANDIDATES
ELECTORAL AND POPULAR VOTES

COMPILED BY

J. M. H. FREDERICK.

1896

PREFACE.

IN the preparation of this little book it has been my aim to supply certain historical information concerning political parties, in a more convenient and more popular form than it has been hitherto presented. From the platforms it will be possible to learn the attitude of any party in a given campaign in which platforms were adopted, and it has been my purpose to allow these to speak for themselves rather than to enter upon an elaborate discussion of them.

Among the works to which I am indebted in collecting the matter from which this book is made, are: Cooper's American Politics, The Writings of Prof. Alexander Johnston, Lalor's Encyclopedia of Political Science, Political Economy and United States History; Stanwood's History of Presidential Elections, The Political Prohibitionist for 1889, the Hand-Book of Prohibition for 1885, and various statistical works and newspaper almanacs.

J. M. H. F.

NATIONAL PARTY PLATFORMS.

THE FIRST PLATFORM.

What is properly considered the first platform of a political party in the United States after the adoption of the Constitution is that enunciation of principles known as the Virginia Resolutions. They were drawn by James Madison and adopted by the Virginia House of Delegates in 1798, and were the direct result of the enactment of the Alien and Sedition Laws by Congress. The Federalists were in power in Congress, and their attempts to form a strong central government and to nationalize the United States met with serious opposition from the Republicans, or anti-Federalists, and especially from the representatives of the new French republic in this country. The latter became a source of much annoyance to the Government, and never missed an opportunity to stir up feeling against it. The Alien and Sedition Laws were designed to put an end to the attempts on the part of the French to make trouble. In creating these laws, the Federalists took their first long stride toward a liberal construction of the Constitution, and the upshot of their action was a declaration of principles by the strict-constructionists, in the Virginia Resolutions. By their transmission to each of the State governments and to the members of both branches of Congress these resolutions came into general notice and became the first definite embodiment of the principles of the strict-constructionist party. On the principles of strict construction embodied in these resolutions the Republicans took their stand, while the Federalists, who believed in greater latitude in interpreting the Constitution, declared in favor of the action of Congress in making laws against the French disturbers.

Virginia Resolutions, 1798.

Resolved, That the General Assembly of Virginia doth unequivocally express a firm resolution to maintain and defend the Constitution of the United States, and the Constitution of this State, against every aggression either foreign or domestic ; and that they will support the government of the United States in all measures warranted by the former.

That this Assembly most solemnly declares a warm attachment to the Union of the States, to maintain which it pledges its powers ; and, that for this end, it is their duty to watch over and oppose every infraction of those principles which constitute the only basis of that Union, because a faithful observance of them can alone secure its existence and the public happiness.

That this Assembly doth explicitly and peremptorily declare, that it views the powers of the Federal Government, as resulting from the compact to which the States are parties, as limited by the plain sense and intention of the instrument constituting that compact, as no farther valid than they are authorized by the grants enumerated in that compact ; and that in case of a deliberate, palpable, and dangerous exercise of other powers, not granted by said compact, the States, who are parties thereto, have the right, and are in duty bound, to interpose, for arresting the progress of the evil, and for maintaining within their respective limits the authorities, rights, and liberties appertaining to them.

That the General Assembly doth also express its deep regret, that a spirit has, in sundry instances, been manifested by the Federal Government, to enlarge its powers by forced constructions of the Constitutional Charter which defines them ; and that indications have appeared of a design to expound certain general phrases (which having been copied from the very limited grant of powers in the former Articles of Confederation, were the less liable to be misconstrued) so as to destroy the meaning and effect of the particular enumeration which necessarily explains, and limits the general phrases, and so as to consolidate the States by degrees into one sovereignty, the obvious tendency and inevitable result of which would be, to transform the present republican system of the United States into an absolute, or at best, a mixed monarchy.

That the General Assembly doth particularly protest against the palpable and alarming infractions of the Constitution, in the two late cases of the "Alien and Sedition Acts," passed at the last session of Congress; the first of which exercises a power nowhere delegated to the Federal Government, and which, by uniting legislative and judicial powers to those of executive, subverts the general principles of free government, as well as particular organization and positive provisions of the Federal Constitution; and the other of which acts exercises, in like manner, a power not delegated by the Constitution, but, on the contrary, expressly and positively forbidden by one of the amendments thereto; a power which, more than any other, ought to produce universal alarm, because it is levelled against the right of freely examining public characters and measures, and of free communication among the people thereon, which has ever been justly deemed the only effectual guardian of every other right.

That this State having by its Convention, which ratified the Federal Constitution, expressly declared, that among other essential rights, "the liberty of conscience and the press cannot be cancelled, abridged, restrained, or modified by any authority of the United States," and from its extreme anxiety to guard these rights from every possible attack of sophistry and ambition, having with other States recommended an amendment for that purpose, which amendment was, in due time, annexed to the Constitution, it would mark a reproachful inconsistency, and criminal degeneracy, if an indifference were now shown to the most palpable violation of one of the rights, thus declared and secured; and to the establishment of a precedent which may be fatal to the other.

That the good people of this commonwealth having ever felt and continuing to feel the most sincere affection for their brethren of the other States; the truest anxiety for establishing and perpetuating the Union of all; and the most scrupulous fidelity to that Constitution, which is the pledge of mutual friendship, and the instrument of mutual happiness; the General Assembly doth solemnly appeal to the like dispositions in the other States, in confidence that they will concur with this commonwealth in declaring, as it does hereby declare, that the acts aforesaid are unconstitutional; and that the necessary and proper measures will be taken by each for co-operating with this State, in maintaining unimpaired the authorities, rights and liberties reserved to the States respectively, or to the people.

That the governor be desired to transmit a copy of the foregoing resolutions to the executive authority of each of the other States, with a request that the same may be communicated to the legislature thereof; and that a copy be furnished to each of the Senators and Representatives representing this State in the Congress of the United States.

Attest, JOHN STEWART.

1798, December 24th. Agreed to by the Senate.

H. BROOK.

A true copy from the original deposited in the office of the General Assembly.

JOHN STEWART,
Keeper of Rolls.

Relation of the Virginia and Kentucky Resolutions.

The Kentucky Resolutions of 1798, although adopted over a month before the Virginia Resolutions were enacted, did not attract general attention until later, and then primarily for their declaration of what may be considered supplementary principles. The Virginia Resolutions were accepted by the anti-Federalists as embodying the fundamental idea of their platform. While the Kentucky Resolutions expressed the same general idea, they are remembered principally for having gone further and assumed a bolder attitude. The Resolutions which passed the Kentucky legislature in 1798, contained the additional declaration, not only that the relation between the States and the Federal Government was a compact, but that the parties thereto were invested with co-equal rights and powers, and that each party had the right to judge of infractions of the agreement and of the proper redress. The resolutions which that body adopted the following year, went even further and pronounced nullification the rightful remedy. It is for these more radical declarations that the Kentucky Resolutions are chiefly remembered.

Kentucky Resolutions.

The following resolutions passed the House of Representatives of Kentucky, Nov. 10, 1798;

1. *Resolved*, That the several States composing the United States of America are not united on the principle of unlimited submission to their General Government; but that by compact under the style and title of a Constitution for the United States, and of amendments thereto, they constituted a General Government for special purposes, delegated to that Government certain definite powers, reserving, each State to itself, the residuary mass of right to their own self-government; and, that whensoever the General Government assumes undelegated powers, its acts are unau-

thoritative, void, and of no force; that to this compact each State acceded as a State, and is an integral party; that this Government, created by this compact, was not made the exclusive or final judge of the extent of the powers delegated to itself; since that would have made its discretion, and not the Constitution, the measure of its powers; but, that as in all other cases of compact among parties having no common judge, each party has an equal right to judge for itself, as well of infractions as of the mode of redress.

2. *Resolved*, That the Constitution of the United States having delegated to Congress a power to punish treason, counterfeiting the securities and current coin of the United States, piracies and felonies committed on the high seas, and offences against the laws of nations, and no other crimes whatever; and it being true, as a general principle, and one of the amendments to the Constitution having also declared, "that the powers not delegated to the United States by the Constitution, nor prohibited by it to the States, are reserved to the States, respectively, or to the people," therefore also the same act of Congress, passed on the 14th day of July, 1798, and entitled "An act in addition to the act entitled An act for the punishment of certain crimes against the United States;" as also the act passed by them on the 27th day of June, 1798, entitled "An act to punish frauds committed on the Bank of the United States," (and all other their acts which assume to create, define or punish crimes other than those enumerated in the Constitution), are altogether void and of no force, and that the power to create, define and punish such other crimes is reserved, and of right appertains solely and exclusively to the respective States, each within its own territory.

3. *Resolved*, That it is true, as a general principle, and is also expressly declared by one of the amendments to the Constitution, that "the powers not delegated to the United States by the Constitution, nor prohibited by it to the States, are reserved to the States, respectively, or to the people;" and that no power over the freedom of religion, freedom of speech, or freedom of the press being delegated to the United States by the Constitution, nor prohibited by it to the States, all lawful powers respecting the same did of right remain, and were reserved to the States or to the people; that thus was manifested their determination to retain to themselves the right of judging how far the licentiousness of speech and of the press may be abridged without lessening their useful freedom, and how far those abuses which cannot be separated from their use should be tolerated rather than the use be destroyed; and thus also they guarded rgainst all abridgment by the United States, of the freedom of religious principles and exercises, and retained to themselves the right of protecting the same,

as this, stated by a law passed on the general demand of its citizens, had already protected them from all human restraint or interference; and that, in addition to this general principle and express declaration, another and more special provision has been made by one of the amendments to the Constitution, which expressly declares, that "Congress shall make no laws respecting an establishment of religion, or prohibiting the free exercise thereof, or abridging the freedom of speech, or of the press," thereby guarding in the same sentence, and under the same words, the freedom of religion, of speech, and of the press, insomuch that whatever violates either, throws down the sanctuary which covers the others; and that libels, falsehood, and defamation, equally with heresy and false religion, are withheld from the cognizance of Federal tribunals. That therefore the act of the Congress of the United States, passed on the 14th day of July, 1798, entitled "An act in addition to the act entitled An act for the punishment of certain crimes against the United States," which does abridge the freedom of the press, is not law, but is altogether void and of no force.

4. *Resolved*, That alien friends are under the jurisdiction and protection of the laws of the State wherein they are; that no power over them has been delegated to the United States, nor prohibited to the individual States distinct from their power over citizens; and it being true, as a general principle, and one of the amendments to the Constitution having also declared, that "the powers not delegated to the United States by the Constitution, nor prohibited by it to the States, are reserved to the States, respectively, or to the people," the act of the Congress of the United States, passed the 22d day of June, 1798, entitled "An act concerning aliens," which assumes power over alien friends not delegated by the Constitution, is not law, but is altogether void and of no force.

5. *Resolved*, That in addition to the general principle as well as the express declaration, that powers not delegated are reserved, another and more special provision inferred in the Constitution, from abundant caution, has declared, "that the migration or importation of such persons as any of the States now existing shall think proper to admit, shall not be prohibited by the Congress prior to the year 1808." That this commonwealth does admit the migration of alien friends described as the subject of the said act concerning aliens; that a provision against prohibiting their migration, is a provision against all acts equivalent thereto, or it would be nugatory; that to remove them when migrated is equivalent to a prohibition of their migration, and is, therefore, contrary to the said provision of the Constitution, and void.

6. *Resolved*, That the imprisonment of a person under the protection of the laws of this commonwealth on his failure to obey the simple order of the President to depart out of the United States as is undertaken by the said act, entitled "An act concerning aliens," is contrary to the Constitution, one amendment in which has provided that "no person shall be deprived of liberty without due process of law," and that another having provided "that in all criminal prosecutions the accused shall enjoy the right to a public trial by an impartial jury, to be informed as to the nature and cause of the accusation, to be confronted with the witnesses against him, to have compulsory process for obtaining witnesses in his favor, and to have assistance of counsel for his defense," the same act undertaking to authorize the President to remove a person out of the United States who is under the protection of the law, on his own suspicion, without jury, without public trial, without confrontation of the witnesses against him, without having witnesses in favor, without defence, without counsel, is contrary to these provisions also of the Constitution, is therefore not law, but utterly void and of no force.

That transferring the power of judging any person who is under the protection of the laws, from the courts to the President of the United States, as is undertaken by the same act concerning aliens, is against the article of the Constitution which provides "that the judicial power of the United States shall be vested in the courts, the judges of which shall hold their office during good behavior," and that the said act is void for that reason also; and it is further to be noted that this transfer of judiciary power is to that magistrate of the General Government who already possesses all the executive and a qualified negative in all the legislative powers.

7. *Resolved*, That the construction applied by the General Government (as is evident by sundry of their proceedings) to those parts of the Constitution of the United States which delegate to Congress power to lay and collect taxes, duties, imposts, excises; to pay the debts and provide for the common defence and general welfare of the United States, and to make all laws which shall be necessary and proper for carrying into execution the powers vested by the Constitution in the Government of the United States or any department thereof, goes to the destruction of all the limits prescribed to their power by the Constitution. That words meant by that instrument to be subsidiary only to the execution of the limited powers ought not to be so construed as themselves to give unlimited powers, nor a part so to be taken as to destroy the whole residue of the instrument. That the proceedings of the General Government under color of these articles will be a fit and necessary subject for revisal and correction at a time of greater tranquillity, while those specified in the preceding resolutions call for immediate redress.

8. *Resolved*, That the preceding resolutions be transmitted to the Senators and Representatives in Congress from this commonwealth, who are enjoined to present the same to their respective Houses and to use their best endeavors to procure at the next session of Congress a repeal of the aforesaid unconstitutional and obnoxious acts.

9. *Resolved, lastly*, That the Governor of this commonwealth be, and is hereby authorized and requested to communicate the preceding resolutions to the legislatures of the several States, to assure them that this commonwealth considers union for special national purposes, and particularly for those specified in their late federal compact, to be friendly to the peace, happiness and prosperity of all the States—that, faithful to that compact, according to the plain intent and meaning in which it was understood and acceded to by the several parties, it is sincerely anxious for its preservation; that it does also believe, that to take from the States all the power of self-government, and transfer them to a general and consolidated Government, without regard to the special delegations and reservations solemnly agreed to in that compact, is not for the peace, happiness or prosperity of these States; and that, therefore, this commonwealth is determined, as it doubts not its co-states are, to submit to undelegated and consequently unlimited powers in no man or body of men on earth; that if the acts before specified should stand, these conclusions would flow from them; that the General Government may place any act they think proper on the list of crimes and punish it themselves, whether enumerated by the Constitution as cognizable by them; that they may transfer its cognizance to the President or any other person, who may himself be the accuser, counsel, judge and jury, whose suspicious may be the evidence, his order the sentence, his officer the executioner, and his breast the sole record of the transaction; that a very numerous and valuable description of the inhabitants of these States, being by this precedent reduced as outlaws to the absolute dominion of one man and the barriers of the Constitution thus swept from us all, no rampart now remains against the passions and the power of a majority of Congress, to protect from a like exportation or other grievous punishment the minority of the same body, the legislators, judges, governors and counsellors of the States, nor their other peaceable inhabitants who may venture to reclaim the Constitutional rights and liberties of the States and people, or who, for other causes, good or bad, may be obnoxious to the view or marked by the suspicions of the President, or to

be thought dangerous to his or their elections or other interests, public or personal; that the friendless alien has been selected as the safest subject of a first experiment, but the citizen will soon follow, or rather has already followed; for, already has a sedition act marked him as a prey; that these and successive acts of the same character, unless arrested on the threshold, may tend to drive these States into revolution and blood, and will furnish new calumnies against republican governments, and new pretexts for those who wish it to be believed, that man cannot be governed but by a rod of iron; that it would be a dangerous delusion were a confidence in the men of our choice to silence our fears for the safety of our rights; that confidence is everywhere the parent of despotism; free government is found in jealousy and not in confidence; it is jealousy and not confidence which prescribes limited constitutions to bind down those whom we are obliged to trust with power; that our Constitution has accordingly fixed the limits to which, and no farther, our confidence may go; and let the honest advocate of confidence read the alien and sedition acts, and say if the Constitution has not been wise in fixing limits to the Government it created, and whether we should be wise in destroying those limits? Let him say what the Government is, if it be not a tyranny which the men of our choice have conferred on the President, and the President of our choice has assented to and accepted over the friendly strangers, to whom the mild spirit of our country and its laws had pledged hospitality and protection; that the men of our choice have more respected the bare suspicions of the President than the solid rights of innocence, the claims of justification, the sacred force of truth, and the forms and substance of law and justice. In questions of power, then, let no more be said of confidence in man, but bind him down from mischief by the chains of the Constitution. That this commonwealth does therefore call on its co-states for an expression of their sentiments on the acts concerning aliens, and for the punishment of certain crimes hereinbefore specified, plainly declaring whether these acts are or are not authorized by the Federal Compact. And it doubts not that their sense will be so announced as to prove their attachment to limited government, whether general or particular, and that the rights and liberties of their co-states will be exposed to no dangers by remaining embarked on a common bottom of their own; but they will concur with this commonwealth in considering the said acts as so palpably against the Constitution as to amount to an undisguised declaration, that the compact is not meant to be the measure of the powers of the General Government, but that it will proceed in the exercise over these States of all powers whatsoever. That they will view this as seizing the rights of the States and consolidating them in the hands of the General Government, with a power assumed to bind the States (not merely in cases made federal), but in all cases whatsoever, by laws made, not with their consent, but by others against their consent; that this would be to surrender the form of government we have chosen, and live under one deriving its power from its own will, and not from our authority; and that the co-states recurring to their natural rights in cases not made federal, will concur in declaring these void and of no force, and will each unite with this commonwealth in requesting their repeal at the next session of Congress.

EDMUND BULLOCK, S. H. R.
JOHN CAMPBELL, S. P. T.

Passed the House of Representatives Nov. 10, 1798.

Attest, THOS. TODD, C. H. R.

In Senate, Nov. 13, 1798.—Unanimously concurred in.

Attest, B. THURSTON, C. S.

Approved Nov. 19, 1798.

JAS. GARRARD, Gov. of Ky.

By the Governor,
HARRY TOULMIN, Sec. of State.

HOUSE OF REPRESENTATIVES,
Thursday, Nov. 14, 1799.

The House, according to the standing order of the day, resolved itself into a committee of the whole House, on the state of the commonwealth, Mr. Desha in the chair; and after some time spent therein, the speaker resumed the chair, and Mr. Desha reported that the committee had taken under consideration sundry resolutions passed by several State legislatures, on the subject of the Alien and Sedition laws, and had come to a resolution thereupon, which he delivered in at the clerk's table, where it was read and unanimously agreed to by the House, as follows:

The representatives of the good people of this commonwealth, in the General Assembly convened, having materially considered the answers of sundry States in the Union, to their resolutions passed the last session, respecting certain unconstitutional laws of Congress, commonly called the Alien and Sedition Laws, would be faithless, indeed, to themselves and to those they represent, were they silently to acquiesce in the principles and doctrines attempted to be maintained in all those answers, that of Virginia only excepted. To again enter the field of argument, and attempt more fully or forcibly to expose the unconstitutionality of those obnoxious laws, would, it is apprehended, be as unnecessary as unavailing. We cannot, however, but lament that, in the discussion of those interesting subjects by sundry of the legislatures of our sister States, unfounded suggestions and uncandid insinuations, derogatory to the true character and principles of this commonwealth, have been substituted in place of fair reasoning and sound argument. Our opinions of these alarming measures of the General Government, together with our reasons for those opinions, were detailed with decency and with temper and submitted to the discussion and judgment of our fellow-citizens throughout the Union. Whether the like decency and temper have been observed in the answers of most of these States, who have denied or attempted to obviate the great truths contained in those resolutions, we have now only to submit to a candid world. Faithful to the true principles of the Federal Union, unconscious of any designs to disturb the harmony of that Union, and anxious only to escape the fangs of despotism, the good people of this commonwealth are regardless of censure or calumniation. Lest, however, the silence of this commonwealth should be construed into an acquiescence in the doctrines and principles advanced and attempted to be maintained by the said answers, or lest those of our fellow-citizens throughout the Union who so widely differ from us on those important subjects, should be deluded by the expectation, that we shall be deterred from what we conceive our duty, or shrink from the principles contained in these resolutions—therefore,

Resolved, That this commonwealth considers the Federal Union, upon the terms and for the purposes specified in the late compact, as conducive to the liberty and happiness of the several States; that it does now unequivocally declare its attachment to the Union, and to that compact, agreeably to its obvious and real intention, and will be among the last to seek its dissolution; that if those who administer the General Government be permitted to transgress the limits fixed by that compact, by a total disregard to the special delegations of power therein contained, an annihilation of State governments and the creation upon their ruins of a general consolidated government, will be the inevitable consequence; that the principle and construction contended for by sundry of the State legislatures, that the General Government is the exclusive judge of the extent of the powers delegated to it, stop nothing short of despotism—since the discretion of those who administer the government, and not the Constitution would be the measure of their powers; that the several States who formed that instrument being sovereign and independent, have the unquestionable right to judge of the infraction, and that a nullification of those sovereignties of all unauthorized acts done under color of that instrument is the rightful remedy; that this commonwealth does, under

the most deliberate reconsideration, declare that the said Alien and Sedition Laws are, in their opinion, palpable violations of the said Constitution; and, however cheerfully it may be disposed to surrender its opinion to a majority of its sister States, in matters of ordinary or doubtful policy, yet in momentous regulations like the present, which so vitally wound the best rights of the citizen, it would consider a silent acquiescence as highly criminal; that although this commonwealth, as a party to the federal compact, will bow to the laws of the Union, yet it does at the same time declare that it will not now or ever hereafter, cease to oppose in a Constitutional manner every attempt at what quarter soever offered, to violate that compact. And, finally, in order that no pretext or arguments may be drawn from a supposed acquiescence on the part of this commonwealth in the Constitutionality of those laws, and be thereby used as precedents for similar future violations of the federal compact, this commonwealth does now enter against them in solemn protest.

Extract, &c.   Attest,

T. TODD, C. H. R.

In Senate, Nov. 22, 1799–Read and concurred in.

Attest,   B. THURSTON, C. S.

Replies to the Virginia Resolutions.

Seven of the States, through their legislatures, replied to the Virginia Resolutions. In every case the sentiments contained therein were denounced, and the construction placed upon the Federal Constitution by the General Government was endorsed and defended.

The Delaware Legislature declared that "they consider the resolutions from the State of Virginia as a very unjustifiable interference with the General Government and constituted authorities of the United States, and of dangerous tendency, and, therefore, not fit subject for the further consideration of the General Assembly."

The Legislature of Rhode Island cited the Constitution, second section of the third article, in support of the action of Congress, and for the reason therein contained "this Legislature, in their public capacity, do not feel themselves authorized to consider and decide on the Constitutionality of the Sedition and Alien Laws (so called); yet they are called upon by the exigency of this occasion to declare that in their private opinions these laws are within the powers delegated to Congress."

The Massachusetts Legislature deemed it "their duty solemnly to declare, that while they hold sacred the principle that consent of the people is the only pure source of just and legitimate power, they cannot admit the right of the State Legislatures to denounce the administration of that Government to which the people themselves, by a solemn compact, have exclusively committed their national concerns."

, The New York Senate resolved "that while the Senate feel themselves constrained to bear unequivocal testimony against such sentiments and doctrines, they deem it a duty no less indispensable, explicitly to declare their incompetency, as a branch of the Legislature of this State, to supervise the acts of the General Government."

The sentiments of the General Assembly of Connecticut are substantially set forth in its resolutions, "that it views with deep regret, and explicitly disavows the principles contained in the aforesaid resolutions, and particularly the opposition to the 'Alien and Sedition Acts'—acts which the Constitution authorized; which the exigency of the country rendered necessary; which the constituted authorities have enacted, and which merit the entire approbation of this Assembly."

The New Hampshire General Assembly considered that "the State Legislatures are not the proper tribunals to determine the Constitutionality of the laws of the General Government; that the duty of such decision is properly and exclusively confided to the Judicial Deparment."

The General Assembly of Vermont in its reply disapproved the Virginia Resolutions "as being unconstitutional in their nature and dangerous in their tendency. It belongs not to the State Legislatures to decide on the Constitutionality of the laws made by the General Government, this power being exclusively vested in Judiciary Courts of the Union."

1800.

A "convention" of Republican Congressmen, held in Philadelphia in 1800, nominated Thomas Jefferson for President and adopted the first national platform ever issued by a political party in a Presidential campaign. The Federalists, among whose leaders a serious rupture had occurred, adopted no platform.

Republican Platform.

1. An inviolable preservation of the Federal Constitution, according to the true sense in which it was adopted by the States, that in which it was advocated by its friends, and not that which its enemies apprehended, who, therefore became its enemies.

2. Opposition to monarchizing its features by the forms of its administration, with a view to conciliate a transition, first, to a President and Senate for life; and, secondly, to an hereditary tenure of those offices, and thus to worm out the elective principle.

3. Preservation to the States of the powers not yielded by them to the Union, and to the Legislature of the Union its Constitutional share in division of powers; and resistance, therefore, to existing movements for transferring all the powers of the States to the General Government, and all of those of that Government to the executive branch.

4. A rigorously frugal administration of the Government and the application of all the possible savings of the public revenue to the liquidation of the public debt; and resistance, therefore, to all measures looking to a multiplication of officers and salaries, merely to create partisans and to augment the public debt, on the principle of its being a public blessing.

5. Reliance for internal defense solely upon the militia, till actual invasion, and for such a naval force only as may be sufficient to protect our coasts and harbors from depredations ; and opposition, therefore, to the policy of a standing army in time of peace which may overawe the public sentiment, and to a navy, which, by its own expenses, and the wars into which it will implicate us, will grind us with public burdens and sink us under them.

6. Free commerce with all nations, political connection with none, and little or no diplomatic establishment.

7. Opposition to linking ourselves, by new treaties, with the quarrels of Europe, entering their fields of slaughter to preserve their balance, or joining in the confederacy of kings to war against the principles of liberty.

8. Freedom of religion, and opposition to all maneuvers to bring about a legal ascendancy of one sect over another.

9. Freedom of speech and of the press ; and opposition, therefore, to all violations of the Constitution, to silence, by force, and not by reason, the complaints or criticisms, just or unjust, of our citizens against the conduct of their public agents.

10. Liberal naturalization laws, under which the well disposed of all nations who may desire to embark their fortunes with us and share with us the public burdens, may have that opportunity, under moderate restrictions, for the development of honest intention, and severe ones to guard against the usurpation of our flag.

11. Encouragement of science and the arts in all their branches, to the end that the American people may perfect their independence of all foreign monopolies, institutions and influences.

1804-8-12

In 1804 and also in 1808 both Republicans and Federalists nominated Presidential candidates in Congressional caucuses, but no platform was adopted in either year. The Republicans followed the Congressional caucus plan of nominations again in 1812, but presented no platform of principles to the country. The Federalists, however, held a convention in New York. It was the first national convention of a representative partisan character held in the United States. It nominated De Witt Clinton for President and adopted what is known as the Clintonian platform.

Clintonian Platform.

1. Opposition to nominations of chief magistrates by Congressional caucuses, as well because such practices are the exercise of undelegated authority, as of their repugnance to the freedom of elections.

2. Opposition to all customs and usages in both the executive and legislative departments which have for their object the maintenance of an official regency to prescribe tenets of political faith, the line of conduct to be deemed fidelity or recreancy to republican principles, and to perpetuate in themselves or families the offices of the Federal Government.

3. Opposition to all efforts on the part of particular States to monopolize the principal offices of the Government, as well because of their certainty to destroy the harmony which ought to prevail amongst all the constituent parts of the Union, as of their leanings toward a form of oligarchy entirely at variance with the theory of republican government; and, consequently, particular opposition to continuing a citizen of Virginia in the executive office another term, unless she can show that she enjoys a corresponding monopoly of talents and patriotism, after she has been honored with the Presidency for twenty out of twenty-four years of our Constitutional existence, and when it is obvious that the practice has arrayed the agricultural against the commercial interests of the country.

4. Opposition to continuing public men for long periods in offices of delicate trust and weighty responsibility as the reward of public services, to the detriment of all or any particular interest in, or section of, the country; and, consequently, to the continuance of Mr. Madison in an office which, in view of our pending difficulties with Great Britain, requires an incumbent of greater decision, energy and efficiency.

5. Opposition to the lingering inadequacy of preparations for the war with Great Britain now about to ensue, and to the measure which allows uninterrupted trade with Spain and Portugal, which, as it cannot be carried on under our flag, gives to Great Britain the means of supplying her armies with provisions, of which they would otherwise be destitute, and thus affording aid and comfort to our enemy.

6. Averment of the existing necessity for placing the country in a condition for aggressive action for the conquest of the British American Provinces and for the defense of our coasts and exposed frontiers; and of the propriety of such a levy of taxes as will raise the necessary funds for the emergency.

7. Advocacy of the election of De Witt Clinton as the surest method of relieving the country from all the evils existing and prospective, for the reason that his great talents and inflexible patriotism guarantee a firm and unyielding maintenance of our national sovereignty, and the protection of those commercial interests which were flagging under the weakness and imbecility of the administration.

1812-30.

After the Clintonian Platform nothing fitting the character of a national platform was presented by any party until 1830, with the single exception of resolutions adopted by the Hartford Convention, which was composed of the Federalists opposed to the War of 1812 with England.

Resolutions Adopted by the Hartford Convention, January 4, 1815.

Resolved, That it be and is hereby recommended to the legislatures of the several States represented in this convention, to adopt all such measures as may be necessary effectually to protect the citizens of said States from the operation and effects of all acts which have been or may be passed by the Congress of the United States, which shall contain provisions subjecting the militia or other citizens to forcible drafts, conscriptions, or impressments not authorized by the Constitution of the United States.

Resolved, That it be and is hereby recommended to the said legislatures, to authorize an immediate and an earnest application to be made to the Government of the United States, requesting their consent to some arrangement whereby the said States may, separately or in concert, be empowered to assume upon themselves the defense of their territory against the enemy, and a reasonable portion of the taxes collected within said States may be paid into the respective treasuries thereof, and appropriated to the balance due said States, and to the future defense of the same. The amount so paid into said treasuries to be credited, and the disbursements made as aforesaid to be charged to the United States.

Resolved, That it be and hereby is recommended to the legislatures of the aforesaid States, to pass laws where it has not already been done, authorizing the governors or commanders-in-chief of their militia to make detachments from the same, or to form voluntary corps, as shall be most convenient and conformable to their Constitutions, and to cause the same to be well armed, equipped, and held in readiness for service, and upon request of the governor of either of the other States, to employ the whole of such detachment or corps, as well as the regular forces of the State, or such part thereof as may be required, and can be spared consistently with the safety of the State, in assisting the State making such request to repel any invasion thereof which shall be made or attempted by the public enemy.

Resolved, That the following amendments of the Constitution of the United States be recommended to the States represented as aforesaid, to be proposed by them for adoption by the State Legislatures, and in such cases as may be deemed expedient by a Constitution chosen by the people of each State. And it is further recommended that the said States shall persevere in their efforts to obtain such amendments until the same shall be effected.

1. Representatives and direct taxes shall be apportioned among the several States which may be included within this Union, according to their respective numbers of free persons, including those bound to serve for a term of years and excluding Indians not taxed, and all other persons.

2. No new State shall be admitted into the Union by Congress, in virtue of the power granted in the Constitution, without the concurrence of two-thirds of both houses.

3. Congress shall not have power to lay an embargo on the ships or vessels of the citizens of the United States in the ports or harbors thereof for more than sixty days.

4. Congress shall not have power, without the concurrence of two-thirds of both houses, to interdict the commercial intercourse between the United States and any foreign nation or the dependencies thereof.

5. Congress shall not make nor declare war nor authorize acts of hostility against any foreign nation without the concurrence of two-thirds of both houses, except such acts of hostility be in defense of the territories of the United States when actually invaded.

6. No person who shall hereafter be naturalized shall be eligible as a member of the Senate or House of Representatives of the United States or capable of holding any civil office under the authority of the United States.

7. The same person shall not be elected President of the United States a second time, nor shall the President be elected from the same State two terms in succession.

Resolved, That if the application of these States to the Government of the United States, recommended in a foregoing resolution, should be unsuccessful and peace should not be concluded, and the defense of these States should be neglected, as it has been since the commencement of the war, it will, in the opinion of this convention, be expedient for the Legislatures of the several States to appoint delegates to another convention, to meet at Boston, in the State of Massachusetts, on the third Monday of June next, with such powers and instructions as the exigency of a crisis so momentous may require.

Resolved, That the Honorable Geo. Cabot, the Honorable Chauncey Goodrich, the Honorable Daniel Lyman, or any two of them, be authorized to call another meeting of this convention, to be holden in Boston at any time before new delegates shall be chosen as recommended in the above resolution, if in their judgment the situation of the country shall urgently require it.

DECLINE OF THE FEDERALISTS.

The mystery which surrounded the Hartford Convention and the ambiguous language in which its resolutions were couched, made the name "Federalist" odious. This in connection with the speedy termination of the war of 1812 completed the downfall of the Federalist party. Since their defeat in 1800 the Federalists had been steadily going over to the Republicans. The difference between the parties had been practically removed, and there remained no important reason for the existence of two parties. Jefferson and Madison, once in power, had broken over the limitations which they had previously declared the Constitution placed upon the Federal Government. The Federalists, on the other hand, being shorn of their power, were not so desirous of a loose construction, especially since their opponents were in position to profit most by it. They did not hesitate to denounce the war, narrow the powers of the General Government and enlarge upon the rights of the States, any more than the Republicans had hesitated to violate the principles which they had pronounced with the utmost emphasis at the time when the Government was in the hands of the Federalists.)

Though the Federalist party was dead and its membership had been absorbed into the all-powerful Republican party, the most of the main principles for which it had stood in the days of power, were still alive. It was impossible that the Republican party should long remain undivided. Henry Clay with his ideas of loose construction of the Constitution was sure to break away from the party which was the legitimate child of Thomas Jefferson. He had either headed or advocated, to use the words of Prof. Johnston, "every attempt to increase the army and navy, to make the tariff protective, to begin a system of general public improvements at national expense, or to make the Federal Government prominent in foreign affairs, as the guardian of the infant republics of South America." The strict constructionists, of course, objected to the principles which Clay advocated, and the breach widened until the election of John Quincy Adams as President. Clay was appointed Secretary of State by Adams, and their respective followings soon united and became known as National Republicans. The followers of Andrew Jackson (who, though receiving a larger number of votes than Adams, was defeated in the House of Representatives) about the same time assumed the name of "Jackson Men," but soon laid this aside and adopted the name of Democrats, by which the members of that party have been known ever since.

ANTI-MASONIC RESOLUTIONS— 1830.

The Anti-Masonic party agreed with the National Republicans on most points, but as Clay was a Free Mason, it was opposed to him personally, and in return was opposed by him and his followers. In September, 1830, the Anti-

Masons having secured a considerable membership in several States, the leaders held a convention in Philadelphia and adopted a resolution recommending "to the people of the United States, opposed to secret societies," to meet in national convention one year later at Baltimore to make suitable nominations for President and Vice-President and to transact such other business as the cause of Anti-Masonry may require.

1832.

In the national campaign of 1832, the National Republicans adopted no platform. The Democrats, however, at a ratification meeting in Washington, May 11, adopted the following:

National Democratic Platform.

✓ *Resolved,* That an adequate protection to American industry is indispensable to the prosperity of the country, and that an abandonment of the policy at this period would be attended with consequences ruinous to the best interests of the nation.

Resolved, That a uniform system of internal improvements, sustained and supported by the General Government, is calculated to secure, in the highest degree, the harmony, the strength and permanency of the republic.

✓ *Resolved,* That the indiscriminate removal of public officers for a mere difference of political opinion is a gross abuse of power, and that the doctrine lately boldly preached in the United States Senate, that "to the victors belong the spoils of the vanquished," is detrimental to the interests, corrupting to the morals and dangerous to the liberties of the country.

THE PARTIES IN 1836.

Preparatory to the Presidential campaign of 1836 the Democrats met in delegate convention at Baltimore, May, 1835, but adopted no platform. In January, 1836, the radical faction, however, in convention at New York, adopted what is known as the "loco-foco" platform. The National Republicans by this time had adopted the name of "Whigs," and in their convention at Albany, February 3, adopted a platform.

"Loco-Foco" Platform.

We hold these truths to be self-evident, that all men were created free and equal; that they are endowed by their Creator with certain inalienable rights, among which are life, liberty and the pursuit of happiness; that the true foundation of republican government is the equal rights of every citizen in his person and property, and in their management; that the idea is quite unfounded that on entering into society we give up our natural rights; that the rightful power of all legislation is to declare and enforce only our natural rights and duties and to take none of them from us; that no man has the natural right to commit aggressions on the equal rights of another, and this is all from which the law ought to restrain him; that every man is under the natural duty of contributing to the necessities of society, and this is all the law should enforce on him; that when the laws have declared and enforced all this they have fulfilled their functions.

We declare unqualified hostility to bank notes and paper money as a circulating medium, because gold and silver is the only safe and Constitutional currency; hostility to any and all monopolies by legislation, because they are violations of equal rights of the people; hostility to the dangerous and unconstitutional creation of vested rights or prerogatives by legislation, because they are usurpations of the people's sovereign rights; no legislative or other authority in the body politic can rightfully by charter or otherwise exempt any man or body of men in any case whatever from trial by jury and the jurisdiction or operation of the laws which govern the community.

We hold that each and every law or act of incorporation passed by preceding legislatures can be rightfully altered and repealed by their successors, and that they should be altered or repealed when necessary for the public good or when required by a majority of the people.

Whig Platform.

Resolved, That in support of our cause we invite all citizens opposed to Martin Van Buren and the Baltimore nominees.

Resolved, That Martin Van Buren, by intriguing with the executive to obtain his influence to elect him to the Presidency, has set an example dangerous to our freedom and corrupting to our free institutions.

Resolved, That the support we render to William H. Harrison is by no means given to him solely on account of his brilliant and successful services as leader of our armies during the last war, but that in him we view also the man of high intellect, the stern patriot, uncontaminated by the machinery of hackneyed politicians—a man of the school of Washington.

Resolved, That in Francis Granger we recognize one of our most distinguished fellow-citizens, whose talents we admire, whose patriotism we trust and whose principles we sanction.

PARTIES IN 1840.

The Abolitionists met in national convention at Warsaw, N. Y., Nov. 13, 1839; nominated a Presidential ticket and adopted a resolution that in their judgment "every consideration of duty and expediency which ought to control the action of Christian freemen, requires of the Abolitionists of the United States to organize a distinct and independent political party, embracing all the necessary means for nominating candidates for office and sustaining them by public suffrage." The nominations made by this convention were confirmed by the convention at Albany, N. Y., April 1, 1840. At the latter convention a platform was adopted favoring abolition of slavery in the District of Columbia and the Territories, of the inter-State slave trade, and, in general, opposition to human slavery to the full extent of Constitutional power. The Whig national convention met at Harrisburg, Pa., December 4, 1839, but adopted no platform. The national convention of Democrats, which met at Baltimore May 5, 1840, on the other hand, adopted a strict constructionist platform.

Democratic Platform.

1. *Resolved*, That the Federal Government is one of limited powers, derived solely from the Constitution, and the grants of power shown therein ought to be strictly construed by all the departments and agents of the Government, and that it is inexpedient and dangerous to exercise doubtful Constitutional powers.

2. *Resolved*, That the Constitution does not confer upon the General Government the power to commence and carry on a general system of international improvements.

3. *Resolved*, That the Constitution does not confer authority upon the Federal Government, directly or indirectly, to assume the debts of the several States, contracted for local internal improvements or other State purposes; nor would such assumption be just or expedient.

4. *Resolved*, That justice and sound policy forbid the Federal Government to foster one branch of industry to the detriment of another, or to cherish the interests of one portion to the injury of another portion of our common country—that every citizen and every section of the country has a right to demand and insist upon an equality of rights and privileges and to complete and ample protection of persons and property from domestic violence or foreign aggression.

5. *Resolved*, That it is the duty of every branch of the Government to enforce and practice the most rigid economy in conducting our public affairs, and that no more revenue ought to be raised than is required to defray the necessary expenses of the Government.

6. *Resolved*, That Congress has no power to charter a United States bank; that we believe such an institution one of deadly hostility to the best interests of the country, dangerous to our republican institutions and the liberties of the people, and calculated to place the business of the country within the control of a concentrated money power and above the laws and the will of the people.

7. *Resolved*, That Congress has no power under the Constitution to interfere with or control the domestic institutions of the several States; and that such States are the sole and proper judges of everything pertaining to their own affairs not prohibited by the Constitution; that all efforts by Abolitionists or others, made to induce Congress to interfere with questions of slavery, or to take incipient steps in relation thereto, are calculated to lead to the most alarming and dangerous consequences, and that all such efforts have an inevitable tendency to diminish the happiness of the people and endanger the stability and permanence of the Union, and ought not to be countenanced by any friend to our political institutions.

8. *Resolved*, That the separation of the moneys of the Government from banking institutions is indispensable for the safety of the funds of the Government and the rights of the people.

9. *Resolved*, That the liberal principles embodied by Jefferson in the Declaration of Independence and sanctioned in the Constitution, which makes ours the land of liberty and the asylum of the oppressed of every nation, have ever been cardinal principles in the Democratic faith; and every attempt to abridge the present privilege of becoming citizens and the owners of soil among us ought to be resisted with the same spirit which swept the Alien and Sedition Laws from our statute books.

WHEREAS, Several of the States which have nominated Martin Van Buren as a candidate for the Presidency, have put in nomination different individuals as candidates for Vice-President, thus indicating a diversity of opinion as to the person best entitled to the nomination; and,

WHEREAS, Some of the said States are not represented in this convention: Therefore,

Resolved, That the convention deem it expedient at the present time not to choose between the individuals in nomination, but to leave the decision to their Republican fellow-citizens in the several States, trusting that before the election shall take place their opinions will become so concentrated as to secure the choice of a Vice-President by the electoral college.

PARTY PLATFORMS IN 1844.

The Abolitionists, or Liberty Party, as they were now called, were the first in the field for the national contest of 1844, having held their convention at Buffalo, August 30, 1843, more than a year before the Presidential election, and adopted a platform consistent with their beliefs. The Whig national convention met in Baltimore, May 1, 1844, and adopted a loose constructionist platform. The Democratic national convention, which met in Baltimore, May 27, adopted a strict constructionist platform.

Liberty Platform.

1. *Resolved*, That human brotherhood is a cardinal principle of true democracy, as well as pure Christianity, which spurns all inconsistent limitations; and neither the political party which repudiates it, nor the political system which is not based upon it, can be truly democratic or permanent.

2. *Resolved*, That the Liberty party, placing itself upon this broad principle, will demand the absolute and unqualified divorce of the General Government from slavery, and also the restoration of equality of rights among men, in every State where the party exists, or may exist.

3. *Resolved*, That the Liberty party has not been organized for any temporary purpose by interested politicians, but has arisen from among the people in consequence of a conviction, hourly gaining ground, that no other party in the country represents the true principles of American liberty, or the true spirit of the Constitution of the United States.

4. *Resolved*, That the Liberty party has not been organized merely for the overthrow of slavery; its first decided effort must, indeed, be directed against slave-holding as the grossest and most revolting manifestation of despotism, but it will also carry out the principle of equal rights into all its practical consequences and applications, and support every just measure conducive to individual and social freedom.

5. *Resolved*, That the Liberty party is not a sectional party but a national party; was not originated in a desire to accomplish a single object, but in a comprehensive regard to the great interests of the whole country; is not a new party, nor a third party, but is the party of 1776, reviving the principles of that memorable era, and striving to carry them into practical application.

6. *Resolved*, That it was understood in the times of the Declaration and the Constitution, that the existence of slavery in some of the States was in derogation of the principles of American liberty, and a deep stain upon the

character of the country, and the implied faith of the States and the Nation was pledged that slavery should never be extended beyond its then existing limits, but should be gradually, and yet, at no distant day, wholly abolished by State authority.

7. *Resolved*, That the faith of the States and the Nation thus pledged, was most nobly redeemed by the voluntary abolition of slavery in several of the States; and by the adoption of the ordinance of 1787, for the government of the territory northwest of the river Ohio, then the only territory in the United States, and consequently the only territory subject in this respect to the control of Congress, by which ordinance slavery was forever excluded from the vast regions which now compose the States of Ohio, Indiana, Illinois, Michigan, and the Territory of Wisconsin, and an incapacity to bear up any other than freemen was impressed on the soil itself.

8. *Resolved*, That the faith of the States and the Nation thus pledged, has been shamefully violated by the omission, on the part of many of the States, to take any measures whatever for the abolition of slavery within their respective limits; by the continuance of slavery in the District of Columbia, and in the Territories of Louisiana and Florida; by the legislation of Congress; by the protection afforded by national legislation and negotiation to slaveholding in American vessels, on the high seas, employed in the coastwise slave traffic; and by the extension of slavery far beyond its original limits, by acts of Congress admitting new slave States into the Union.

9. *Resolved*, That the fundamental truths of the Declaration of Independence, that all men are endowed by their Creator with certain inalienable rights, among which are life, liberty and the pursuit of happiness, was made the fundamental law of our National Government, by that amendment of the Constitution which declares that no person shall be deprived of life, liberty, or property, without due process of law.

10. *Resolved*, That we recognize as sound the doctrine maintained by slaveholding jurists, that slavery is against natural rights, and strictly local, and that its existence and continuance rest on no other support than State legislation, and not on any authority of Congress.

11. *Resolved*, That the General Government has under the Constitution no power to establish or continue slavery anywhere, and therefore that all treaties and acts of Congress establishing, continuing or favoring slavery in the District of Columbia, in the Territory of Florida, or on the high seas, are unconstitutional, and all attempts to hold men as property within the limits of exclusive national jurisdiction ought to be prohibited by law.

12. *Resolved*, That the provision of the Constitution of the United States which confers extraordinary political powers on the owners of slaves, and thereby constituting the two hundred and fifty thousand slaveholders in the slave States a privileged aristocracy; and the provisions for the reclamation of fugitive slaves from service, are anti-republican in their character, dangerous to the liberties of the people and ought to be abrogated.

13. *Resolved*, That the practical operation of the second of these provisions is seen in the enactment of the act of Congress respecting persons escaping from their masters, which act, if the construction given to it by the Supreme Court of the United States in the case of Prigg vs. Pennsylvania be correct, nullifies the habeas corpus acts of all the States, takes away the whole legal security of personal freedom and ought, therefore, to be immediately repealed.

14. *Resolved*, That the peculiar patronage and support hitherto extended to slavery and slaveholding by the General Government ought to be immediately withdrawn, and the example and influence of national authority ought to be arrayed on the side of liberty and free labor.

15. *Resolved*, That the practice of the General Government, which prevails in the slave States, of employing slaves upon the public works instead of free laborers and paying aristocratic masters, with a view to secure or reward political services, is utterly indefensible and ought to be abandoned.

16. *Resolved*, That freedom of speech and of the press and the right of petition and the right of trial by jury are sacred and inviolable, and that all rules, regulations and laws in derogation of either are oppressive, unconstitutional and not to be endured by a free people.

17. *Resolved*, That we regard voting in an eminent degree as a moral and religious duty, which, when exercised, should be by voting for those who will do all in their power for immediate emancipation.

18. *Resolved*, That this convention recommend to the friends of liberty in all those free States where any inequality of rights and privileges exists on account of color, to employ their utmost energies to remove all such remnants and effects of the slave system.

WHEREAS, The Constitution of the United States is a series of agreements, covenants or contracts between the people of the United States, each with all and all with each; and,

WHEREAS, It is a principle of universal morality, that the moral laws of the Creator are paramount to all human laws; or, in the language of an Apostle, that "we ought to obey God rather than men;" and,

WHEREAS, The principle of common law—that any contract, covenant or agreement to do an act derogatory to natural right is vitiated and annulled by its inherent immorality—has been recognized by one of the justices of the Supreme Court of the United States, who, in a recent case, expressly holds that "*any* contract that rests upon such a basis is *void;*" and,

WHEREAS, The third clause of the second section of the fourth article of the Constitution of the United States, when construed as providing for the surrender of a fugitive slave, *does* "rest upon such a basis," in that it is a contract to rob a man of a natural right—namely, his natural right to his own liberty—and is therefore absolutely *void:* Therefore,

19. *Resolved*, That we hereby give it to be distinctly understood by this Nation and the world that, as Abolitionists, considering that the strength of our cause lies in its righteousness, and our hope for it, in our conformity to the laws of God and our respect for the rights of man, we owe it to the Sovereign Ruler of the Universe, as a proof of our allegiance to Him, in all our civil relations and offices, whether as private citizens or public functionaries sworn to support the Constitution of the United States, to regard and to treat the third clause of the fourth article of that instrument, whenever applied to the case of a fugitive slave, as utterly null and void, and consequently as forming no part of the Constitution of the United States whenever we are called upon or sworn to support it.

20. *Resolved*, That the power given to Congress by the Constitution to provide for calling out the militia to suppress insurrection does not make it the duty of the Government to maintain slavery by military force, much less does it make it the duty of the citizens to form a part of such military force; when freemen unsheathe the sword it should be to strike for liberty, not for despotism.

21. *Resolved*, That to preserve the peace of the citizens and secure the blessings of freedom, the Legislature of each of the free States ought to keep in force suitable statutes, rendering it penal for any of its inhabitants to transport or aid in transporting from such State any person sought to be thus transported, merely because subject to the slave laws of any other State; this remnant of independence being accorded to the free States by the decision of the Supreme Court in the case of Prigg vs. The State of Pennsylvania.

Whig Platform.

1. *Resolved*, That these principles may be summed as comprising a well-regulated national currency; a tariff for revenue to defray the necessary expenses of the Government and discriminating with special reference to the protection of the domestic labor of the country; the distribution of the proceeds from the sales of the public lands; a single term for the Presidency;

a reform of executive usurpations; and generally such an administration of the affairs of the country as shall impart to every branch of the public service the greatest practical efficiency, controlled by a well-regulated and wise economy.

Democratic Platform.

Resolutions 1, 2, 3, 4, 5, 6, 7, 8 and 9 of the platform of 1840 were reaffirmed, to which were added the following:

10. *Resolved*, That the proceeds of the public lands ought to be sacredly applied to the national objects specified in the Constitution, and that we are opposed to the laws lately adopted, and to any law for the distribution of such proceeds among the States, as alike inexpedient in policy and repugnant to the Constitution.

11. *Resolved*, That we are decidedly opposed to taking from the President the qualified veto power by which he is enabled, under restrictions and responsibilities amply sufficient to guard the public interest, to suspend the passage of a bill whose merits cannot secure the approval of two-thirds of the Senate and House of Representatives, until the judgment of the people can be obtained thereon, and which has thrice saved the American people from the corrupt and tyrannical domination of the Bank of the United States.

12. *Resolved*, That our title to the whole of the Territory of Oregon is clear and unquestionable; that no portion of the same ought to be ceded to England or any other power, and that the reoccupation of Oregon and the reannexation of Texas at the earliest practicable period are great American measures, which this convention recommends to the cordial support of the Democracy of the Union.

ATTITUDE OF PARTIES IN 1848.

The Democrats opened the battle of 1848 by their convention at Baltimore, May 22, of that year, in which they renewed in their platform their adherence to the strict constructionist idea. The Whigs held their convention in Philadelphia June 7, but adopted no platform. On June 9, however, the resolutions given below were adopted at a Whig ratification meeting in Philadelphia. The Free Soilers, a branch of the Democratic party, who were opposed to any further extension of slavery into the Territories, met in convention at Buffalo August 9 and adopted the so-called "Buffalo platform." The Free Soilers were joined by the members of the old Liberty party.

Democratic Platform.

1. *Resolved*, That the American Democracy place their trust in the intelligence, the patriotism and the discriminating justice of the American people.

2. *Resolved*, That we regard this as a distinctive feature of our political creed, which we are proud to maintain before the world as the great moral element in a form of government, springing from and upheld by the popular will; and contrast it with the creed and practice of Federalism, under whatever name or form, which seeks to palsy the will of the constituent, and which conceives no imposture too monstrous for the popular credulity.

3. *Resolved*, Therefore, that entertaining these views, the Democratic party of this Union, through the delegates assembled in general conventions of the States coming together in a spirit of concord of devotion to the doctrines and faith of a free representative government, and appealing to their fellow-citizens for the rectitude of their intentions, renew and reassert before the American people, the declaration of principles avowed by them on a former occasion, when in general convention they presented their candidates for the popular suffrage.

Resolutions 1, 2, 3 and 4 of the platform of 1840 were reaffirmed.

8. *Resolved*, That it is the duty of every branch of the Government to enforce and practice the most rigid economy in conducting our public affairs, and that no more revenue ought to be raised than is required to defray the necessary expenses of the Government and for the gradual but certain extinction of the debt created by the prosecution of a just and necessary war.

Resolution 5 of the platform of 1840 was enlarged by the following:

And that the result of Democratic legislation in this and all other financial measures upon which issues have been made between the two political parties of the country have demonstrated to careful and practical men of all parties, their soundness, safety and utility in all business pursuits.

Resolutions 7, 8 and 9 of the platform of 1840 were here inserted.

13. *Resolved*, That the proceeds of the public lands ought to be sacredly applied to the National objects specified in the Constitution; and that we are opposed to any law for the distribution of such proceeds among the States as alike inexpedient in policy and repugnant to the Constitution.

14. *Resolved*, That we are decidedly opposed to taking from the President the qualified veto power by which he is enabled, under restrictions and responsibilities amply sufficient to guard the public interests, to suspend the passage of a bill whose merits cannot secure the approval of two-thirds of the Senate and House of Representatives until the judgment of the people can be obtained thereon, and which has saved the American people from the corrupt and tyrannical domination of the Bank of the United States, and from a corrupting system of general internal improvements.

15. *Resolved*, That the war with Mexico, provoked on her part by years of insult and injury, was commenced by her army crossing the Rio Grande, attacking the American troops, and invading our sister State of Texas, and upon all the principles of patriotism and the laws of nations, it is a just and necessary war on our part, in which every American citizen should have shown himself on the side of his country, and neither morally nor physically by word or by deed, have given "aid and comfort to the enemy."

16. *Resolved*, That we would be rejoiced at the assurance of peace with Mexico, founded on the just principles of indemnity for the past and security for the future; but that while the ratification of the liberal treaty offered to Mexico remains in doubt it is the duty of the country to sustain the administration and to sustain the country in every measure necessary to provide for the vigorous prosecution of the war, should that treaty be rejected.

17. *Resolved*, That the officers and soldiers who have carried the arms of their country into Mexico, have crowned it with imperishable glory. Their unconquerable courage, their daring enterprise, their unfaltering perseverance and fortitude when assailed on all sides by innumerable foes and that more formidable enemy —the diseases of the climate—exalt their devoted patriotism into the highest heroism, and give them a right to the profound gratitude of their country, and the admiration of the world.

18. *Resolved*, That the Democratic national convention of thirty States composing the American Republic, tender their fraternal congratulations to the national convention of the Republic of France, now assembled as the free suffrage representative of the sovereignty of thirty-five millions of republicans, to establish government on those eternal principles of equal rights, for which their La Fayette and our Washington fought side by side in the struggle for our national independence; and we would especially convey to them, and to the whole people of France, our earnest wishes for the consolidation of their liberties, through the wisdom that shall guide their councils, on the basis of a democratic Constitution, not derived from the grants or concessions of kings or dynasties, but originating from the only true source of political power recognized in the States of this Union—

the inherent and inalienable right of the people in their sovereign capacity to make and to amend their forms of government in such manner as the welfare of the community may require.

19. *Resolved*, That in view of the recent development of this grand political truth, of the sovereignty of the people and their capacity and power of self-government, which is prostrating thrones and erecting republics on the ruins of despotism in the Old World, we feel that a high and sacred duty is devolved, with increased responsibility, upon the Democratic party of this country, as the party of the people, to sustain and advance among us Constitutional liberty, equality, and fraternity, by continuing to resist all monopolies and exclusive legislation for the benefit of the few at the expense of the many, and by a vigilant and constant adherence to those principles and compromises of the Constitution, which are broad enough and strong enough to embrace and uphold the Union as it was, the Union as it is, and the Union as it shall be, in the full expansion of the energies and capacity of this great and progressive people.

20. *Resolved*, That a copy of these resolutions be forwarded, through the American minister at Paris, to the national convention of the Republic of France.

21. *Resolved*, That the fruits of the great political triumph of 1844, which elected James K. Polk and George M. Dallas, President and Vice-President of the United States, have fulfilled the hopes of the Democracy of the Union in defeating the declared purposes of their opponents in creating a national bank; in preventing the corrupt and unconstitutional distribution of the land proceeds from the common treasury of the Union for local purposes; in protecting the currency and labor of the country from ruinous fluctuations, and guarding the money of the country for the use of the people by the establishment of the Constitutional treasury; in the noble impulse given to the cause of free trade by the repeal of the tariff of '42, and the creation of the more equal, honest, and productive tariff of 1846; and that in our opinion, it would be a fatal error to weaken the bands of a political organization by which these great reforms have been achieved, and risk them in the hands of their known adversaries, with whatever delusive appeals they may solicit our surrender of that vigilance which is the only safeguard of liberty.

22. *Resolved*, That the confidence of the Democracy of the Union in the principles, capacity, firmness and integrity of James K. Polk, manifested by his nomination and election in 1844, has been signally justified by the strictness of his adherence to sound Democratic doctrines, by the purity of purpose, the energy and ability, which have characterized his administration in all our affairs at home and abroad; that we tender to him our cordial congratulations upon the brilliant success which has hitherto crowned his patriotic efforts, and assure him in advance, that at the expiration of his Presidential term he will carry with him to his retirement the esteem, respect and admiration of a grateful country.

23. *Resolved*, That this convention hereby present to the people of the United States, Lewis Cass, of Michigan, as the candidate of the Democratic party for the office of President, and William O. Butler, of Kentucky, for Vice-President of the United States.

Whig Resolutions.

1. *Resolved*, That the Whigs of the United States, here assembled by their representatives, heartily ratify the nomination of General Zachary Taylor as President, and Millard Fillmore as Vice-President of the United States, and pledge themselves to their support.

2. *Resolved*, That in the choice of General Taylor as the Whig candidate for President, we are glad to discover sympathy with a great popular sentiment throughout the Nation—a sentiment which, having its origin in admiration of great military success, has been strengthened by the development, in every action and every word, of sound conservative opinions, and of true fidelity to the great example of former days, and to the principles of the Constitution as administered by its founders.

3. *Resolved*, That General Taylor in saying that, had he voted in 1844, he would have voted the Whig ticket, gives us the assurance—and no better is needed from a consistent and truth-speaking man—that his heart was with us at the crisis of our political destiny, when Henry Clay was our candidate, and when not only Whig principles were well defined and clearly asserted, but Whig measures depended on success. The heart that was with us then is with us now, and we have a soldier's word of honor, and a life of public and private virtue, as the security.

4. *Resolved*, That we look on General Taylor's administration of the government as one conducive of peace, prosperity and union; of peace, because no one better knows, or has greater reason to deplore, what he has seen sadly on the field of victory, the horrors of war, and especially of a foreign and aggressive war; of prosperity, now more than ever needed to relieve the Nation from a burden of debt, and restore industry—agricultural, manufacturing and commercial—to its accustomed and peaceful functions and influences; of union because we have a candidate whose very position as a Southwestern man, reared on the banks of the great stream whose tributaries, natural and artificial, embrace the whole Union, render the protection of the interests of the whole country his first trust, and

whose various duties in past life have been rendered, not on the soil or under the flag of any State or section, but over the wide frontier, and under the broad banner of the Nation.

5. *Resolved*, That standing, as the Whig party does, on the broad and firm platform of the Constitution, braced up by all its inviolable and sacred guarantees and compromises and cherished in the affections, because protective of the interests of the people, we are proud to have as the exponent of our opinions one who is pledged to construe it by the wise and generous rules which Washington applied to it and who has said—and no Whig desires any other assurance—that he will make Washington's administration his model.

6. *Resolved*, That, as Whigs and Americans, we are proud to acknowledge our gratitude for the great military services, which, beginning at Palo Alto and ending at Buena Vista, first awakened the American people to a just estimate of him who is now our Whig Candidate. In the discharge of a painful duty—for his march into the enemy's country was a reluctant one; in the command of regulars at one time and volunteers at another and of both combined; in the decisive though punctual discipline of his camp, where all respected and loved him; in the negotiation of terms for a dejected and desperate enemy; in the exigency of actual conflict when the balance was perilously doubtful—we have found him the same—brave, distinguished and considerate, no heartless spectator of bloodshed, no trifler with human life or human happiness; and we do not know which to admire most, his heroism in withstanding the assaults of the enemy in the most hopeless fields of Buena Vista—mourning in general sorrow over the graves of Ringgold, of Clay, of Hardin—or in giving in the heat of battle terms of merciful capitulation to the vanquished foe at Monterey, and not being ashamed to avow that he did it to spare women and children, helpless infancy and more helpless age, against whom no American soldier wars. Such a military man, whose triumphs are neither remote nor doubtful, whose virtues these trials have tested, we are proud to make our candidate.

7. *Resolved*, That in support of this nomination we ask our Whig friends throughout the Nation to unite, to co-operate zealously, resolutely, with earnestness, in behalf of our candidate, whom calumny cannot reach, and with respectful demeanor to our adversaries, whose candidates have yet to prove their claims on the gratitude of the Nation.

Buffalo Platform.

WHEREAS, We have assembled in convention as a union of freemen, for the sake of freedom, forgetting all political difference in a common resolve to maintain the rights of free labor against the aggression of the slave power, and to secure free soil to a free people; and,

WHEREAS, The political conventions recently assembled at Baltimore and Philadelphia—the one stifling the voice of a great constituency, entitled to be heard in its deliberations, and the other abandoning its distinctive principles for mere availability—have dissolved the national party organization heretofore existing, by nominating for the chief magistracy of the United States, under the slaveholding dictation, candidates, neither of whom can be supported by the opponents of slavery extension, without a sacrifice of consistency, duty and self-respect; and,

WHEREAS, These nominations so made, furnish the occasion, and demonstrate the necessity of the union of the people under the banner of free Democracy, in a solemn and formal declaration of their independence of the slave power, and of their fixed determination to rescue the Federal Government from its control:

1. *Resolved*, Therefore, that we, the people here assembled, remembering the example of our fathers in the days of the first Declaration of Independence, putting our trust in God for the triumph of our cause, and invoking His guidance in our endeavors to advance it, do now plant ourselves upon the national platform of freedom, in opposition to the sectional platform of slavery.

2. *Resolved*, That slavery in the several States of this Union which recognize its existence, depends upon the State laws alone, which cannot be repealed or modified by the Federal Government, and for which laws that Government is not responsible. We therefore propose no interference by Congress with slavery within the limits of any State.

3. *Resolved*, That the proviso of Jefferson to prohibit the existence of slavery after 1800 in all the Territories of the United States, Southern and Northern; the votes of six States and sixteen delegates in Congress of 1784, for the proviso, to three States and seven delegates against it; the actual exclusion of slavery from the Northwestern Territory, by the ordinance of 1787, unanimously adopted by the States in Congress; and the entire history of that period, clearly show that it was the settled policy of the Nation not to extend, nationalize or encourage, but to limit, localize and discourage slavery; and to this policy, which should never have been departed from, the Government ought to return.

4. *Resolved*, That our fathers ordained the Constitution of the United States, in order, among other great national objects, to establish justice, promote the general welfare, and secure the blessings of liberty; but expressly denied to the Federal Government which they created, all

Constitutional power to deprive any person of life, liberty, or property without due legal process.

5. *Resolved*, That in the judgment of this convention, Congress has no more power to make a slave than to make a king; no more power to institute or establish slavery than to institute or establish a monarchy; no such power can be found among those specifically conferred by the Constitution, or derived by just implication from them.

6. *Resolved*, That it is the duty of the Federal Government to relieve itself from all responsibility for the existence or continuance of slavery wherever the Government possesses Constitutional power to legislate on that subject, and it is thus responsible for its existence.

7. *Resolved*, That the true, and in the judgment of this convention, the only safe measures of preventing the extension of slavery into the Territory now free, is to prohibit its extension in all such Territory by an act of Congress.

8. *Resolved*, That we accept the issue which the slave power has forced upon us; and to their demand for more slave States, and more slave territory, our calm but final answer is, No more slave States and no more slave territory. Let the soil of our extensive domains be kept free for the hardy pioneers of our own land, and the oppressed and banished of other lands, seeking homes of comfort and fields of enterprise in the New World.

9. *Resolved*, That the bill lately reported by the committee of eight in the Senate of the United States, was no compromise, but an absolute surrender of the rights of the non-slaveholders of all the States; and while we rejoice to know that a measure which, while opening the door for the introduction of slavery into the Territories now free, would also have opened the door to litigation and strife among the future inhabitants thereof, to the ruin of their peace and prosperity, was defeated in the House of Representatives, its passage, in hot haste, by a majority embracing several Senators who voted in open violation of the known will of their constituents, should warn the people to see to it that their representatives be not suffered to betray them. There must be no more compromises with slavery; if made, they must be repealed.

10. *Resolved*, That we demand freedom and established institutions for our brethren in Oregon, now exposed to hardships, peril and massacre, by the reckless hostility of the slave power to the establishment of free government and free territories; and not only for them but for our brethren in California and New Mexico.

11. *Resolved*, It is due not only to this occasion, but to the whole people of the United States, that we should also declare ourselves on certain other questions of national policy: Therefore,

12. *Resolved*, That we demand cheap postage for the people; a retrenchment of the expenses and patronage of the Federal Government; the abolition of all unnecessary offices and salaries; and the election by the people of all civil officers in the service of the Government, so far as the same may be practicable.

13. *Resolved*, That river and harbor improvements, when demanded by the safety and convenience of commerce with foreign nations, or among the several States, are objects of national concern, and that it is the duty of Congress, in the exercise of its Constitutional power, to provide therefor.

14. *Resolved*, That the free grant to actual settlers, in consideration of the expenses they incur in making settlements in the wilderness, which are usually fully equal to their actual cost, and of the public benefits resulting therefrom, of reasonable portions of the public lands, under suitable limitations, is a wise and just measure of public policy, which will promote in various ways the interest of all the States of this Union; and we, therefore, recommend it to the favorable consideration of the American people.

15. *Resolved*, That the obligations of honor and patriotism require the earliest practical payment of the national debt; and we are, therefore, in favor of such a tariff of duties as will raise revenue adequate to defray the expenses of the Federal Government, and to pay annual installments of our debt and the interest thereon.

16. *Resolved*, That we inscribe on our banner "Free Soil, Free Speech, Free Labor and Free Men," and under it we will fight on, and fight ever until a triumphant victory shall reward our exertions.

IN 1852.

There was little notable change in 1852 from the attitude of the parties to the issues of the day four years previous. The Democratic National Convention at Baltimore June 1, 1852, adopted a platform framed on the principle of strict construction. The Whig convention, which met in the same city June 16, adhered to the liberal ideas of its party and adopted a loose constructionist platform. The Free Soil Democrats met in convention in Pittsburgh August 11 of the same year and presented their principles formulated in the customary platform.

Democratic Platform.

Resolutions, 1, 2, 3, 4, 5, 6 and 7 of the platform of 1848 were reaffirmed, to which were added the following:

8. *Resolved*, That it is the duty of every branch of the Government to enforce and practice the most rigid economy in conducting our public affairs, and that no more revenue ought to be raised than is required to defray the necessary expenses of the Government and for the gradual but certain extinction of the public debt.

9. *Resolved*, That Congress has no power to charter a National Bank; that we believe such an institution one of deadly hostility to the best interests of the country, dangerous to our republican institutions and the liberties of the people, calculated to place the business of the country within the control of a concentrated money power, and that above the laws and will of the people; and that the results of Democratic legislation in this and all other financial measures upon which issues have been made between the two political parties of the country, have demonstrated to candid and practical men of all parties their soundness, safety and utility in all business pursuits.

10. *Resolved*, That the separation of the moneys of the Government from banking institutions is indispensable for the safety of the funds of the Government and the rights of the people.

11. *Resolved*, That the liberal principles embodied by Jefferson in the Declaration of Independence and sanctioned in the Constitution, which makes ours the land of liberty and the asylum of the oppressed of every nation, have ever been cardinal principles in the Democratic faith; and every attempt to abridge the privilege of becoming citizens and the owners of the soil among us ought to be resisted with the same spirit that swept the Alien and Sedition laws from our statute books.

12. *Resolved*, That Congress has no power under the Constitution to interfere with or control the domestic institutions of the several States, and that such States are the sole and proper judges of everything appertaining to their own affairs not prohibited by the Constitution; that all efforts of the Abolitionists or others, made to induce Congress to interfere with questions of slavery, or to take incipient steps in relation thereto, are calculated to lead to the most alarming and dangerous consequences; and that all such efforts have an inevitable tendency to diminish the happiness of the people and endanger the stability and permanency of the Union, and ought not to be countenanced by any friend of our political institutions.

13. *Resolved*, That the foregoing proposition covers and is intended to embrace the whole subject of slavery agitation in Congress; and, therefore, the Democratic party of the Union, standing on this national platform, will abide by and adhere to a faithful execution of the acts known as the Compromise measures settled by the last Congress, "the act for reclaiming fugitives from service labor" included; which act, being designed to carry out an express provision of the Constitution, cannot, with fidelity thereto, be repealed nor so changed as to destroy or impair its efficiency.

14. *Resolved*, That the Democratic party will resist all attempts at renewing in Congress or out of it the agitation of the slavery question under whatever shape or color the attempt may be made.

[Here resolutions 13 and 14 of the platform of 1848 were inserted.]

17. *Resolved*, That the Democratic party will faithfully abide by and uphold the principles laid down in the Kentucky and Virginia resolutions of 1792 and 1798, and in the report of Mr. Madison to the Virginia Legislature in 1799; that it adopts those principles as constituting one of the main foundations of its political creed and is resolved to carry them out in their obvious meaning and import.

18. *Resolved*, That the war with Mexico, upon all the principles of patriotism and the law of nations, was a just and necessary war on our part, in which no American citizen should have shown himself opposed to his country, and neither morally nor physically, by word or deed, given aid and comfort to the enemy.

19. *Resolved*, That we rejoice at the restoration of friendly relations with our sister Republic of Mexico, and earnestly desire for her all the blessings and prosperity which we enjoy under republican institutions; and we congratulate the American people on the results of that war, which have so manifestly justified the policy and conduct of the Democratic party and insured the United States indemnity for the past and security for the future.

20. *Resolved*, That in view of the condition of popular institutions in the Old World, a high and sacred duty is devolved with increased responsibility upon the Democracy of this country as the party of the people, to uphold and maintain the rights of every State, and thereby the union of States, and to sustain and advance among them Constitutional liberty, by continuing to resist all monopolies and exclusive legislation for the benefit of the few at the expense of the many, and by a vigilant and constant adherence to those principles and compromises of the Constitution which are broad enough and strong enough to embrace and uphold the Union as it is and the Union as it should be, in the full expansion of the energies and capacity of this great and progressive people.

Whig Platform

The Whigs of the United States, in convention assembled, adhering to the great conservative principles by which they are controlled and governed, and now as ever relying upon the intelligence of the American people, with an abiding confidence in their capacity for self-government and their devotion to the Constitution and the Union, do proclaim the following as the political sentiments and determination for the establishment and maintenance of which their national organization as a party was effected:

1. The Government of the United States is of a limited character, and is confined to the exercise of powers expressly granted by the Constitution and such as may be necessary and proper for carrying the granted powers into full execution, and that powers not granted or necessarily implied are reserved to the States, respectively, and to the people.

2. The State governments should be held secure to their reserved rights, and the General Government sustained in its Constitutional powers, and that the Union should be revered and watched over as the palladium of our liberties.

3. That while struggling freedom everywhere enlists the warmest sympathy of the Whig party, we still adhere to the doctrines of the Father of his Country, as announced in his farewell address, of keeping ourselves from all entangling alliances with foreign countries, and of never quitting our own to stand upon foreign ground; that our mission as a republic is not to propagate our opinions, or impose on other countries our form of government, by artifice or force, but to teach by example, and show by our success, moderation and justice, the blessings of self-government, and the advantages of free institutions.

4. That, as the people make and control the Government, they should obey its Constitution, laws, and treaties as they would retain their self-respect and the respect which they claim and will enforce from foreign powers.

5. Governments should be conducted on the principles of the strictest economy; and revenue sufficient for the expenses thereof, in time of peace, ought to be derived mainly from a duty on imports, and not from direct taxes; and on laying such duties sound policy requires a just discrimination, and, when practicable, by specific duties, whereby suitable encouragement may be afforded to American industry, equally to all classes and to all portions of the country.

6. The Constitution vests in Congress the power to open and repair harbors and remove obstructions from navigable rivers, whenever such improvements are necessary for the common defense, and for the protection and facility of commerce with foreign nations or among the States, said improvements being in every instance national and general in their character.

7. The Federal and State governments are parts of one system, alike necessary for the common prosperity, peace and security, and ought to be regarded alike with a cordial, habitual and immovable attachment. Respect for the authority of each, and acquiescence in the just Constitutional measures of each, are duties required by the plainest considerations of National, State and individual welfare.

8. That the series of acts of the 32nd Congress, the act known as the Fugitive Slave Law included, are received and acquiesced in by the Whig party of the United States as a settlement in principle and substance of the dangerous and exciting questions which they embrace, and so far as they are concerned, we will maintain them, and insist upon their strict enforcement, until time and experience shall demonstrate the necessity of further legislation to guard against the evasion of the laws on the one hand and the abuse of their powers on the other—not impairing their present efficiency; and we deprecate all further agitation of the question thus settled as dangerous to our peace, and will discountenance all efforts to continue or renew such agitation whenever, wherever or however the attempt may be made; and we will maintain the system as essential to the nationality of the Whig party and the integrity of the Union. .

Free-Soil Platform.

Having assembled in national convention as the free Democracy of the United States, united by a common resolve to maintain right against wrong, and freedom against slavery; confiding in the intelligence, patriotism and discriminating justice of the American people; putting our trust in God for the triumph of our cause, and invoking His guidance in our endeavor to advance it, we now submit to the candid judgment of all men the following declaration of principles and measures:

1. That governments deriving their just powers from the consent of the governed, are instituted among men to secure to all those inalienable rights of life, liberty and the pursuit of happiness, with which they are endowed by their Creator, and of which none can be deprived by valid legislation, except for crime.

2. That the true mission of American Democracy is to maintain the liberties of the people, the sovereignty of the States, and the perpetuity of the Union, by the impartial application to public affairs, without sectional discriminations, of the fundamental principles of human rights, strict justice and an economical administration.

3. That the Federal Government is one of limited powers, derived solely from the Constitution, and the grants of power therein ought to be strictly construed by all the departments and agents of the Government, and it is inexpedient and dangerous to exercise doubtful Constitutional powers.

4. That the Constitution of the United States, ordained to form a more perfect union, to estab-

lish justice, and secure the blessings of liberty, expressly denies to the General Government all power to deprive any person of life, liberty or property, without due process of law; and, therefore, the Government, having no more power to make a slave than to make a king, and no more power to establish slavery than to establish a monarchy, should at once proceed to relieve itself from all responsibility for the existence of slavery wherever it possesses Constitutional power to legislate for its extinction.

5. That to the persevering and importunate demands of the slave power for more slave States, new slave territories, and the nationalization of slavery, our distinct and final answer is, No more slave States, no slave territory, no nationalized slavery, and no national legislation for the extradition of slaves.

6. That slavery is a sin against God, and a crime against man, which no human enactment or usage can make right; and that Christianity, humanity and patriotism alike demand its abolition.

7. That the Fugitive Slave act of 1850 is repugnant to the Constitution, to the principles of the common law, to the spirit of Christianity, and to the sentiments of the civilized world; we, therefore, deny its binding force on the American people and demand its immediate and total repeal.

8. That the doctrine that any human law is a finality, and not subject to modification or repeal, is not in accordance with the creed of the founders of our Government, and is dangerous to the liberties of the people.

9. That the acts of Congress, known as the compromise measures of 1850, by making the admission of a sovereign State contingent upon the adoption of other measures demanded by the special interests of slavery; by their omission to guarantee freedom in the free Territories; by their attempt to impose unconstitutional limitations on the powers of Congress and the people to admit new States; by their provisions for the assumption of five millions of the State debt of Texas, and for the payment of five millions more, and the cession of large territory to the same State under menace, as an inducement to the relinquishment of a groundless claim; and by their invasion of the sovereignty of the States and the liberties of the people, through the enactment of an unjust, oppressive, and unconstitutional fugitive slave law, are proved to be inconsistent with all the principles and maxims of Democracy, and wholly inadequate to the settlement of the questions of which they are claimed to be an adjustment.

10. That no permanent settlement of the slavery question can be looked for except in the practical recognition of the truth that slavery is sectional and freedom national; by the total

separation of the General Government from slavery, and the exercise of its legitimate and Constitutional influence on the side of freedom; and by leaving to the States the whole subject of slavery and the extradition of fugitives from service.

11. That all men have a natural right to a portion of the soil; and that as the use of the soil is indispensable to life, the right of all men to the soil is as sacred as their right to life itself.

12. That the public lands of the United States belong to the people and should not be sold to individuals nor granted to corporations, but should be held as a sacred trust for the benefit of the people, and should be granted in limited quantities, free of cost, to landless settlers.

13. That due regard for the Federal Constitution, a sound administrative policy, demand that the funds of the General Government be kept separate from banking institutions; that inland and ocean postage should be reduced to the lowest possible point; that no more revenue should be raised than is required to defray the strictly necessary expenses of the public service and to pay off the public debt; and that the power and patronage of the Government should be diminished by the abolition of all unnecessary offices, salaries and privileges, and by the election of the people of all civil officers in the service of the United States, so far as may be consistent with the prompt and efficient transaction of the public business.

14. That river and harbor improvements, when necessary to the safety and convenience of commerce with foreign nations, or among the several States, are objects of national concern; and it is the duty of Congress in the exercise of its Constitutional powers, to provide for the same.

15. That emigrants and exiles from the Old World should find a cordial welcome to homes of comfort and fields of enterprise in the New; and every attempt to abridge their privilege of becoming citizens and owners of soil among us ought to be resisted with inflexible determination.

16. That every nation has a clear right to alter or change its own government and to administer its own concerns in such manner as may best secure the rights and promote the happiness of the people; and foreign interference with that right is a dangerous violation of the law of nations, against which all independent governments should protest and endeavor by all proper means to prevent; and especially is it the duty of the American Government, representing the chief republic of the world, to protest against and by all proper means to prevent, the intervention of kings and emperors against nations seeking to establish for themselves republican or constitutional governments.

17. That the independence of Hayti ought to be recognized by our Government, and our com-

mercial relations with it placed on the footing of the most favored nations.

18. That as by the Constitution, "the citizens of each State shall be entitled to all the privileges and immunities of citizens in the several States," the practice of imprisoning colored seamen of other States, while the vessels to which they belong lie in port, and refusing the exercise of the right to bring such cases before the Supreme Court of the United States, to test the legality of such proceedings, is a flagrant violation of the Constitution, and an invasion of the rights of the citizens of other States, utterly inconsistent with the profession made by the slaveholders, that they wish the provisions of the Constitution faithfully observed by every State in the Union.

19. That we recommend the introduction into all treaties hereafter to be negotiated between the United States and foreign nations, of some provision for the amicable settlement of difficulties by a resort to decisive arbitrations.

20. That the Free Democratic party is not organized to aid either the Whig or Democratic wing of the great slave compromise party of the nation, but to defeat them both; and that repudiating and denouncing both as hopelessly corrupt and utterly unworthy of confidence, the purpose of the Free Democracy is to take possession of the Federal Government and administer it for the better protection of the rights and interests of the whole people.

21. That we inscribe on our banner Free Soil, Free Speech, Free Labor, and Free Men, and under it will fight on and fight ever, until a triumphant victory shall reward our exertions.

22. That upon this platform the convention presents to the American people, as a candidate for the office of President of the United States, John P. Hale, of New Hampshire, and as a candidate for the office of Vice-President of the United States, George W. Julian, of Indiana, and earnestly commend them to the support of all freemen and all parties.

PLATFORMS OF 1856.

In the national campaign of 1856 a new party made its appearance. The Northern Whigs had previously assumed the name of Anti-Nebraska Men, and now they adopted the name Republican party. The new party was thus little more than the Northern branch of the old Whig party, adhering to the same general principles with the addition of more pronounced views on the slavery question. Its first platform was adopted at the National Convention, which met in Philadelphia June 17, 1856. The Democratic National

Convention had met in Cincinnati the 2d of the same month, and on the 6th had adopted a platform. The American or Know-Nothing Convention met February 21 in Philadelphia and made the usual platform declarations. The name of Whig was kept alive after the Northern branch of the party bearing that name had become known as Republicans by the Southern wing of the old party. Its platform of this year was adopted at the National Convention held at Baltimore September 13.

The American Platform.

1. An humble acknowledgment to the Supreme Being for His protecting care vouchsafed to our fathers in their successful revolutionary struggle and hitherto manifested to us, their descendants, in the preservation of the liberties, the independence and the union of these States.

2. The perpetuation of the Federal Union and Constitution as the palladium of our civil and religious liberties, and the only sure bulwarks of American independence.

3. *Americans must rule America;* and to this end *native*-born citizens should be selected for all State, Federal and municipal offices of Government employment, in preference to all others. *Nevertheless,*

4. Persons born of American parents residing temporarily abroad should be entitled to all the rights of native-born citizens.

5. No person should be selected for political station (whether of native or foreign birth) who recognizes any allegiance or obligation of any description to any foreign prince, potentate or power, or who refuses to recognize the Federal and State Constitutions (each within its sphere) as paramount to all other laws, as rules of political action.

6. The unequivocal recognition and maintenance of the reserved rights of the several States and the cultivation of harmony and fraternal good will between the citizens of the several States, and to this end, non-interference by Congress with questions appertaining solely to the individual States and non-intervention by each State with the affairs of any other State.

7. The recognition of the right of native-born and naturalized citizens of the United States, permanently residing in any Territory thereof, to frame their Constitution and laws and to regulate their domestic and social affairs in their own mode, subject only to the provisions of the Federal Constitution, with the privilege of admission into the Union whenever they have the requisite population for one Representative in Congress: *Provided, always,* That none but those who are citizens of the United States under

the Constitution and laws thereof, and who have a fixed residence in any such Territory, ought to participate in the formation of the Constitution or in the enactment of laws for said Territory or State.

8. An enforcement of the principle that no State or Territory ought to admit others than citizens to the right of suffrage or of holding political offices of the United States.

9. A change in the laws of naturalization, making a continued residence of twenty-one years of all not heretofore provided for an indispensable requisite for citizenship hereafter, and excluding all paupers and persons convicted of crime from landing upon our shores; but no interference with the vested rights of foreigners.

10. Opposition to any union between church and state; no interference with religious faith or worship, and no test oaths for office.

11. Free and thorough investigation into any and all alleged abuses of public functionaries and a strict economy in public expenditures.

12. The maintenance and enforcement of all laws constitutionally enacted until said laws shall be repealed or shall be declared null and void by competent judicial authority.

13. Opposition to the reckless and unwise policy of the present administration in the general management of our national affairs, and more especially as shown in removing "Americans" (by designation) and conservatives in principle from office and placing foreigners and ultraists in their places; as shown in a truckling subserviency to the stronger and an insolent and cowardly bravado towards the weaker powers; as shown in reopening sectional agitation by the repeal of the Missouri Compromise; as shown in granting to unnaturalized foreigners the right of suffrage in Kansas and Nebraska; as shown in its vacillating course on the Kansas and Nebraska question; as shown in the corruptions which pervade some of the departments of the Government; as shown in disgracing meritorious naval officers through prejudice or caprice, and as shown in the blundering mismanagement of our foreign relations.

14. Therefore, to remedy existing evils and prevent the disastrous consequences otherwise resulting therefrom, we would build up the "American Party" upon the principles hereinbefore stated.

15. That each State council should have authority to amend their several constitutions, so as to abolish the several degrees and substitute a pledge of honor, instead of other obligations, for fellowship and admission into the party.

16. A free and open discussion of all political principles embraced in our platform.

Democratic Platform.

Resolved, That the American Democracy place their trust in the intelligence, the patriotism, and discriminating justice of the American people.

Resolved, That we regard this as a distinctive feature of our political creed, which we are proud to maintain before the world as a great moral element in a form of government springing from and upheld by the popular will; and we contrast it with the creed and practice of federalism, under whatever name or form, which seeks to palsy the will of the constituent, and which conceives no imposture too monstrous for the popular credulity.

Resolved, therefore, That entertaining these views, the Democratic party of this Union, through their delegates assembled in national convention, coming together in a spirit of concord, of devotions to the doctrines and faith of a free representative government, and appealing to their fellow-citizens for the rectitude of their intentions, renew and reassert before the American people, the declaration of principles avowed by them, when, on former occasions, in general convention, they have presented their candidates for the popular suffrage.

1. That the Federal Government is one of limited power, derived solely from the Constitution, and the grants of power made therein ought to be strictly construed by all the departments and agents of the Government, and that it is inexpedient and dangerous to exercise doubtful Constitutional powers.

2. That the Constitution does not confer upon the General Government the power to commence and carry on a general system of internal improvements.

3. That the Constitution does not confer authority upon the Federal Government, directly or indirectly, to assume the debts of the several States, contracted for local and internal improvements or other State purposes; nor would such assumption be just or expedient.

4. That justice and sound policy forbid the Federal Government to foster one branch of industry to the detriment of another, or to cherish the interests of one portion of our common country; that every citizen and every section of the country has a right to demand and insist upon an equality of rights and privileges, and a complete and ample protection of persons and property from domestic violence and foreign aggression.

5. That it is the duty of every branch of the Government to enforce and practice the most rigid economy in conducting our public affairs, and that no more revenue ought to be raised than is required to defray the necessary expenses of the Government and gradual but certain extinction of the public debt.

6. That the proceeds of the public lands ought to be sacredly applied to the national objects specified in the Constitution, and that we are

opposed to any law for the distribution of such proceeds among the States, as alike inexpedient in policy and repugnant in the Constitution.

7. That Congress has no power to charter a national bank; that we believe such an institution one of deadly hostility to the best interests of the country, dangerous to our republican institutions and the liberties of the American people, and calculated to place the business of the country within the control of a concentrated money power and above the laws and will of the people; and the results of the Democratic legislation in this and all other financial measures upon which issues have been made between the two political parties of the country, have demonstrated to candid and practical men of all parties their soundness, safety, and utility in all business pursuits.

8. That the separation of the moneys of the Government from banking institutions is indispensable to the safety of the funds of the Government and the rights of the people.

9. That we are decidedly opposed to taking from the President the qualified veto power, by which he is enabled, under restrictions and responsibilities amply sufficient to guard the public interests, to suspend the passage of a bill whose merits cannot secure the approval of two-thirds of the Senate and House of Representatives, until the judgment of the people can be obtained thereon, and which has saved the American people from the corrupt and tyrannical dominion of the Bank of the United States, and from a corrupting system of internal improvements.

10. That the liberal principles embodied by Jefferson in the Declaration of Independence, and sanctioned in the Constitution, which makes ours the land of liberty and the asylum of the oppressed of every nation, have ever been cardinal principles in the Democratic faith; and every attempt to abridge the privilege of becoming citizens and owners of soil among us ought to be resisted with the same spirit which swept the Alien and Sedition laws from our statute books; and,

WHEREAS, Since the foregoing declaration was uniformly adopted by our predecessors in national conventions, an adverse, political and religious test has been secretly organized by a party claiming to be exclusively Americans, and it is proper that the American Democracy should clearly define its relation thereto, and declare its determined opposition to all secret political societies by whatever name they may be called,

Resolved, That the foundation of the Union of States having been laid in, and its prosperity, expansion and pre-eminent example in free government built upon, entire freedom of matters of religious concernment, and no respect of persons in regard to rank or place of birth, no party

can justly be deemed National, Constitutional or in accordance with American principles, which bases its exclusive organization upon religious opinions and accidental birth-place. And hence a political crusade in the nineteenth century and in the United States of America against Catholics and foreign born is neither justified by the past history or future prospects of the country, nor in unison with the spirit of toleration and enlightened freedom which peculiarly distinguishes the American system of popular government.

Resolved, That we reiterate with renewed energy of purpose the well considered declarations of former conventions upon the sectional issue of domestic slavery and concerning the reserved rights of the States—

1. That Congress has no power under the Constitution to interfere with or control the domestic institutions of the several States, and that all such States are the sole and proper judges of everything appertaining to their own affairs not prohibited by the Constitution; that all efforts of the Abolitionists or others made to induce Congress to interfere with questions of slavery or to take incipient steps in relation thereto are calculated to lead to the most alarming and dangerous consequences, and that all such efforts have an inevitable tendency to diminish the happiness of the people and endanger the stability and permanency of the Union and ought not to be countenanced by any friend of our political institutions.

2. That the foregoing proposition covers and was intended to embrace the whole subject of slavery agitation in Congress, and therefore the Democratic party of the Union, standing on this national platform, will abide by and adhere to a faithful execution of the acts known as the Compromise measures, settled by the Congress of 1850—"the act for reclaiming fugitives from service or labor" included; which act, being designed to carry out an express provision of the Constitution, cannot, with fidelity thereto, be repealed or so changed as to destroy or impair its efficiency.

3. That the Democratic party will resist all attempts at renewing in Congress or out of it the agitation of the slavery question under whatever shape or color the attempt may be made.

4. That the Democratic party will faithfully abide by and uphold the principles laid down in the Kentucky and Virginia resolutions of 1792 and 1798 and in the report of Mr. Madison to the Virginia legislature in 1799, that it adopts these principles as constituting one of the main foundations of its political creed and is resolved to carry them out in their obvious meaning and import.

And that we may more distinctly meet the issue on which a sectional party, subsisting exclusively on slavery agitation, now relies to test the fidelity of the people, North and South, to the Constitution and the Union,

1. *Resolved*, That claiming fellowship with and desiring the co-operation of all who regard the preservation of the Union under the Constitution as the paramount issue and repudiating all sectional parties and platforms concerning domestic slavery which seek to embroil the States and incite to treason and armed resistance to law in the Territories, and whose avowed purpose, if consummated, must end in civil war and disunion, the American Democracy recognize and adopt the principles contained in the organic laws establishing the Territories of Nebraska and Kansas as embodying the only sound and safe solution of the slavery question, upon which the great national idea of the people of this whole country can repose in its determined conservation of the Union, and non-interference of Congress with slavery in the Territories or in the District of Columbia.

2. That this was the basis of the compromise of 1850, confirmed by both the Democratic and Whig parties in national conventions, ratified by the people in the election of 1852 and rightly applied to the organization of the Territories in 1854.

3. That by the uniform application of the Democratic principle to the organization of Territories and the admission of new States, with or without domestic slavery, as they may elect, the equal rights of all the States will be preserved intact, the original compacts of the Constitution maintained inviolate, and the perpetuity and expansion of the Union insured to its utmost capacity of embracing in peace and harmony every future American State that may be constituted or annexed with a republican form of government.

Resolved, That we recognize the right of the people of all the Territories, including Kansas and Nebraska, acting through the legally and fairly expressed will of the majority of the actual residents, and whenever the number of their inhabitants justifies it, to form a Constitution, with or without domestic slavery, and be admitted into the Union upon terms of perfect equality with the other States.

Resolved, finally, That in view of the condition of the popular institutions in the Old World (and the dangerous tendencies of sectional agitation, combined with the attempt to enforce civil and religious disabilities against the rights of acquiring and enjoying citizenship in our own land) a high and sacred duty is devolved, with increased responsibility, upon the Democratic party of this country, as the party of the Union, to uphold and maintain the rights of every State, and thereby the union of the States, and to sustain and advance among us Constitutional liberty, by continuing to resist all monopolies and exclusive legislation for the benefit of the few at the expense of the many, and by a vigilant and constant adherence to these principles and compromises of the Constitution which are broad enough and strong enough to embrace and uphold the Union as it was, the Union as it is, and the Union as it shall be, in the full expression of the energies and capacity of this great and progressive people.

1. *Resolved*, That there are questions connected with the foreign policy of this country which are inferior to no domestic questions whatever. The time has come for the people of the United States to declare themselves in favor of free seas and progressive free trade throughout the world, and by solemn manifestations, to place their moral influence at the side of their successful example.

2. *Resolved*, That our geographical and political position with reference to the other States of this continent, no less than the interest of our commerce and the development of our growing power, requires that we should hold sacred the principles involved in the Monroe Doctrine. Their bearing and import admit of no misconstruction, and should be applied with unbending rigidity.

3. *Resolved*, That the great highway which nature, as well as the assent of States most immediately interested in its maintenance, has marked out for free communication between the Atlantic and Pacific oceans, constitutes one of the most important achievements realized by the spirit of modern times, in the unconquerable energy of our people; and that result would be secured by a timely and efficient exertion of the control which we have the right to claim over it; and no power on earth should be suffered to impede or clog its progress by any interference with relations that may suit our policy to establish between our Government and the governments of the States within whose dominions it lies; we can under no circumstances surrender our preponderance in the adjustment of all questions arising out of it.

4. *Resolved*, That in view of so commanding an interest, the people of the United States cannot but sympathize with the efforts which are being made by the people of Central America to regenerate that portion of the continent which covers the passage across the interoceanic isthmus.

5. *Resolved*, That the Democratic party will expect of the next administration that every proper effort be made to insure our ascendancy in the Gulf of Mexico, and to maintain permanent protection to the great outlets through which are emptied into its waters the products raised out of the soil and the commodities created by the industry of the people of our western valleys and of the Union at large.

6. *Resolved*, That the administration of Franklin Pierce has been true to Democratic principles, and, therefore, true to the great interests of the country; in the face of violent opposition he has maintained the laws at home and vindicated the rights of American citizens abroad, and, therefore, we proclaim our unqualified admiration of his measures and policy.

Republican Platform.

This convention of delegates, assembled in pursuance of a call addressed to the people of the United States, without regard to past political differences or divisions, who are opposed to the repeal of the Missouri Compromise, to the policy of the present administration, to the extension of slavery into free territory; in favor of admitting Kansas as a free State, of restoring the action of the Federal Government to the principles of Washington and Jefferson; and who propose to unite in presenting candidates for the offices of President and Vice-President, do resolve as follows:

Resolved, That the maintenance of the principles promulgated in the Declaration of Independence, and embodied in the Federal Constitution, is essential to the preservation of our Republican institutions, and that the Federal Constitution, the rights of the States, and the Union of the States shall be preserved.

Resolved, That with our republican fathers we hold it to be a self-evident truth that all men are endowed with the inalienable rights to life, liberty, and the pursuit of happiness, and that the primary object and ulterior design of our Federal Government were to secure these rights to all persons within its exclusive jurisdiction; that as our republican fathers, when they had abolished slavery in all our national territory, ordained that no person should be deprived of life, liberty, or property, without due process of law, it becomes our duty to maintain this provision of the Constitution against all attempts to violate it for the purpose of establishing slavery in any Territory of the United States, by positive legislation, prohibiting its existence or extension therein. That we deny the authority of Congress, of a territorial legislature, of any individual or association of individuals, to give legal existence to slavery in any Territory of the United States, while the present Constitution shall be maintained.

Resolved, That the Constitution confers upon Congress sovereign power over the Territories of the United States for their Government, and that in the exercise of this power it is both the right and the imperative duty of Congress to prohibit in the Territories those twin relics of barbarism, polygamy and slavery.

Resolved, That while the Constitution of the United States was ordained and established, in order to form a more perfect union, establish justice, insure domestic tranquillity, provide for the common defense, promote the general welfare, and secure the blessings of liberty, and contains ample provisions for the protection of the life, liberty and property of every citizen, the dearest Constitutional rights of the people of Kansas have been fraudulently and violently taken from them; their Territory has been invaded by an armed force; spurious and pretended legislative, judicial and executive officers have been set over them, by whose usurped authority, sustained by the military power of the Government, tyrannical an unconstitutional laws have been enacted and enforced; the rights of the people to keep and bear arms have been infringed; test oaths of an extraordinary and entangling nature have been imposed, as a condition of exercising the right of suffrage and holding office; the right of an accused person to a speedy and public trial by an impartial jury has been denied; the right of the people to be secure in their persons, houses, papers, and effects against unreasonable searches and seizures, has been violated; they have been deprived of life, liberty and property without due process of law; that the freedom of speech and of the press has been abridged; the right to choose their representatives has been made of no effect; murders, robberies and arsons have been instigated or encouraged, and the offenders have been allowed to go unpunished; that all these things have been done with the knowledge, sanction, and procurement of the present national administration, and that for this high crime against the Constitution, the Union and humanity, we arraign the administration, the President, his advisers, agents, supporters, apologists and accessories, either before or after the facts, before the country and before the world, and that it is our fixed purpose to bring the actual perpetrators of these atrocious outrages and their accomplices, to a sure and condign punishment hereafter.

Resolved, That Kansas should be immediately admitted as a State of the Union with her present free Constitution, as at once the most effectual way of securing to her citizens the enjoyment of the rights and privileges to which they are entitled, and of ending the civil strife now raging in her territory.

Resolved, That the highwayman's plea that "might makes right," embodied in the Ostend Circular, was in every respect unworthy of American diplomacy, and would bring shame and dishonor upon any government or people who gave it their sanction.

Resolved, That a railroad to the Pacific ocean, by the most central and practicable route, is imperatively demanded by the interests of the whole country, and that the Federal Government ought to render immediate and efficient aid in its construction, and, as an auxiliary thereto, the immediate construction of an emigrant route on the line of the railroad.

Resolved, That appropriations of Congress for the improvement of rivers and harbors of a national character, required for the accommodation and security of our existing commerce, are authorized by the Constitution, and justified by the obligation of the government to protect the lives and property of citizens.

Resolved, That we invite the affiliation and co-operation of the men of all parties, however differing from us in other respects, in support of the principles herein declared; and believing that the spirit of our institutions, as well as the Constitution of our country, guarantees liberty of conscience and equality of rights among citizens, we oppose all prospective legislation affecting their security.

Whig Platform.

Resolved, That the Whigs of the United States, now here assembled, hereby declare their reverence for the Constitution of the United States, their unalterable attachment to the national Union, and a fixed determination to do all in their power to preserve them for themselves and their posterity. They have no new principles to announce; no new platform to establish; but are content to broadly rest — where their fathers rested — upon the Constitution of the United States, wishing no safer guide, no higher law.

Resolved, That we regard with the deepest interest and anxiety the present disordered condition of our national affairs—a portion of the country ravaged by civil war, large sections of our population embittered by mutual recriminations; and we distinctly trace these calamities to the culpable neglect of duty by the present national administration.

Resolved, That the Government of the United States was formed by the conjunction in political unity of widespread geographical sections, materially differing, not only in climate and products, but in social and domestic institutions; and that any cause that shall permanently sway the different sections of the Union in political hostility and organize parties founded only on geographical distinctions, must inevitably prove fatal to a continuance of the national Union.

Resolved, That the Whigs of the United States declare, as a fundamental article of political faith, an absolute necessity for avoiding geographical parties. The danger so clearly discerned by the Father of his Country has now become fearfully apparent in the agitation now convulsing the Nation, and must be arrested at once if we would preserve our Constitution and our Union from dismemberment and the name of America from being blotted out from the family of civilized nations.

Resolved, That all who revere the Constitution and the Union must look with alarm at the parties in the field in the present Presidential campaign—one claiming only to represent sixteen Northern States and the other appealing mainly to the passions and prejudices of the Southern States; that the success of either faction must add fuel to the flame which now threatens to wrap our dearest interests in a common ruin.

Resolved, That the only remedy for an evil so appalling is to support a candidate pledged to neither of the geographical sections nor arrayed in political antagonism, but holding both in a just and legal regard. We congratulate the friends of the Union that such a candidate exists in Millard Fillmore.

Resolved, That without adopting or referring to the peculiar doctrines of the party which has already selected Mr. Fillmore as a candidate, we look to him as a well-tried and faithful friend of the Constitution and the Union, eminent alike for his wisdom and firmness, for his justice and moderation in our foreign relations—calm and pacific temperament, so well becoming the head of a great nation—for his devotion to the Constitution in its true spirit—his inflexibility in executing the laws, but beyond all these attributes, in possessing the one transcendent merit of being a representative of neither of the two sectional parties now struggling for political supremacy.

Resolved, That in the present exigency of political affairs we are not called upon to discuss the subordinate questions of administration in the exercising of the Constitutional powers of the Government. It is enough to know that a civil war is raging and that the Union is in peril; and we proclaim the conviction that the restoration of Mr. Fillmore to the Presidency will furnish the best if not the only means of restoring peace.

PLATFORMS OF 1860.

The Democratic party met in delegate convention at Charleston, S. C., April 23, 1860, but owing to a wide divergence of opinion between the Northern and Southern wings the result was a split of the party into two distinct factions. The Southern faction at once organized a new convention and adopted a platform, but did not nominate a Presidential ticket until it reassembled at Baltimore on June 28. The Northern Democrats met in Baltimore June 18 and adopted what is known as the Douglas platform. The American, now calling itself the Constitutional Union party, held its national convention in

Baltimore May 9. The Republican party met in national convention at Chicago May 16 and on the following day adopted a platform.

Constitutional Union Platform.

WHEREAS, Experience has demonstrated that platforms adopted by the partisan conventions of the country have had the effect to mislead and deceive the people, and at the same time to widen the political divisions of the country by the elevation and encouragement of geographical and sectional parties: Therefore,

Resolved, That it is both the part of patriotism and of duty to *recognize* no political principles other than the CONSTITUTION OF THE COUNTRY, THE UNION OF THE STATES AND THE ENFORCEMENT OF THE LAWS; and that as representatives of the Constitutional Union men of the country, in national convention assembled, we hereby pledge ourselves to maintain, protect and defend, separately and unitedly, these great principles of public liberty and national safety against all enemies at home and abroad, believing that thereby peace may once more be restored to the country, the rights of the people and of the States re-established and the Government again placed in that condition of justice, fraternity and equality which under the example and Constitution of our fathers has solemnly bound every citizen of the United States to maintain a more perfect union, establish justice, insure domestic tranquillity, provide for the common defense, promote the general welfare and secure the blessings of liberty to ourselves and our posterity.

Republican Platform.

Resolved, That we, the delegated representatives of the Republican electors of the United States, in convention assembled, in discharge of the duty we owe to our constituents and our country, unite in the following declarations:

1. That the history of the Nation, during the last four years, has fully established the propriety and necessity of the organization and perpetuation of the Republican party, and that the causes which called it into existence are permanent in their nature, and now, more than ever before, demand its peaceful and Constitutional triumph.

2. That the maintenance of the principles promulgated in the Declaration of Independence and embodied in the Federal Constitution, "That all men are created equal; that they are endowed by their Creator with certain inalienable rights; that among these are life, liberty and the pursuit of happiness; that to secure these rights, governments are instituted among men, deriving their just powers from the consent of the governed," is essential to the preservation of our republican institutions; and that the Federal Constitution, the rights of the States, and the Union of the States, must and shall be preserved.

3. That to the union of the States this Nation owes its unprecedented increase in population, its surprising development of material resources, its rapid augmentation of wealth, its happiness at home and its honor abroad; and we hold in abhorrence all schemes for disunion, come from whatever source they may; and we congratulate the country that no Republican member of Congress has uttered or countenanced the threats of disunion so often made by Democratic members without rebuke and with applause from their political associates; and we denounce those threats of disunion, in case of a popular overthrow of their ascendancy, as denying the vital principles of free government, and as an avowal of contemplated treason, which it is the imperative duty of an indignant people sternly to rebuke and forever silence.

4. That the maintenance inviolate of the rights of the States, and especially the right of each State to order and control its own domestic institutions according to its own judgment exclusively, is essential to that balance of powers on which the perfection and endurance of our political fabric depends; and we denounce the lawless invasion, by armed force, of the soil of any State or Territory, no matter under what pretext, as among the gravest of enemies.

5. That the present Democratic administration has far exceeded our worst apprehensions, in its measureless subserviency to the exactions of a sectional interest; as especially evinced in its desperate exertions to force the infamous Lecompton constitution upon the protesting people of Kansas; in construing the personal relations between master and servant to involve an unqualified property in persons; in its attempted enforcement, everywhere, on land and sea, through the intervention of Congress and of the Federal courts, of the extreme pretensions of a purely local interest; and in its general and unvarying abuse of the power entrusted to it by a confiding people.

6. That the people justly view with alarm the reckless extravagance which pervades every department of the Federal Government; that a return to rigid economy and accountability is indispensable to arrest the systematic plunder of the public treasury by favored partisans; while the recent startling developments of frauds and corruptions at the Federal metropolis, show that an entire change of administration is imperatively demanded.

7. That the new dogma that the Constitution, of its own force, carries slavery into any or all of the Territories of the United States, is a dangerous political heresy at variance with explicit provisions of the instrument itself, with con-

temporaneous exposition, and with legislative and judicial precedent—is revolutionary in its tendency, and subversive of the peace and harmony of the country.

8. That the normal condition of all the territory of the United States is that of freedom; that as our Republican fathers when they had abolished slavery in all our national territory, ordained that " no person shall be deprived of life, liberty or property, without due process of law," it becomes our duty by legislation, whenever such legislation is necessary, to maintain this provision of the Constitution against all attempts to violate it; and we deny the authority of Congress, of a Territorial legislature, or of any individuals, to give legal existence to slavery in any territory of the United States.

9. That we brand the recent reopening of the African slave trade, under the cover of our national flag, aided by perversions of judicial power, as a crime against humanity and a burning shame to our country and age; and we call upon Congress to take prompt and efficient measures for the total and final suppression of that execrable traffic.

10. That in the recent vetoes, by their Federal governors, of the acts of the legislatures of Kansas and Nebraska, prohibiting slavery in those Territories, we find a practical illustration of the boasted Democratic principle of non-intervention and popular sovereignty, embodied in the Kansas-Nebraska bill, and a demonstration of the deception and fraud involved therein.

11. That Kansas should, of right, be immediately admitted as a State under the Constitution recently formed and adopted by her people, and accepted by the House of Representatives.

12. That, while providing revenue for the support of the General Government by duties on imports, sound policy requires such an adjustment of these imports as to encourage the development of the industrial interest of the whole country; and we commend that policy of national exchanges which secures to the working men liberal wages, to agriculture remunerative prices, to mechanics and manufacturers an adequate reward for their skill, labor, and enterprise, and to the Nation commercial prosperity and independence.

13. That we protest against any sale or alienation to others of the public lands held by actual settlers, and against any view of the homestead policy which regards the settlers as paupers or suppliants for public bounty; and we demand the passage by Congress of the complete and satisfactory homestead measure which has already passed the House.

14. That the Republican party is opposed to any change in our naturalization laws or any State legislation by which the rights of citizenship hitherto accorded to immigrants from foreign lands shall be abridged or impaired; and in favor of giving a full and efficient protection to the rights of all classes of citizens, whether native or naturalized, both at home and abroad.

15. That appropriations by Congress for river and harbor improvements of a national character, required for the accommodation and security of an existing commerce, are authorized by the Constitution and justified by the obligations of government to protect the lives and property of its citizens.

16. That a railroad to the Pacific ocean is imperatively demanded by the interest of the whole country; that the Federal Government ought to render immediate and efficient aid in its construction; and that as preliminary thereto, a daily overland mail should be promptly established.

17. Finally, having thus set forth our distinctive principles and views, we invite the co-operation of all citizens, however differing on other questions, who substantially agree with us in our affirmance and support.

Democratic (Douglas) Platform.

1. *Resolved,* That we, the Democracy of the Union, in convention assembled, hereby declare our affirmance of the resolutions unanimously adopted and declared as a platform of principles by the Democratic convention at Cincinnati, in the year 1856, believing that Democratic principles are unchangeable in their nature when applied to the same subject-matters; and we recommend, as the only further resolutions, the following:

Inasmuch as differences of opinion exist in the Democratic party as to the nature and extent of the powers of a Territorial legislature, and as to the powers and duties of Congress, under the Constitution of the United States, over the institution of slavery within the Territories,

2. *Resolved,* That the Democratic party will abide by the decisions of the Supreme Court of the United States on the question of Constitutional law.

3. *Resolved,* That it is the duty of the United States to afford ample and complete protection to all its citizens, whether at home or abroad, and whether native or foreign.

4. *Resolved,* That one of the necessities of the age, in a military, commercial, and postal point of view, is speedy communication between the Atlantic and Pacific States; and the Democratic party pledge such Constitutional Government aid as will insure the construction of a railroad to the Pacific coast at the earliest practicable period.

5. *Resolved,* That the Democratic party are in favor of the acquisition of the Island of Cuba, on such terms as shall be honorable to ourselves and just to Spain.

6. *Resolved*, That the enactments of State legislatures to defeat the faithful execution of the Fugitive Slave law are hostile in character, subversive of the Constitution, and revolutionary in their effect.

7. *Resolved*, That it is in accordance with the true interpretation of the Cincinnati platform, that, during the existence of the Territorial Governments, the measure of restriction, whatever it may be, imposed by the Federal Constitution on the power of the Territorial legislature over the subject of domestic relations, as the same has been, or shall hereafter be, finally determined by the Supreme Court of the United States, shall be respected by all good citizens, and enforced with promptness and fidelity by every branch of the General Government.

Democratic (Breckinridge) Platform.

Resolved, That the platform adopted by the Democratic party at Cincinnati be affirmed, with the following explanatory resolutions:

1. That the government of a Territory, organized by an act of Congress, is provisional and temporary; and, during its existence, all citizens of the United States have an equal right to settle, with their property in the Territory, without their rights, either of person or property, being destroyed or impaired by Congressional or Territorial legislation.

2. That it is the duty of the Federal Government in all its departments to protect when necessary the rights of persons and property in the Territories and wherever else its Constitutional authority extends.

3. That when the settlers in a Territory having an adequate population form a State Constitution in pursuance of law, the right of sovereignty commences, and, being consummated by admission into the Union, they stand on an equal footing with the people of the other States, and the State thus organized ought to be admitted into the Federal Union whether its Constitution prohibits or recognizes the institution of slavery.

4. That the Democratic party are in favor of the acquisition of the Island of Cuba on such terms as shall be honorable to ourselves and just to Spain at the earliest practicable moment.

5. That the enactments of State Legislatures to defeat the faithful execution of the Fugitive Slave law are hostile in character, subversive of the Constitution and revolutionary in their effect.

6. That the Democracy of the United States recognize it as the imperative duty of this Government to protect the naturalized citizens in all their rights, whether at home or in foreign lands, to the same extent as its native born citizens.

Whereas, One of the greatest necessities of the age in a political, commercial, postal and military point of view, is a speedy communication between the Pacific and Atlantic coasts: Therefore, be it

Resolved, That the Democratic party do hereby pledge themselves to use every means in their power to secure the passage of some bill to the extent of the Constitutional authority of Congress for the construction of a Pacific railroad from the Mississippi River to the Pacific Ocean at the earliest practicable moment.

PLATFORMS OF 1864.

In the campaign of 1864 only the loyal States took part. Three parties—Radical, Republican and Democratic—took part in the political contest of this year. The Radicals, who wished to deal with rebellion and rebels more harshly, met in Cleveland May 31 and adopted a platform. The Republican party platform was framed and adopted in the national convention which assembled in Baltimore June 7. The Democratic convention met in Chicago August 29 and adopted the "peace" platform.

Radical Platform.

1. That the Federal Union shall be preserved.

2. That the Constitution and laws of the United States must be observed and obeyed.

3. That the Rebellion must be suppressed by force of arms and without compromise.

4. That the rights of free speech, free press and the *habeas corpus* be held inviolate, save in districts where martial law has been proclaimed.

5. That the Rebellion has destroyed slavery; and the Federal Constitution should be so amended as to prohibit its re-establishment and to secure to all men absolute equality before the law.

6. That integrity and economy are demanded at all times in the administration of the Government, and that in time of war the want of them is criminal.

7. That the right of asylum, except for crime and subject to law, is a recognized principle of American liberty, and that any violation of it cannot be overlooked and must not go unrebuked.

8. That the national policy known as the "Monroe Doctrine" has become a recognized principle, and that the establishment of an anti-republican government on this continent by any foreign power cannot be tolerated.

9. That the gratitude and support of the Nation are due to the faithful soldiers and the earnest leaders of the Union army and navy, for their heroic achievements and deathless valor in defense of our imperiled country and of civil liberty.

10. That the one-term policy for the Presidency adopted by the people is strengthened by the force of the existing crisis, and should be maintained by Constitutional amendment.

11. That the Constitution should be so amended that the President and Vice-President shall be elected by a direct vote of the people.

12. That the question of the reconstruction of the rebellious States belongs to the people, through their representatives in Congress, and not to the Executive.

13. That the confiscation of the lands of the rebels and their distribution among the soldiers and actual settlers is a measure of justice.

Republican Platform.

Resolved, That it is the highest duty of every American citizen to maintain against all their enemies, the integrity of the Union, and the paramount authority of the Constitution and laws of the United States; and that, laying aside all differences of political opinions, we pledge ourselves as Union men, animated by a common sentiment and aiming at a common object, to do everything in our power to aid the Government in quelling, by force of arms, the Rebellion now raging against its authority, and in bringing to the punishment due to their crimes the rebels and traitors arrayed against it.

Resolved, That we approve the determination of the Government of the United States not to compromise with rebels, nor to offer them any terms of peace, except such as may be based upon an "unconditional surrender" of their hostility and a return to their allegiance to the Constitution and laws of the United States; and that we call upon the Government to maintain this position, and to prosecute the war with the utmost possible vigor to the complete suppression of the Rebellion, in full reliance upon the self-sacrificing patriotism, the heroic valor, and the undying devotion of the American people to the country and its free institutions.

Resolved, That as slavery was the cause, and now constitutes the strength of this Rebellion, and as it must be always and everywhere hostile to the principles of republican government, justice and the national safety demand its utter and complete extirpation from the soil of the Republic; and that we uphold and maintain the acts and proclamations by which the Government, in its own defence, has aimed a death-blow at the gigantic evil. We are in favor, furthermore, of such an amendment to the Constitution, to be made by the people in conformity with its provisions, as shall terminate and forever prohibit the existence of slavery within the limits or the jurisdiction of the United States.

Resolved, That the thanks of the American people are due to the soldiers and sailors of the army and navy who have periled their lives in defense of their country and in vindication of the honor of its flag; that the Nation owes to them some permanent recognition of their patriotism and their valor, and ample and permanent provision for those of their survivors who have received disabling and honorable wounds in the service of the country; and that the memories of those who have fallen in its defense shall be held in grateful and everlasting remembrance.

Resolved, That we approve and applaud the practical wisdom, the unselfish patriotism, and the unswerving fidelity to the Constitution and the principles of American liberty with which Abraham Lincoln has discharged, under circumstances of unparalleled difficulty, the great duties and responsibilities of the Presidential office; that we approve and indorse, as demanded by the emergency and essential to the preservation of the Nation, and as within the provisions of the Constitution, the measures and acts which he has adopted to defend the Nation against its open and secret foes; that we approve, especially, the Proclamation of Emancipation and the employment, as Union soldiers, of men heretofore held in slavery; and that we have full confidence in his determination to carry these and all other Constitutional measures essential to the salvation of the country, into full and complete effect.

Resolved, That we deem it essential to the general welfare that harmony should prevail in the national councils, and we regard as worthy of public confidence and official trust those only who cordially indorse the principles proclaimed in these resolutions, and which should characterize the administration of the Government.

Resolved, That the Government owes to all men employed in its armies, without regard to distinction of color, the full protection of the laws of war; and that any violation of these laws or of the usages of civilized nations in the time of war, by the rebels now in arms, should be made the subject of prompt and full redress.

Resolved, That foreign immigration, which in the past has added so much to the wealth, development of resources, and increase of power to this Nation—the asylum of the oppressed of all nations—should be fostered and encouraged by a liberal and just policy.

Resolved, That we are in favor of the speedy construction of the railroad to the Pacific coast.

Resolved, That the national faith, pledged for the redemption of the public debt, must be kept inviolate, and that for this purpose we recommend economy and rigid responsibility in the public expenditures and a vigorous and just system of taxation; and that it is the duty of every loyal State to sustain the credit and promote the use of the national currency.

Resolved, That we approve the position taken by the Government, that the people of the

United States can never regard with indifference the attempt of any European power to overthrow by force, or to supplant by fraud the institutions of any republican government on the western continent, and that they will view with extreme jealousy, as menacing to the peace and independence of this, our country, the efforts of any such power to obtain new footholds for monarchical governments, sustained by a foreign military force, in near proximity to the United States.

Democractic Platform.

Resolved, That in the future, as in the past, we will adhere with unswerving fidelity to the Union under the Constitution, as the only solid foundation of our strength, security and happiness as a people, and as a framework of government equally conducive to the welfare and prosperity of all the States, both Northern and Southern.

Resolved, That this convention does explicitly declare, as the sense of the American people, that, after four years of failure to restore the Union by the experiment of war, during which, under the pretense of a military necessity of a war power higher than the Constitution, the Constitution itself has been disregarded in every part, and public liberty and private right alike trodden down, and the material prosperity of the country essentially impaired, justice, humanity, liberty, and the public welfare demand that immediate efforts be made for a cessation of hostilities, with a view to an ultimate convention of all the States, or other peaceable means, to the end that at the earliest practicable moment peace may be restored on the basis of the federal union of all the States.

Resolved, That the direct interference of the military authority of the United States in the recent elections held in Kentucky, Maryland, Missouri and Delaware was a shameful violation of the Constitution; and the repetition of such acts in the approaching election will be held as revolutionary and resisted with all the means and power under our control.

Resolved, That the aim and object of the Democratic party is to preserve the Federal Union and the rights of the States unimpaired; and they hereby declare that they consider the administrative usurpation of extraordinary and dangerous powers not granted by the Constitution; the subversion of the civil by the military law in States not in insurrection; the arbitrary military arrest, imprisonment, trial and sentence of American citizens in States where civil law exists in full force; the suppression of freedom of speech and of the press; the denial of the right of asylum; the open and avowed disregard of State rights; the employment of unusual test oaths, and the interference with and denial of the rights of the people to bear arms in their defense as calculated to prevent a restoration of the Union and the perpetuation of a government deriving its just powers from the consent of the governed.

Resolved, That the shameful disregard of the administration to its duty in respect to our fellow-citizens who now are and long have been prisoners of war, in a suffering condition, deserves the severest reprobation on the score alike of public policy and common humanity.

Resolved, That the sympathy of the Democratic party is heartily and earnestly extended to the soldiery of our army and the sailors of our navy, who are and have been in the field and on the sea under the flag of their country; and, in the event of our attaining power, they will receive all the care and protection, regard and kindness, that the brave soldiers of the Republic have so nobly earned.

THE PARTIES IN 1868.

Only two parties presented platforms for endorsement by the people in 1868. The Republican National Convention met in Chicago May 20, and adopted its reconstruction platform. The Democratic platform, which demanded that the Southern States should immediately and unconditionally be given representation in Congress and other power granted to the loyal States, was adopted in the party national convention, which met in New York City July 4.

Republican Platform.

1. We congratulate the country on the assured success of the reconstruction policy of Congress, as evinced by the adoption in the majority of the States lately in rebellion, of constitutions securing equal civil and political rights to all; and it is the duty of the Government to sustain those institutions and to prevent the people of such States from being remitted to a state of anarchy.

2. The guarantee of Congress of equal suffrage to all loyal men at the South was demanded by every consideration of public safety, of gratitude and of justice, and must be maintained; while the question of suffrage in all the loyal States properly belongs to the people of those States.

3. We denounce all forms of repudiation as a national crime, and the national honor requires the payment of the public indebtedness in the utmost good faith to all creditors at home and abroad, not only according to the letter, but the spirit of the laws under which it was contracted.

4. It is due to the labor of the Nation that taxation should be equalized and reduced as rapidly as the national faith will permit.

5. The national debt, contracted as it has been for the preservation of the Union for all time to come, should be extended over a fair period for redemption; and it is the duty of Congress to reduce the rate of interest thereon whenever it can be honestly done.

6. That the best policy to diminish our burden of debts is to so improve our credit that capitalists will seek to loan us money at lower rates of interest than we now pay, and must continue to pay, so long as repudiation, partial or total, open or covert, is threatened or suspected.

7. The Government of the United States should be administered with the strictest economy, and the corruptions which have been so shamefully nursed and fostered by Andrew Johnson call loudly for radical reform.

8. We profoundly deplore the tragic death of Abraham Lincoln, and regret the accession to the Presidency of Andrew Johnson, who has acted treacherously to the people who elected him and the cause he was pledged to support; who has usurped high legislative and judicial functions; who has refused to execute the laws; who has used his high office to induce other officers to ignore and violate the laws; who has employed his executive powers to render insecure the property, the peace, liberty and life of the citizens; who has abused the pardoning power; who has denounced the national legislature as unconstitutional; who has persistently and corruptly resisted, by every means in his power, every proper attempt at the reconstruction of the States lately in rebellion; who has perverted the public patronage into an engine of wholesale corruption, and who has been justly impeached for high crimes and misdemeanors, and properly pronounced guilty thereof by the vote of thirty-five Senators.

9. The doctrine of Great Britain and other European powers, that because a man is once a subject he is always so, must be resisted at every hazard by the United States, as a relic of feudal times, not authorized by the laws of nations, and at war with our national honor and independence. Naturalized citizens are entitled to protection in all their rights of citizenship as though they were native born; and no citizen of the United States, native or naturalized, must be liable to arrest and imprisonment by any foreign power for acts done or words spoken in this country; and if so arrested and imprisoned, it is the duty of the Government to interfere in his behalf.

10. Of all who were faithful in the trials of the late war, there were none entitled to more special honor than the brave soldiers and seamen who endured the hardships of campaign and cruise, and imperiled their lives in the service of the country. The bounties and pensions provided by the laws for these brave defenders of the Nation are obligations never to be forgotten; the widows and orphans of the gallant dead are the wards of the people—a sacred legacy bequeathed to the Nation's protecting care.

11. Foreign immigration, which in the past has added so much to the wealth, development, resources, and increase of power to this Republic, the asylum of the oppressed of all nations, should be fostered and encouraged by a liberal and just policy.

12. This convention declares itself in sympathy with all oppressed people who are struggling for their rights.

13. That we highly commend the spirit of magnanimity and forbearance with which men who have served in the Rebellion, but who now frankly and honestly co-operate with us in restoring the peace of the country and reconstructing the Southern State governments upon the basis of impartial justice and equal rights, are received back into the communion of the loyal people; and we favor the removal of the disqualifications and restrictions imposed upon the late rebels, in the same measure as the spirit of disloyalty shall die out, and as may be consistent with the safety of the loyal people.

14. That we recognize the great principles laid down in the immortal Declaration of Independence as the true foundation of democratic government; and we hail with gladness every effort toward making these principles a living reality on every inch of American soil.

Democratic Platform.

The Democratic party in national convention assembled, reposing its trust in the intelligence, patriotism and discriminating justice of the people, standing upon the Constitution as the foundation and limitation of the powers of the Government and the guarantee of the liberties of the citizen, and recognizing the questions of slavery and secession as having been settled, for all time to come, by the war or voluntary action of the Southern States in constitutional conventions assembled, and never to be revived or agitated, do, with the return of peace, demand—

1. Immediate restoration of all the States to their rights in the Union under the Constitution, and of civil government to the American people.

2. Amnesty for all past political offenses, and the regulation of the elective franchise in the States by their citizens.

3. Payment of all the public debt of the United States as rapidly as practicable—all money drawn from the people by taxation, except so much as is requisite for the necessities of the Government, economically administered, being honestly applied to such payment; and when the obligations of the Government do not expressly state upon their face, or the law under which they were issued does not provide that

they shall be paid in coin, they ought, in right and in justice, to be paid in the lawful money of the United States.

4. Equal taxation of every species of property according to its real value, including Government bonds and other public securities.

5. One currency for the Government and the people, the laborer and the office-holder, the pensioner and the soldier, the producer and the bond-holder.

6. Economy in the administration of the Government; the reduction of the standing army and navy; the abolition of the Freedman's Bureau and all political instrumentalities designed to secure negro supremacy; simplification of the system and discontinuance of inquisitorial modes of assessing and collecting internal revenue; that the burden of taxation may be equalized and lessened, and the credit of the Government and the currency made good; the repeal of all enactments for enrolling the State militia into national forces in times of peace; and a tariff for revenue upon foreign imports, and such equal taxation under the internal revenue laws as will afford incidental protection to domestic manufactures, and as will, without impairing the revenue, impose the least burden upon, and best promote and encourage the great industrial interests of the country.

7. Reform of abuses in the administration; the expulsion of corrupt men from office; the abrogation of useless offices; the restoration of rightful authority to, and the independence of, the executive and judicial departments of the Government; the subordination of the military to the civil power, to the end that the usurpations of Congress and the despotism of the sword may cease.

8. Equal rights and protection for naturalized and native born citizens, at home and abroad; the assertion of American nationality which shall command the respect of foreign powers, and furnish an example and encouragement to people struggling for national integrity, constitutional liberty and individual rights; and the maintenance of the rights of naturalized citizens against the absolute doctrine of immutable allegiance and the claims of foreign powers to punish them for alleged crimes committed beyond their jurisdiction.

In demanding these measures and reforms, we arraign the Radical party for its disregard of right and the unparalleled oppression and tyranny which have marked its career. After the most solemn and unanimous pledge of both houses of Congress to prosecute the war exclusively for the maintenance of the Government and the preservation of the Union under the Constitution, it has repeatedly violated the most sacred pledge under which alone was rallied that noble volunteer army which carried our flag to victory. Instead of restoring the Union, it has, so far as in its power, dissolved it, and subjected ten States, in time of profound peace, to military despotism and negro supremacy. It has nullified there the right of trial by jury; it has abolished the *habeas corpus*, that most sacred writ of liberty; it has overthrown the freedom of speech and press; it has substituted arbitrary seizures and arrests, and military trials and secret star-chamber inquisitions, for the Constitutional tribunals; it has disregarded, in time of peace, the right of the people to be free from searches and seizures; it has entered the post and telegraph offices, and even the private rooms of individuals, and seized their private papers and letters, without any specific charge or notice of affidavit, as required by the organic law. It has converted the American Capitol into a bastile; it has established a system of spies and official espionage to which no constitutional monarchy of Europe would now dare to resort. It has abolished the right of appeal on important Constitutional questions to the supreme judicial tribunals, and threatens to curtail or destroy its original jurisdiction, which is irrevocably vested by the Constitution; while the learned Chief Justice has been subjected to the most atrocious calumnies, merely because he would not prostitute his high office to the support of the false and partisan charges preferred against the President. Its corruption and extravagance have exceeded anything known in history; and, by its frauds and monopolies, it has nearly doubled the burden of the debt created by the war. It has stripped the President of his Constitutional power of appointment, even of his own Cabinet. Under its repeated assaults the pillars of the Government are rocking on their base; and should it succeed in November next, and inaugurate its President we will meet, as a subjected and conquered people, amid the ruins of liberty and the scattered fragments of the Constitution.

And we do declare and resolve that ever since the people of the United States threw off all subjection to the British crown, the privilege and trust of suffrage have belonged to the several States, and have been granted, regulated, and controlled exclusively by the political powers of each State respectively; and that any attempt by Congress, on any pretext whatsoever, to deprive any State of this right, or interfere with its exercise, is a flagrant usurpation of power which can find no warrant in the Constitution, and if sanctioned by the people, will subvert our form of government, and can only end in a single, centralized, and consolidated government, in which the separate existence of the States will be entirely absorbed, and an unqualified despotism be established in place of a Federal Union of coequal States. And that we regard the construction acts (so-called) of Congress as usurpations and unconstitutional, revolutionary and void.

That our soldiers and sailors, who carried the flag of our country to victory against the most gallant and determined foe, must ever be gratefully remembered, and all the guarantees given in their favor must be faithfully carried into execution.

That the public lands should be distributed as widely as possible among the people, and should be disposed of either under the pre-emption of homestead lands or sold in reasonable quantities, and to none but actual occupants, at the minimum price established by the Government. When grants of public lands may be allowed, necessary for the encouragement of important public improvements, the proceeds of the sale of such lands, and not the lands themselves, should be so applied.

That the President of the United States, Andrew Johnson, in exercising the power of his high office in resisting the aggressions of Congress upon the Constitutional rights of the States and the people, is entitled to the gratitude of the whole American people; and, on behalf of the Democratic party, we tender him our thanks for his patriotic efforts in that regard.

Upon this platform, the Democratic party appeal to every patriot, including all the conservative element and all who desire to support the Constitution and restore the Union, forgetting all past differences of opinion, to unite with us in the present great struggle for the liberties of the people; and that to all such, to whatever party they may have heretofore belonged, we extend the right hand of fellowship, and hail all such, co-operating with us, as friends and brethren.

Resolved, That this convention sympathizes cordially with the workingmen of the United States, in their efforts to protect the rights and interests of the laboring classes of the country.

Resolved, That the thanks of the convention are tendered to Chief Justice Salmon P. Chase, for the justice, dignity and impartiality with which he presided over the court of impeachment on the trial of President Andrew Johnson.

THE SITUATION IN 1872.

The platforms presented to the voters of the United States in 1872 were unusually numerous. On February 21 of that year the Labor Reform platform was adopted by a convention held at Columbus, Ohio. On the following day and in the same city the Prohibition party met in national convention and adopted a platform. The Republicans this year were divided, and what is known as the Liberal Republican platform was adopted by a convention held at Cincinnati, May 1. This action was ratified by the regular Democratic convention which met at Baltimore, July 9. The straight-out Republicans held their convention and adopted a platform at Philadelphia, June 5. Those Democrats who looked with disfavor upon the action of the Baltimore convention in ratifying the action of the Liberal Republican convention, met in Louisville, Ky., September 3, and presented a platform for the favor of the voters of America.

Labor Reform Platform.

We hold that all political power is inherent in the people, and free government founded on their authority and established for their benefit; that all citizens are equal in political rights, entitled to the largest religious and political liberty compatible with the good order of society, as also the use and enjoyment of the fruits of their labor and talents; and no man or set of men is entitled to exclusive separable endowments and privileges or immunities from the Government, but in consideration of public services; and any laws destructive of these fundamental principles are without moral binding force, and should be repealed. And believing that all the evils resulting from unjust legislation now affecting the industrial classes can be removed by the adoption of the principles contained in the following declaration: Therefore,

Resolved, That it is the duty of the Government to establish a just standard of distribution of capital and labor, by providing a purely national circulating medium, based on the faith and resources of the Nation, issued directly to the people without the intervention of any system of banking corporations, which money shall be legal tender in the payment of all debts, public and private, and interchangeable, at the option of the holder, for Government bonds bearing a rate of interest not to exceed 3.65 per cent., subject to future legislation by Congress.

2. That the national debt should be paid in good faith, according to the original contract, at the earliest option of the Government, without mortgaging the property of the people or the future exigencies of labor to enrich a few capitalists at home and abroad.

3. That justice demands that the burdens of Government should be so adjusted as to bear equally on all classes, and that the exemption from taxation of Government bonds bearing extravagant rates of interest, is a violation of all just principles of revenue laws.

4. That the public lands of the United States belong to the people, and should not be sold to

individuals nor granted to corporations, but should be held as a sacred trust for the benefit of the people, and should be granted to the landless settlers only, in amounts not exceeding one hundred and sixty acres of land.

5. That Congress should modify the tariff so as to admit free such articles of common use as we can neither produce nor grow, and lay duties for revenue mainly upon articles of luxury and upon such articles of manufacture as will, we having the raw materials, assist in further developing the resources of the country.

6. That the presence in our country of Chinese laborers, imported by capitalists in large numbers for servile use, is an evil entailing want and its attendant train of misery and crime on all classes of the American people, and should be prohibited by legislation.

7. That we ask for the enactment of a law by which all mechanics and day laborers employed by or on behalf of the Government, whether directly or indirectly, through persons, firms or corporations, contracting with the State, shall conform to the reduced standard of eight hours per day, recently adopted by Congress for national employes; and also for an amendment to the acts of incorporation for cities and towns by which all laborers and mechanics employed at their expense shall conform to the same number of hours.

8. That the enlightened spirit of the age demands the abolition of the system of contract labor in our prisons and other reformatory institutions.

9. That the protection of life, liberty and property are the three cardinal principles of government, and the first two are more sacred than the latter; therefore, money needed for prosecuting wars should, as it is required, be assessed and collected from the wealthy of the country and not entailed as a burden on posterity.

10. That it is the duty of the Government to exercise its rights over railroads and telegraph corporations, that they shall not in any case be privileged to exact such rates of freight, transportation or charges, by whatever name, as may bear unduly or unequally upon the producer or consumer.

11. That there should be such a reform in the civil service of the National Government as will remove it beyond all partisan influence and place it in the charge and under the direction of intelligent and competent business men.

12. That as both history and experience teach us that power ever seeks to perpetuate itself by every and all means, and that its prolonged possession in the hands of one person is always dangerous to the interests of a free people, and believing that the spirit of our organic laws and the stability and safety of our free institutions are best obeyed on the one hand and secured on the other by a regular Constitutional change in the chief of the country at each election; therefore we are in favor of limiting the occupancy of the Presidential chair to one term.

13. That we are in favor of granting general amnesty and restoring the Union at once on the basis of equality of rights and privileges to all, the impartial administration of justice being the only true bond of union to bind the States together and restore the Government of the people.

14. That we demand the subjection of the military to the civil authorities, and the confinement of its operations to national purposes alone.

15. That we deem it expedient for Congress to supervise the patent laws so as to give labor more fully the benefit of its own ideas and inventions.

16. That fitness and not political or personal considerations should be the only recommendation to public office, either appointive or elective; and any and all laws looking to the establishment of this principle are heartily approved.

Prohibition Platform.

The preamble recites that protection and allegiance are reciprocal duties, and every citizen who yields obediently to the full commands of government should be protected in all enjoyment of personal security, personal liberty and private property. That the traffic in intoxicating drinks greatly impairs the personal security and personal liberty of a great mass of citizens, and renders private property insecure. That all political parties are hopelessly unwilling to adopt an adequate policy on this question. Therefore, as a national convention, we adopt the following declaration of principles:

That while we acknowledge the true patriotism and profound statesmanship of those patriots who laid the foundation of this Government, securing at once the rights of the States severally and in their inseparable union by the Federal Constitution, we would not merely garnish the sepulchres of our republican fathers, but we do hereby renew our pledges of solemn fealty to the imperishable principles of civil and religious liberty embodied in the Declaration of Independence and our Federal Constitution.

That the traffic in intoxicating beverages is a dishonor to Christian civilization, a political wrong of unequaled enormity, subversive of ordinary objects of government, not capable of being regulated or restrained by any system of license whatever, and imperatively demands for its suppression effective legal prohibition both by State and national legislation.

That there can be no greater peril to a nation than existing party competition for the liquor vote. That any party not opposed to the traffic, experience shows, will engage in this competition —will court the favor of criminal classes, will barter away the public morals, the purity of the ballot and every object of good government for party success.

That as Prohibitionists we will individually use all efforts to persuade men from the use of intoxicating liquors, and we invite all persons to assist in this movement.

That competence, honesty and sobriety are indispensable qualifications for holding office.

That removals from public office for mere political differences of opinion are wrong.

That fixed and moderate salaries of public officers should take the place of fees and perquisites, and that all means should be taken to prevent corruption and encourage economy.

That the President and Vice-President should be elected directly by the people.

That we are in favor of a sound national currency, adequate to the demands of business, and convertible into gold and silver at the will of the holder, and the adoption of every measure compatible with justice and public safety to appreciate our present currency to the gold standard.

That the rates of ocean and inland postage, and railroad telegraph lines and water transportation should be made as low as possible by law.

That we are opposed to all discrimination in favor of capital against labor, as well as all monopoly and class legislation.

That the removal of the burdens imposed in the traffic in intoxicating drinks will emancipate labor, and will practically promote labor reform.

That suffrage should be granted to all persons without regard to sex.

That the fostering and extension of common schools is a primary duty of the Government.

That a liberal policy should be pursued to promote foreign emigration.

Liberal Republican Platform.

We, the Liberal Republicans of the United States, in national convention assembled at Cincinnati, proclaim the following principles as essential to just government:

1. We recognize the equality of all men before the law, and hold that it is the duty of government in its dealings with the people, to mete out equal and exact justice to all, of whatever nativity, race, color or persuasion, religious or political.

2. We pledge ourselves to maintain the Union of these States, emancipation and enfranchisement, and to oppose any reopening of the questions settled by thirteenth, fourteenth and fifteenth amendments of the Constitution.

3. We demand the immediate and absolute removal of all disabilities imposed on account of the Rebellion, which was finally subdued seven years ago, believing that universal amnesty will result in complete pacification in all sections of the country.

4. Local self-government, with impartial suffrage, will guard the rights of all citizens more securely than any centralized power. The public welfare requires the supremacy of the civil over the military authority, and the freedom of person under the protection of the *habeas corpus*. We demand for the individual the largest liberty consistent with public order, for State self-government, and for the Nation a return to the methods of peace and the Constitutional limitations of power.

5. The civil service of the Government has become a mere instrument of partisan tyranny and personal ambition, and an object of selfish greed. It is a scandal and reproach upon free institutions, and breeds a demoralization dangerous to the perpetuity of republican government. We, therefore, regard a thorough reform of the civil service as one of the most pressing necessities of the hour; that honesty, capacity and fidelity constitute the only valid claims to public employment; that the offices of the Government cease to be a matter of arbitrary favoritism and patronage, and that public station shall become again a post of honor. To this end it is imperatively required that no President shall be a candidate for re-election.

6. We demand a system of Federal taxation which shall not unnecessarily interfere with the industry of the people, and which shall provide the means necessary to pay the expenses of the Government, economically administered, the pensions, the interest on the public debt, and a moderate reduction annually of the principal thereof; and recognizing that there are in our midst honest and irreconcilable differences of opinion with regard to the respective systems of protection and free trade. We remit the discussion of the subject to the people in their Congressional districts and the decision of Congress thereon, wholly free from executive interference or dictation.

7. The public credit must be sacredly maintained, and we denounce repudiation in every form and guise.

8. A speedy return to the specie payment is demanded alike by the highest considerations of commercial morality and honest government.

9. We remember with gratitude the heroism and sacrifices of the soldiers and sailors of the Republic; and no act of ours shall ever detract from their justly earned fame or the full rewards of their patriotism.

10. We are opposed to all further grants of lands to railroads or other corporations. The public domain should be held sacred to actual settlers.

11. We hold that it is the duty of the Government, in its intercourse with foreign nations, to cultivate the friendships of peace, by treating with all on fair and equal terms, regarding it

alike dishonorable either to demand what is not right or submit to what is wrong.

12. For the promotion and success of these vital principles and the support of the candidates nominated by this convention, we invite and cordially welcome the co-operation of all patriotic citizens, without regard to previous political affiliations.

Democratic Platform.

We, the Democratic electors of the United States, in convention assembled, do present the following principles, already adopted at Cincinnati, as essential to just government:

[Liberal Republican platform adopted at Cincinnati follows the above introduction.]

Republican Platform.

The Republican party of the United States, assembled in national convention in the city of Philadelphia, on the 5th and 6th days of June, 1872, again declares its faith, appeals to its history and announces its position upon the questions before the country:

1. During eleven years of supremacy it has accepted, with grand courage, the solemn duties of the time. It suppressed a gigantic rebellion, emancipated four millions of slaves, decreed the equal citizenship of all, and established universal suffrage, exhibiting unparalleled magnanimity; it criminally punished no man for political offenses, and warmly welcomed all who proved their loyalty by obeying the laws and dealing justly with their neighbors. It has steadily decreased, with firm hand, the resultant disorders of a great war, and initiated a wise and humane policy toward the Indians. The Pacific railroad and similar vast enterprises have been generously aided and successfully conducted, the public lands freely given to actual settlers, immigration protected and encouraged, and a full acknowledgment of naturalized citizens' rights secured from European powers. A uniform national currency has been provided, repudiation frowned down, the national credit sustained under the most extraordinary burdens, and new bonds negotiated at lower rates. The revenues have been carefully collected and honestly applied. Despite annual large reductions of the rates of taxation, the public debt has been reduced during General Grant's Presidency at the rate of a hundred millions a year, great financial crises have been avoided, and peace and plenty prevail throughout the land. Menacing foreign difficulties have been peacefully and honorably compromised, and the honor and power of the Nation kept in high respect throughout the world. This glorious record of the past is the party's best pledge for the future. We believe the people will not entrust the Government to any party or combination of men composed chiefly of those who have resisted every step of this beneficent progress.

2. The recent amendments to the national Constitution should be cordially sustained because they are right, not merely tolerated because they are law, and should be carried out according to their spirit by appropriate legislation, the enforcement of which can safely be entrusted only to the party that secured those amendments.

3. Complete liberty and exact equality in the enjoyment of all civil, political, and public rights should be established and effectually maintained throughout the Union by efficient and appropriate State and Federal legislation. Neither the law nor its administration should admit any discrimination in respect to citizens by reason of race, creed, color, or previous condition of servitude.

4. The National Government should seek to maintain honorable peace with all nations, protecting its citizens everywhere, and sympathizing with all peoples who strive for greater liberty.

5. Any system of civil service under which the subordinate positions of the Government are considered rewards for mere party zeal is fatally demoralizing; and we, therefore, favor a reform of the system, by laws which shall abolish the evils of patronage, and make honesty, efficiency, and fidelity the essential qualifications for public positions, without practically creating a life tenure of office.

6. We are opposed to further grants of the public lands to corporations and monopolies, and demand that the national domain be set apart for free homes for the people.

7. The annual revenue after paying current expenditures, pensions and the interest on the public debt, should furnish a moderate balance for the reduction of the principal; and that revenue, except so much as may be derived from a tax upon tobacco and liquors, should be raised by duties upon importations, the details of which should be so adjusted as to aid in securing remunerative wages to labor, and promote the industries, prosperity, and growth of the whole country.

8. We hold in undying honor the soldiers and sailors whose valor saved the Union. Their pensions are a sacred debt of the Nation, and the widows and orphans of those who died for their country are entitled to the care of a generous and grateful people. We favor such additional legislation as will extend the bounty of the Government to all our soldiers and sailors who were honorably discharged, and who in the line of duty became disabled, without regard to the length of service or the cause of such discharge.

9. The doctrine of Great Britain and other European powers concerning allegiance—"once a subject always a subject"—having at last,

through the efforts of the Republican party, been abandoned, and the American idea of the individual's right to transfer allegiance having been accepted by European nations, it is the duty of our Government to guard with jealous care the rights of adopted citizens against the assumption of unauthorized claims by their former governments, and we urge continued careful encouragement and protection of voluntary immigration.

10. The franking privilege ought to be abolished, and a way prepared for a speedy reduction in the rates of postage.

11. Among the questions which press for attention is that which concerns the relations of capital and labor; and the Republican party recognizes the duty of so shaping legislation as to secure full protection and the amplest field for capital, and for labor, the creator of capital, the largest opportunities and a just share of the mutual profits of these two great servants of civilization.

12. We hold that Congress and the President have only fulfilled an imperative duty in their measures for the suppression of violence and treasonable organizations in certain lately rebellious regions and for the protection of the ballot box, and therefore they are entitled to the thanks of the Nation.

13. We denounce repudiation of the public debt in any form or disguise as a national crime. We witness with pride the reduction of the principal of the debt and of the rates of interest upon the balance, and confidently expect that our excellent national currency will be perfected by a speedy resumption of specie payment.

14. The Republican party is mindful of its obligations to the loyal women of America for their noble devotion to the cause of freedom. Their admission to wider fields of usefulness is viewed with satisfaction; and the honest demand of any class of citizens for additional rights should be treated with respectful consideration.

15. We heartily approve the action of Congress in extending amnesty to those lately in rebellion, and rejoice in the growth of peace and fraternal feeling throughout the land.

16. The Republican party proposes to respect the rights reserved by the people to themselves as carefully as the powers delegated by them to the States and to the Federal Government. It disapproves of the resort to unconstitutional laws for the purpose of removing evils, by interference with rights not surrendered by the people to either State or National Government.

17. It is the duty of the general Government to adopt such measures as may tend to encourage and restore American commerce and ship-building.

18. We believe that the modest patriotism, the earnest purpose, the sound judgment, the practical wisdom, the incorruptible integrity and the illustrious services of Ulysses S. Grant have commended him to the heart of the American people; and with him at our head we start to-day upon a new march to victory.

19. Henry Wilson, nominated for the Vice-Presidency, known to the whole land from the early days of the great struggle for liberty as an indefatigable laborer in all campaigns, an incorruptible legislator and representative man of American institutions, is worthy to associate with our great leader and share the honors which we pledge our best efforts to bestow upon them.

Democratic Platform (Straightout).

WHEREAS, A frequent recurrence to first principles and eternal vigilance against abuses are the wisest provisions for liberty, which is the source of progress and fidelity to our Constitutional system is the only protection for either: Therefore,

Resolved, That the original basis of our whole political structure is consent in every part thereof. The people of each State voluntarily created their State, and the States voluntarily formed the Union; and each State provided by its written Constitution for everything a State could do for the protection of life, liberty and property within it; and each State, jointly with the others, provided a Federal Union for foreign and interstate relations.

Resolved, That all governmental powers, whether State or Federal, are trust powers coming from the people of each State, and that they are limited to the written letter of the Constitution and the laws passed in pursuance of it, which powers must be exercised in the utmost good faith, the Constitution itself stating in what manner they may be altered and amended.

Resolved, That the interests of labor and capital should not be permitted to conflict, but should be harmonized by judicious legislation. While such a conflict continues, labor, which is the parent of wealth, is entitled to paramount consideration.

Resolved, That we proclaim to the world that principle is to be preferred to power; that the Democratic party is held together by the cohesion of time-honored principles, which they will never surrender in exchange for all the offices which President's can confer. The pangs of the minorities are doubtless excruciating, but we welcome an eternal minority under the banner inscribed with our principles rather than an almighty and everlasting majority purchased by their abandonment.

Resolved, That having been betrayed at Baltimore into a false creed and a false leadership by the convention, we repudiate both, and appeal to the people to approve our platform and to rally to the polls and support the true platform and the candidates who embody it.

GREENBACK PROPOSITIONS, 1874.

The proposal to resume specie payment was the occasion of a Greenback convention at Indianapolis, Nov. 25, 1874, at which resolutions were adopted embodying these three propositions: 1, that the currency of all banks and corporations should be withdrawn; 2, that paper money issued by the Government, "based on the faith and resources of the Nation," and exchangeable on demand for bonds bearing interest at 3.65 per cent., should be the only currency; and, 3, that coin should be paid only for interest on the present national debt, and for that portion of the principal for which coin had been specifically promised:

THE CONTEST OF 1876.

The political field in 1876 was again considerably cut up by differing parties. The American National Platform was adopted as early as June, 1875, on the 9th of which month its framers met in mass convention in Pittsburg. On May 17, 1876, the Prohibition Reform Party met in convention in Cleveland, Ohio; and on the same day the Independent Party (Greenback) met in Indianapolis, Ind. Each party adopted a platform embodying its views. The Republican national convention assembled in Cincinnati, June 14, and the Democratic national convention met in St. Louis the 28th of the same month. The customary platform was adopted at each convention.

American National Platform.

We hold:

1. That ours is a Christian and not a heathen Nation, and that the God of the Christian Scriptures is the author of civil government.
2. That God requires and man needs a Sabbath.
3. That the prohibition of the importation, manufacture, and sale of intoxicating drinks as a beverage, is the true policy on the temperance question.
4. That charters of all secret lodges granted by our Federal and State legislatures should be withdrawn, and their oaths prohibited by law.
5. That the civil equality secured to all American citizens by articles 13th, 14th and 15th of our

amended Constitution should be preserved inviolate.

6. That arbitration of differences with nations is the most direct and sure method of securing and perpetuating a permanent peace.
7. That to cultivate the intellect without improving the morals of men is to make mere adepts and experts; therefore, the Bible should be associated with books of science and literature in all our educational institutions.
8. That land and other monopolies should be discountenanced.
9. That the Government should furnish the people with an ample and sound currency and a return to specie payment as soon as practicable.
10. The maintenance of the public credit, protection to all loyal citizens and justice to Indians, are essential to the honor and safety of our Nation.
11. And, finally, we demand for the American people the abolition of electoral colleges, and a direct vote for President and Vice-President of the United States.

Prohibition Reform Platform.

The Prohibition Reform party of the United States, organized in the name of the people, to revive, enforce and perpetuate in the Government the doctrines of the Declaration of Independence, submit, in this centennial year of the Republic, for the suffrages of all good citizens, the following platform of national reforms and measures:

1. The legal prohibition in the District of Columbia, the Territories, and in every other place subject to the laws of Congress, of the importation, exportation, manufacture, and traffic of all alcoholic beverages, as high crime against society; an amendment of the National Constitution, to render these prohibitory measures universal and permanent; and the adoption of treaty stipulations with foreign powers, to prevent the importation and exportation of all alcoholic beverages.
2. The abolition of class legislation, and of special privileges in the Government, and the adoption of equal suffrage and eligibility to office, without distinction of race, religious creed, property or sex.
3. The appropriation of the public lands, in limited quantities, to actual settlers only; the reduction of the rates of inland and ocean postage; of telegraph communication; of railroad and water transportation and travel, to the lowest practical point, by force of laws, wisely and justly framed, with reference, not only to the interest of capital employed, but to the higher claims of the general good.
4. The suppression by laws of lotteries and gambling in gold, stocks, produce, and every form of money and property, and the penal

inhibition of the use of the public mails for advertising schemes of gambling and lotteries.

5. The abolition of those foul enormities, polygamy and the social evil; and the protection of purity, peace and happiness of homes, by ample and efficient legislation.

6. The national observance of the Christian Sabbath, established by laws prohibiting ordinary labor and business in all departments of public service and private employment (works of necessity, charity and religion excepted) on that day.

7. The establishment, by mandatory provisions in national and State constitutions, and by all necessary legislation, of a system of free public schools for the universal and forced education of all the youth of the land.

8. The free use of the Bible, not as a ground of religious creeds, but as a text-book of the purest morality, the best liberty, and the noblest literature, in our public schools, that our children may grow up in its light, and that its spirit and principles may pervade our Nation.

9. The separation of the Government in all its departments and institutions, including the public schools and all funds for their maintenance, from the control of every religious sect or other association, and the protection alike of all sects by equal laws, with entire freedom of religious faith and worship.

10. The introduction into all treaties hereafter negotiated with foreign governments of a provision for the amicable settlement of international difficulties by arbitration.

11. The abolition of all barbarous modes and instruments of punishment; the recognition of the laws of God and the claims of humanity in the discipline of jails and prisons, and of that higher and wiser civilization worthy of our age and Nation, which regards the reform of criminals as a means for the prevention of crime.

12. The abolition of executive and legislative patronage, and the election of President, Vice-President, United States Senators, and of all civil officers, so far as practicable, by the direct vote of the people.

13. The practice of a friendly and liberal policy to immigrants from all nations, the guarantee to them of ample protection, and of equal rights and privileges.

14. The separation of the money of the Government from all banking institutions. The National Government only should exercise the high prerogative of issuing paper money, and that should be subject to prompt redemption on demand, in gold and silver, the only equal standards of value recognized by the civilized world.

15. The reduction of the salaries of public officers in a just ratio with the decline of wages and market prices; the abolition of sinecures, unnecessary offices, and official fees and perquisites; the practice of strict economy in Government expenses, and a free and thorough investigation into any and all alleged abuses of public trusts.

Independent Platform (Greenback).

The Independent party is called into existence by the necessities of the people whose industries are prostrated, whose labor is deprived of its just reward by a ruinous policy which the Republican and Democratic parties refuse to change; and, in view of the failure of these parties to furnish relief to the depressed industries of the country, thereby disappointing the just hopes and expectations of a suffering people, we declare our principles, and invite all independent and patriotic men to join our ranks in this movement for financial reform and industrial emancipation.

1. We demand the immediate and unconditional repeal of the specie resumption act of January 14, 1875, and the rescue of our industries from ruin and disaster resulting from its enforcement; and we call upon all patriotic men to organize in every Congressional district of the country, with a view of electing representatives to Congress who will carry out the wishes of the people in this regard and stop the present suicidal and destructive policy of contraction.

2. We believe that a United States note, issued directly by the Government, and convertible, on demand, into United States obligations, bearing a rate of interest not exceeding one cent a day on each one hundred dollars and exchangeable for United States notes at par, will afford the best circulating medium ever devised. Such United States notes should be full legal tenders for all purposes, except for the payment of such obligations as are, by existing contracts, especially made payable in coin; and we hold that it is the duty of the Government to provide such a circulating medium, and insist, in the language of Thomas Jefferson, that "bank paper must be suppressed, and the circulation restored to the Nation, to whom it belongs."

3. It is the paramount duty of the Government, in all its legislation, to keep in view the full development of all legitimate business, agricultural, mining, manufacturing and commercial.

4. We most earnestly protest against any further issue of gold bonds for sale in foreign markets, by which we would be made, for a long period, "hewers of wood and drawers of water" to foreigners, especially as the American people would gladly and promptly take at par all bonds the Government may need to sell, provided they are made payable at the option of the holder, and bearing interest at 3.65 per cent. per annum, or even a lower rate.

5. We further protest against the sale of Government bonds for the purpose of purchasing silver to be used as a substitute for our more convenient and less fluctuating fractional currency, which, although well calculated to enrich owners of silver mines, yet in operation it will still further oppress, in taxation, an already overburdened people.

Republican Platform.

When, in the economy of Providence, this land was to be purged of human slavery, and when the strength of the Government of the people, by the people and for the people, was to be demonstrated, the Republican party came into power. Its deeds have passed into history, and we look back to them with pride. Incited by their memories to high aims for the good of our country and mankind, and looking to the future with unfaltering courage, hope and purpose, we, the representatives of the party, in national convention assembled, make the following declaration of principles:

1. The United States of America is a nation, not a league. By the combined workings of the National and State Governments, under their respective constitutions, the rights of every citizen are secured at home and abroad and the common welfare promoted.

2. The Republican party has preserved these governments to the hundredth anniversary of the Nation's birth, and they are now embodiments of the great truths spoken at its cradle—"That all men are created equal; that they are endowed by their Creator with certain inalienable rights, among which are life, liberty and the pursuit of happiness; that for the attainment of these ends governments have been instituted among men, deriving their just powers from the consent of the governed." Until these truths are cheerfully obeyed, or, if need be, vigorously enforced, the work of the Republican party is unfinished.

3. The permanent pacification of the Southern section of the Union and the complete protection of all its citizens in the free enjoyment of all their rights is a duty to which the Republican party stands sacredly pledged. The power to provide for the enforcement of the principles embodied in the recent Constitutional amendments is vested, by those amendments, in the Congress of the United States; and we declare it to be the solemn obligation of the legislative and executive departments of the Government to put into immediate and vigorous exercise all their Constitutional powers for removing any just causes of discontent on the part of any class, and for securing to every American citizen complete liberty and exact equality in the exercise of all civil, political and public rights. To this end we imperatively demand a Congress and a Chief Executive whose courage and fidelity to these duties shall not falter until these results are placed beyond dispute or recall.

4. In the first act of Congress signed by President Grant the National Government assumed to remove any doubt of its purpose to discharge all just obligations to the public creditors and "solemnly pledged its faith to make provision at the earliest practicable period for the redemption of the United States notes in coin." Commercial prosperity, public morals and national credit demand that this promise be fulfilled by a continuous and steady progress to specie payment.

5. Under the Constitution the President and heads of departments are to make nominations for office, the Senate is to advise and consent to appointments and the House of Representatives is to accuse and prosecute faithless officers. The best interest of the public service demand that these distinctions be respected; that Senators and Representatives who may be judges and accusers should not dictate appointments to office. The invariable rule in appointment should have reference to the honesty, fidelity and capacity of the appointees, giving to the party in power those places when harmony and vigor of administration require its policy to be represented, but permitting all others to be filled by persons selected with sole reference to the efficiency of the public service and the right of all citizens to share in the honor of rendering faithful service to the country.

6. We rejoice in the quickened conscience of the people concerning political affairs, and will hold all public officers to a rigid responsibility, and engage that the prosecution and punishment of all who betray official trusts shall be swift, thorough and unsparing.

7. The public school system of the several States is the bulwark of the American Republic, and with a view to its security and permanence we recommend an amendment to the Constitution of the United States, forbidding the application of any public funds or property for the benefit of any schools or institutions under sectarian control.

8. The revenue necessary for current expenditures and the obligations of the public debt must be largely derived from duties upon importations, which, so far as possible, should be adjusted to promote the interests of American labor and advance the prosperity of the whole country.

9. We reaffirm our opposition to further grants of the public lands to corporations and monopolies, and demand that the national demain be devoted to free homes for the people.

10. It is the imperative duty of the Government so to modify existing treaties with European governments, that the same protection

shall be afforded to the adopted American citizen that is given to the native-born; and that all necessary laws should be passed to protect emigrants, in the absence of power in the States, for that purpose.

11. It is the immediate duty of Congress to fully investigate the effect of the immigration and importation of Mongolians upon the moral and material interest of the country.

12. The Republican party recognizes with approval the substantial advances recently made toward the establishment of equal rights for women by the many important amendments effected by Republican legislatures in the laws which concern the personal and property relations of wives, mothers, and widows, and by the appointment and election of women to the superintendence of education, charities and other public trusts. The honest demands of this class of citizens for additional rights, privileges, and immunities, should be treated with respectful consideration.

13. The Constitution confers upon Congress sovereign powers over the Territories of the United States for their Government; and in the exercise of this power it is the right and duty of Congress to prohibit and extirpate, in the Territories, that relic of barbarism—polygamy; and we demand such legislation as shall secure this end and the supremacy of American institutions in all the Territories.

14. The pledges which the Nation has given to her soldiers and sailors must be fulfilled, and a grateful people will always hold those who imperiled their lives for the country's preservation in the kindest remembrance.

15. We sincerely deprecate all sectional feeling and tendencies. We, therefore, note with deep solicitude that the Democratic party counts, as its chief hope of success, upon the electoral vote of a united South, secured through the efforts of those who were recently arrayed against the Nation; and we invoke the earnest attention of the country to the grave truth that a success thus achieved would reopen sectional strife and imperil national honor and human rights.

16. We charge the Democratic party with being the same in character and spirit as when it sympathized with treason; with making its control of the House of Representatives the triumph and opportunity of the Nation's recent foes; with reasserting and applauding in the National Capitol, the sentiments of irrepentant rebellion; with sending Union soldiers to the rear, and promoting Confederate soldiers to the front; with deliberately proposing to repudiate the plighted faith of the Government; with being equally false and imbecile upon the overshadowing financial questions; with thwarting the ends of justice by its partisan mismanagement and obstruction of investigation; with proving itself through the period of its ascendancy in the lower house of Congress utterly incompetent to administer the Government; and we warn the country against trusting a party thus alike unworthy, recreant and incapable.

17. The national administration merits commendation for its honorable work in the management of domestic and foreign affairs, and President Grant deserves the continued hearty gratitude of the American people for his patriotism and his eminent services in war and in peace.

18. We present, as our candidates for President and Vice-President of the United States, two distinguished statesmen of eminent ability and character, and conspicuously fitted for those high offices, and we confidently appeal to the American people to entrust the administration of their public affairs to Rutherford B. Hayes and William A. Wheeler.

Democratic Platform.

We, the delegates of the Democratic party of the United States, in national convention assembled, do hereby declare the administration of the Federal Government to be in urgent need of immediate reform; do hereby enjoin upon the nominees of this convention and of the Democratic party in each State, a zealous effort and co-operation to this end; and do hereby appeal to our fellow-citizens of every former political connection to undertake, with us, this first and most pressing patriotic duty.

For the Democracy of the whole country we do here reaffirm our faith in the permanence of the Federal Union, our devotion to the Constitution of the United States, with its amendments, universally accepted as a final settlement of the controversies that engineered civil war, and do here record our steadfast confidence in the perpetuity of republican self-government.

In absolute acquiescence in the will of a majority—the vital principle of republics; in the supremacy of the civil over the military authority; in the total separation of church and State, for the sake alike of civil and religious freedom; in the equality of all citizens before just laws of their own enactment; in the liberty of individual conduct, unvexed by sumptuary laws; in the faithful education of the rising generation, that they may preserve, enjoy and transmit these best conditions of human happiness and hope—we behold the noblest products of a hundred years of changeful history; but while upholding the bond of our Union and great charter of these our rights, it behooves a free people to practice also that eternal vigilance which is the price of liberty.

Reform is necessary to rebuild and establish in the hearts of the whole people the Union, eleven years ago happily rescued from the danger of a secession of States, but now to be saved from a corrupt centralism which, after inflicting upon ten States the rapacity of carpet-bag tyranny, has honeycombed the offices of the Federal Government itself with incapacity, waste and fraud; infected States and municipalities with the contagion of misrule, and locked fast the prosperity of an industrious people in the paralysis of "hard times."

Reform is necessary to establish a sound currency, restore the public credit, and maintain the national honor.

We denounce the failure, for all these eleven years of peace, to make good the promise of the legal tender notes, which are a changing standard of value in the hands of the people, and the non-payment of which is a disregard of the plighted faith of the Nation.

We denounce the improvidence which, in eleven years of peace, has taken from the people, in federal taxes, thirteen times the whole amount of the legal-tender notes, and squandered four times their sum in useless expense without accumulating any reserve for their redemption.

We denounce the financial imbecility and immorality of that party which, during eleven years of peace, has made no advance toward resumption, no preparation for resumption, but, instead, has obstructed resumption by wasting our resources and exhausting all our surplus income; and, while annually professing to intend a speedy return to specie payments, has annually enacted fresh hindrances thereto. As such hindrance we denounce the resumption clause of 1875, and we here demand its repeal.

We demand a judicious system of preparation, by public economies, by official retrenchments, and by wise finance, which shall enable the Nation soon to assure the whole world of its perfect ability and of its perfect readiness to meet any of its promises at the call of the creditor entitled to payment. We believe such a system, well devised and, above all, entrusted to competent hands for execution, creating at no time an artificial scarcity of currency, and at no time alarming the public mind into a withdrawal of that vaster machinery of credit by which 95 per cent. of all business transactions are performed; a system open, public, and inspiring general confidence, would, from the day of its adoption, bring healing on its wings to all war harassed industries—set in motion the wheels of commerce, manufactures, and the mechanic arts—restore employment to labor—and renew, in all its natural sources, the prosperity of the people.

Reform is necessary in the sense and modes of Federal taxation, to the end that capital may be set free from distrust and labor lightly burdened.

We denounce the present tariff, levied upon nearly four thousand articles, as a masterpiece of injustice, inequality and false pretense. It yields a dwindling, not a yearly rising, revenue. It has impoverished many industries, to subsidize a few. It prohibits imports that might purchase products of American labor. It has degraded American commerce from the first to an inferior rank on the high seas. It has cut down the sales of American manufactures at home and abroad, and depleted the returns of American agriculture—an industry followed by half our people. It costs the people five times more than it produces to the Treasury, obstructs the processes of production, and wastes the fruits of labor. It promotes fraud, fosters smuggling, enriches dishonest officials, and bankrupts honest merchants. We demand that all custom-house taxation shall be only for revenue.

Reform is necessary in the scale of public expense—Federal, State and municipal. Our Federal taxation has swollen from sixty millions gold, in 1860, to four hundred and fifty millions currency, in 1870; our aggregate taxation from one hundred and fifty-four millions gold, in 1860, to seven hundred and thirty millions currency, in 1870—or, in one decade, from less than five dollars per head to more than eighteen dollars per head. Since the peace, the people have paid to their tax-gatherers more than thrice the sum of the national debt, and more than twice that sum for the Federal Government alone. We demand a vigorous frugality in every department and from every officer of the Government.

Reform is necessary to put a stop to the profligate waste of public lands, and their diversion from actual settlers, by the party in power, which has squandered 200,000,000 of acres upon railroads alone, and, out of more than thrice that aggregate, has disposed of less than a sixth directly to tillers of the soil.

Reform is necessary to correct the omission of a Republican Congress, and the errors of our treaties and our diplomacy which have stripped our fellow-citizens of foreign birth and kindred race, recrossing the Atlantic, of the shield of American citizenship, and have exposed our brethren of the Pacific coast to the incursions of a race not sprung from the same great parent stock, and in fact now, by law, denied citizenship through naturalization, as being neither accustomed to the traditions of a progressive civilization nor exercised in liberty under equal laws. We denounce the policy which thus discards the liberty-loving German and tolerates a revival of the coolie trade in Mongolian women, imported for immoral purposes, and Mongolian men, held to perform servile labor contracts, and demand such modification of the treaty with the Chinese Empire, or such legislation within Constitutional limitations, as shall prevent further importation or immigration of the Mongolian race.

Reform is necessary and can never be effected but by making it the controlling issue of the elections and lifting it above the two false issues with which the office-holding class and the party in power seek to smother it.

1. The false issue with which they would enkindle sectarian strife in respect to the public schools, of which the establishment and support belong exclusively to the several States and which the Democratic party has cherished from their foundation, and is resolved to maintain without prejudice or preference for any class, sect or creed and without largesses from the Treasury to any.

2. The false issue by which they seek to light anew the dying embers of sectional hate between kindred peoples once estranged, but now united in one indivisible Republic and a common destiny.

Reform is necessary in the civil service. Experience proves that efficient, economical conduct of the governmental business is not possible if its civil service be subject to change at every election, be a prize fought for at the ballot-box, be a brief reward of party zeal, instead of posts of honor assigned for proved competency and held for fidelity in the public employ; that the dispensing of patronage should neither be a tax upon the time of all our public men nor the instrument of their ambition. Here again promises, falsified in the performance, attest that the party in power can work out no practical or salutary reform.

Reform is necessary even more in the higher grades of the public service, President, Vice-President, judges, Senators, Representatives, Cabinet officers—these and all others in authority—are the people's servants. Their offices are not a private perquisite; they are a public trust. When the annals of this Republic show the disgrace and censure of a Vice-President; a late Speaker of the House of Representatives marketing his rulings as a presiding officer; three Senators profiting secretly by their votes as lawmakers; five chairmen of the leading committees of the late House of Representatives exposed in jobbery; a late Secretary of the Treasury forcing balances in the public accounts; a late Attorney General misappropriating public funds; a Secretary of the Navy enriched or enriching friends by percentages levied off the profits of contractors with his department; an ambassador to England concerned in a dishonorable speculation; the President's private secretary barely escaping conviction upon trial for guilty complicity in frauds upon the revenue; the Secretary of War impeached for high crimes and misdemeanors—the demonstration is complete, that the first step in reform must be the people's choice of honest men from another party, lest the disease of one political organization infect the body politic,

and lest by making no change of men or parties we get no change of measures and no real reform.

All these abuses, wrongs and crimes—the product of sixteen years' ascendency of the Republican party—create a necessity for reform, confessed by the Republicans themselves; but their reformers are voted down in convention and displaced from the Cabinet. The party's mass of honest voters is powerless to resist the 80,000 office-holders, its leaders and guides.

Reform can only be had by a peaceful civic revolution. We demand a change of system, a change of administration, a change of parties that we may have a change of measures and of men.

Resolved, That this convention, representing the Democratic party of the United States, do cordially endorse the action of the present House of Representatives in reducing and curtailing the expenses of the Federal Government in cutting down salaries and extravagant appropriations and in abolishing useless offices and places not required by the public necessities; and we shall trust to the firmness of the Democratic members of the House that no committee of conference and no misinterpretation of the rules will be allowed to defeat these wholesome measures of economy demanded by the country.

Resolved, That the soldiers and sailors of the Republic and the widows and orphans of those who have fallen in battle have a just claim upon the care, protection and gratitude of their fellow-citizens.

PLATFORMS OF 1880.

The first convention preparatory to the campaign of 1880 was that held by the National party at Toledo, Ohio, February 22, 1878. Other National party conventions were held as follows: National Liberal, at Cincinnati, Ohio, September 14, 1879; Republican, at Chicago, Ill., June 2, 1880; National (Greenback), at Chicago, Ill., June 9, 1880; Prohibition, at Cleveland, Ohio, June 17, 1880; Democratic, at Cincinnati, Ohio, June 22, 1880. The so-called Independent Republicans also presented a declaration of principles in this campaign.

National Platform.

WHEREAS, Throughout our entire country the value of real estate is depreciated, industry paralyzed, trade depressed, business incomes and wages reduced, unparalleled distress inflicted upon the poorer and middle ranks of our people, the land filled with fraud, embezzlement, bankruptcy, crime, suffering, pauperism and starvation; and,

WHEREAS, This state of things has been brought about by legislation in the interest of, and dictated by, money-lenders, bankers and bond-holders; and,

WHEREAS, While we recognize the fact that the men in Congress connected with the old political parties have stood up manfully for the rights of the people, and met the threats of the money power, and the ridicule of an ignorant and subsidized press, yet neither the Republican nor the Democratic parties, in their policies, propose remedies for the existing evils; and,

WHEREAS, The Independent Greenback party and other associations more or less effective, have been unable hitherto to make a formidable opposition to old party organizations; and,

WHEREAS, The limiting of the legal tender quality of the greenbacks, the changing of currency bonds into coin bonds, the demonetization of the silver dollar, the exempting of bonds from taxation, the contraction of the circulating medium, the proposed forced resumption of specie payments, and the prodigal waste of the public lands, were crimes against the people; and, as far as possible, the results of these criminal acts must be counteracted by judicious legislation:

Therefore, We assemble in national convention and make a declaration of our principles, and invite all patriotic citizens to unite in an effort to secure financial reform and industrial emancipation. The organization shall be known as the "National Party," and under this name we will perfect, without delay, national, State and local associations, to secure the election to office of such men only as will pledge themselves to do all in their power to establish these principles:

1. It is the exclusive function of the General Government to coin and create money and regulate its value. All bank issues designed to circulate as money should be suppressed. The circulating medium, whether of metal or paper, shall be issued by the Government, and made a full legal tender for all debts, duties and taxes in the United States, at its stamped value.

2. There shall be no privileged class of creditors. Official salaries, pensions, bonds, and all other debts and obligations, public and private, shall be discharged in the legal tender money of the United States strictly according to the stipulations of the laws under which they were contracted.

3. The coinage of silver shall be placed on the same footing as that of gold.

4. Congress shall provide said money adequate to the full employment of labor, the equitable distribution of its products, and the requirement of business, fixing a minimum amount per capita of the population as near as may be, and otherwise regulating its value by wise and equitable provisions of law, so that the rate of interest will secure to labor its just reward.

5. It is inconsistent with the genius of popular government that any species of private property should be exempt from bearing its proper share of the public burdens. Government bonds and money should be taxed precisely as other property, and a graduated income tax should be levied for the support of the Government and the payment of its debts.

6. Public lands are the common property of the whole people, and should not be sold to speculators nor granted to railroads or other corporations, but should be donated to actual settlers in limited quantities.

7. The Government should by general enactments, encourage the development of our agricultural, mineral, mechanical, manufacturing, and commercial resources, to the end that labor may be fully and profitably employed; but no monopolies should be legalized.

8. All useless offices should be abolished, the most rigid economy favored in every branch of the public service, and severe punishment inflicted upon public officers who betray the trusts reposed in them.

9. As educated labor has devised means for multiplying productions by inventions and discoveries, and as their use requires the exercise of mind as well as body, such legislation should be had that the number of hours of daily toil will be reduced, giving to the working classes more leisure for mental improvement and their several enjoyments, and saving them from premature decay and death.

10. The adoption of an American monetary system, as proposed herein, will harmonize all differences in regard to tariff and federal taxation, reduce and equalize the cost of transportation by land and water, distribute equitably the joint earnings of capital and labor, secure to the producers of wealth the results of their labor and skill, and muster out of service the vast army of idlers, who, under the existing system, grow rich upon the earnings of others, that every man and woman may, by their own efforts, secure a competency, so that overgrown fortunes and extreme poverty will be seldom found within the limits of our Republic.

11. Both national and State governments should establish bureaus of labor and industrial statistics, clothed with the power of gathering and publishing the same.

12. The contract system of employing labor in our prisons and reformatory institutions works great injustice to our mechanics and artisans, and should be prohibited.

13. The importation of servile labor into the United States from China is a problem of the

most serious importance, and we recommend legislation looking to its suppression.

We believe in the supremacy of law over and above all perishable material, and in the necessity of a party of united people that will rise above old party lines and prejudices. We will not affiliate in any degree with any of the old parties, but, in all cases and localities, will organize anew, as united National men—nominate for office and official positions only such persons as are clearly believers in and identified with this our sacred cause; and, irrespective of creed, color, place of birth, or past condition of political or other servitude, vote only for men who entirely abandon old party lines and organizations.

National Liberal Platform.

1. Total separation of Church and State, to be guaranteed by amendment of the United States Constitution; including the equitable taxation of church property, secularization of the public schools, abrogation of Sabbatarian laws, abolition of chaplaincies, prohibition of public appropriations for religious purposes, and all measures necessary to the same general end.

2. National protection for national citizens in their equal civil, political and religious rights, to be guaranteed by amendment of the United States Constitution and afforded through the United States courts.

3. Universal education, the basis of universal suffrage in this secular Republic, to be guaranteed by amendment of the United States Constitution, requiring every State to maintain a thoroughly secularized public school system, and to permit no child within its limits to grow up without a good elementary education.

Independent Republican Principles.

I. Independent Republicans adhere to the Republican principles of national supremacy, sound finances, and civil service reform, expressed in the Republican platform of 1876, in the letter of acceptance of President Hayes, and in his message of 1879; and they seek the realization of those principles in practical laws and their efficient administration. This requires,

1. The continuance on the statute book of laws protecting the rights of voters at national elections. But national supremacy affords no pretext for interference with the local rights of communities; and the development of the South from its present defective civilization can be secured only under Constitutional methods, such as those of President Hayes.

2. The passage of laws which shall deprive greenbacks of their legal tender quality, as a first step toward their ultimate withdrawal and cancellation, and shall maintain all coins made legal tender at such weight and fineness as will enable them to be used without discount in the commercial transactions of the world.

3. The repeal of the acts which limit the terms of office of certain government officials to four years; the repeal of the tenure-of-office acts, which limit the power of the executive to remove for cause; the establishment of a permanent civil service commission, or equivalent measures, to ascertain, by open competition, and certify to the President, or other appointing power, the fitness of applicants for nomination or appointment to all non-political offices.

II. Independent Republicans believe that local issues should be independent of party. The words Republican and Democrat should have no weight in determining whether a school or city shall be administered on business principles by capable men. With a view to this, legislation is asked which shall prescribe for the voting for local and for State officers upon separate ballots.

III. Independent Republicans assert that a political party is a co-operation of voters to secure the practical enactment into legislation of political convictions set forth as its platform. Every voter accepting that platform is a member of that party; any representative of that party opposing the principles or evading the promises of its platform forfeits the support of its voters. No voter should be held by the action or nomination of any caucus or convention of his party against his private judgment. It is his duty to vote against bad measures and unfit men, as the only means of obtaining good ones; and if his party no longer represents its professed principles in its practical workings, it is his duty to vote against it.

IV. Independent Republicans seek good nominations through participation in the primaries and through the defeat of bad nominees; they will labor for the defeat of any local Republican candidate, and, in co-operation with those holding like views elsewhere, for the defeat of any general Republican candidate whom they do not deem fit.

Republican Platform.

The Republican party, in national convention assembled, at the end of twenty years since the Federal Government was first committed to its charge, submits to the people of the United States its brief report of its administration.

It suppressed a rebellion which had armed nearly a million of men to subvert the national authority. It reconstructed the Union of the States with freedom instead of slavery, as its cornerstone. It transformed four millions of human beings from the likeness of things to the rank of citizens. It relieved Congress from the infamous work of hunting fugitive slaves, and charged it to see that slavery does not exist.

It has raised the value of our paper currency from thirty-eight per cent. to the par of gold. It has restored upon a solid basis payment in coin for all the national obligations, and has given us a currency absolutely good and equal in every part of our extended country. It has lifted the credit of the Nation from the point where six per cent. bonds sold at eighty-six to that where four per cent. bonds are eagerly sought at a premium.

Under its administration railways have increased from 31,000 miles in 1860 to more than 82,000 miles in 1870.

Our foreign trade has increased from $700,-000,000 to $1,150,000,000 in the same time; and our exports, which were $20,000,000 less than our imports in 1860, were $264,000,000 more than our imports in 1870.

Without resorting to loans, it has, since the war closed, defrayed the ordinary expenses of government, besides the accruing interest on the public debt, and disbursed annually over $30,-000,000 for soldiers' pensions. It has paid $888,-000,000 of the public debt, and by refunding the balance at lower rates has reduced the annual interest charge from nearly $151,000,000 to less than $89,000,000.

All the industries of the country have revived, labor is in demand, wages have increased, and throughout the entire country there is evidence of a coming prosperity greater than we have ever enjoyed.

Upon this record the Republican party asks for the continued confidence and support of the people; and this convention submits for their approval the following statement of the principles and purposes which will continue to guide and inspire its efforts:

1. We affirm that the work of the last twenty years has been such as to commend itself to the favor of the Nation, and that the fruits of the costly victories which we have achieved through immense difficulties should be preserved; that the peace regained should be cherished; that the dissevered Union, now happily restored, should be perpetuated, and that the liberties secured to this generation should be transmitted undiminished to future generations; that the order established and the credit acquired should never be impaired; that the pensions promised should be paid; that the debt so much reduced should be extinguished by the full payment of every dollar thereof; that the reviving industries should be further promoted, and that the commerce, already so great, should be steadily encouraged.

2. The Constitution of the United States is a supreme law, and not a mere contract; out of confederate States it made a sovereign Nation. Some powers are denied to the Nation, while others are denied to States; but the boundary between the powers delegated and those reserved is to be determined by national and not by the State tribunals.

3. The work of popular education is one left to the care of the several States, but it is the duty of the National Government to aid that work to the extent of its Constitutional ability. The intelligence of the Nation is but the aggregate of the intelligence in the several States, and the destiny of the Nation must be guided, not by the genius of any one State, but by the average genius of all.

4. The Constitution wisely forbids Congress to make any law respecting an establishment of religion, but it is idle to hope that the Nation can be protected against the influences of sectarianism while each State is exposed to its domination. We, therefore, recommend that the Constitution be so amended as to lay the same prohibition upon the Legislature of each State, to forbid the appropriation of public funds to the support of sectarian schools.

5. We reaffirm the belief avowed in 1876 that the duties levied for the purpose of revenue should so discriminate as to favor American labor; that no further grant of the public domain should be made to any railway or other corporation; that slavery having perished in the States, its twin barbarity—polygamy—must die in the Territories; that everywhere the protection accorded to citizens of American birth must be secured to citizens by American adoption; that we esteem it the duty of Congress to develop and improve our water-courses and harbors, but insist that further subsidies to private persons or corporations must cease; that the obligations of the Republic to the men who preserved its integrity in the day of battle are undiminished by the lapse of fifteen years since their final victory —to do them perpetual honor is and shall forever be the grateful privilege and sacred duty of the American people.

6. Since the authority to regulate immigration and intercourse between the United States and foreign nations rests with the Congress of the United States and its treaty-making powers, the Republican party, regarding the unrestricted immigration of the Chinese as an evil of great magnitude, invoke the exercise of that power to restrain and limit that immigration by the enactment of such just, humane and reasonable provisions as will produce that result.

7. That the purity and patriotism which characterized the early career of Rutherford B. Hayes in peace and war, and which guided the thoughts of our immediate predecessors to select him for a Presidential candidate, have continued to inspire him in his career as chief executive, and that history will accord to his administration the honors which are due to an efficient, just and courteous discharge of the public business, and

will honor his interposition between the people and proposed partisan laws.

8. We charge upon the Democratic party the habitual sacrifice of patriotism and justice to a supreme and insatiable lust for office and patronage. That to obtain possession of the national and State governments, and the control of place and positions, they have obstructed all efforts to promote the purity and to conserve the freedom of suffrage; have devised fraudulent certifications and returns; have labored to unseat lawfully elected members of Congress to secure, at all hazards, the vote of a majority of the States in the House of Representatives; have endeavored to occupy by force and fraud the places of trust given to others by the people of Maine, and rescued by the courageous action of Maine's patriotic sons; have, by methods vicious in principle and tyrannical in practice, attached partisan legislation to appropriation bills, upon whose passage the very movements of government depend; have crushed the rights of the individual; have advocated the principle and sought the favor of rebellion against the Nation, and have endeavored to obliterate the sacred memories of the war, and to overcome its inestimably valuable results of nationality, personal freedom and individual equality. Equal, steady and complete enforcement of the laws and protection of all our citizens in the enjoyment of all privileges and immunities guaranteed by the Constitution, are the first duties of the Nation. The danger of a solid South can only be averted by a faithful performance of every promise which the Nation made to the citizen. The execution of the laws, and the punishment of all those who violate them, are the only safe methods by which an enduring peace can be secured, and genuine prosperity established throughout the South. Whatever promises the Nation makes, the Nation must perform; and the Nation cannot with safety relegate this duty to the States. The solid South must be divided by the peaceful agencies of the ballot, and all opinions must there find free expression; and to this end honest voters must be protected against terrorism, violence or fraud. And we affirm it to be the duty and the purpose of the Republican party to use all legitimate means to restore all the States of this Union to the most perfect harmony which may be practicable; and we submit to the practical, sensible people of the United States to say whether it would not be dangerous to the dearest interests of our country, at this time, to surrender the administration of the national Government to a party which seeks to overthrow the existing policy, under which we are so prosperous, and thus bring distrust and confusion where there is now order, confidence and hope.

9. The Republican party, adhering to a principle affirmed by its last national convention, of respect for the Constitutional rule covering appointments to office, adopts the declaration of President Hayes, that the reform of the civil service should be thorough, radical and complete. To this end it demands the co-operation of the legislative with the executive department of the Government, and that Congress shall so legislate that fitness, ascertained by proper practical tests, shall admit to the public service; and that the power of removal for cause, with due responsibility for the good conduct of subordinates, shall accompany the power of appointment.

National Platform (Greenback).

The civil Government should guarantee the divine right of every laborer to the results of his toil, thus enabling the producers of wealth to provide themselves with the means for physical comfort, and facilities for mental, social and moral culture; and we condemn, as unworthy of our civilization, the barbarism which imposes upon wealth-producers a state of drudgery as the price of a bare animal existence. Notwithstanding the enormous increase of productive power by the universal introduction of labor-saving machinery and the discovery of new agents for the increase of wealth, the task of the laborer is scarcely lightened, the hours of toil are but little shortened, and few producers are lifted from poverty into comfort and pecuniary independence. The associated monopolies, the international syndicates, and other income classes demand dear money, cheap labor, and a strong government, and, hence a weak people. Corporate control of the volume of money has been the means of dividing society into hostile classes of an unjust distribution of the products of labor, and of building up monopolies of associated capital endowed with power to confiscate private property. It has kept money scarce; and the scarcity of money enforces debt trade, and public and corporate loans; debt engenders usury, and usury ends in the bankruptcy of the borrower. Other results are deranged markets, uncertainty in manufacturing enterprises and agriculture, precarious and intermittent employment for the laborer, industrial war, increasing pauperism and crime, and the consequent intimidation and disfranchisement of the producer, and a rapid declension into corporate feudalism. Therefore, we declare,

1. That the right to make and issue money is a sovereign power, to be maintained by the people for their common benefit. The delegation of this right to corporations is a surrender of the central attribute of sovereignty, void of Constitutional sanction and conferring upon a subordinate and irresponsible power an absolute dominion over industry and commerce. All money, whether metallic or paper, should be issued and its volume controlled by the Govern-

ment and not by or through banking corporations, and when so issued should be a full legal tender for all debts, public and private.

2. That the bonds of the United States should not be refunded, but paid as rapidly as practicable, according to contract. To enable the Government to meet these obligations legal tender currency should be substituted for the notes of the national banks, the national banking system abolished and the unlimited coinage of silver, as well as gold, established by law.

3. That labor should be so protected by national and State authority as to equalize its burdens and insure a just distribution of the results. The eight hour law of Congress should be enforced, the sanitary condition of industrial establishments placed under rigid control, the competition of contract convict labor abolished, a bureau of labor statistics established, factories, mines and workshops inspected, the employment of children under fourteen years of age forbidden, and wages paid in cash.

4. Slavery being simply cheap labor and cheap labor being simply slavery, the importation and presence of Chinese serfs necessarily tends to brutalize and degrade American labor; therefore immediate steps should be taken to abrogate the Burlingame treaty.

5. Railroad land grants forfeited by reason of non-fulfillment of contract should be immediately reclaimed by the Government, and henceforth the public domain reserved exclusively as homes for actual settlers.

6. It is the duty of Congress to regulate interstate commerce. All lines of communication and transportation should be brought under such legislative control as shall secure moderate, fair and uniform rates for passenger and freight traffic.

7. We denounce as destructive to property and dangerous to liberty the action of the old parties in fastening and sustaining gigantic land, railroad and money corporations and monopolies invested with and exercising powers belonging to the Government and yet not responsible to it for the manner of their exercise.

8. That the Constitution in giving Congress the power to borrow money, to declare war, raise and support armies, to provide and maintain a navy never intended that the men who loaned their money for an interest consideration should be preferred to the soldiers and sailors who periled their lives and shed their blood on land and sea in defense of their country; and we condemn the cruel class legislation of the Republican party, which, while professing great gratitude to the soldier, has most unjustly discriminated against him and in favor of the bondholder.

9. All property should bear its just proportion of taxation and we demand a graduated income tax.

10. We denounce as dangerous the efforts everywhere manifested to restrict the right of suffrage.

11. We are opposed to an increase of the standing army in time of peace and the insidious scheme to establish an enormous military power under the guise of militia laws.

12. We demand absolute democratic rules for the government of Congress, placing all representatives of the people upon an equal footing and taking away from committees a veto power greater than that of the President.

13. We demand a government of the people, by the people and for the people instead of a government of the bondholder, by the bondholder and for the bondholder; and we denounce every attempt to stir up sectional strife as an effort to conceal monstrous crimes against the people.

14. In the furtherance of these ends we ask the co-operation of all fair-minded people. We have no quarrel with individuals, wage no war on classes, but only against vicious institutions. We are not content to endure further discipline from our present actual rulers, who, having dominion over money, over transportation, over land and labor, over the press and the machinery of government, wield unwarrantable power over our institutions and over life and property.

Prohibition Reform Platform.

The Prohibition Reform party of the United States, organized in the name of the people to revive, enforce and perpetuate in the Government the doctrines of the Declaration of Independence, submit for the suffrage of all good citizens the following platform of national reforms and measures:

In the examination and discussion of the temperance question it has been proven and it is an accepted truth that alcoholic drinks, whether fermented, brewed or distilled, are poisonous to the healthy human body, the drinking of which is not only needless but hurtful, necessarily tending to form intemperate habits, increasing greatly the number, severity and fatal termination of diseases, weakening and deranging the intellect, polluting the affections, hardening the heart and corrupting the morals, depriving many of reason and still more of its healthful exercise and annually bringing down large numbers to untimely graves, producing, in the children of many who drink, a predisposition to intemperance, insanity, and various bodily and mental diseases, causing diminution of strength, feebleness of vision, fickleness of purpose and premature old age, and inducing, in all future generations, deterioration of moral and physical character. Alcoholic drinks are thus the implacable foe of man as an individual.

1. The legalized importation, manufacture, and sale of intoxicating drinks ministers to their use, and teaches the erroneous and destructive sentiment that such use is right, thus tending to produce and perpetuate the above-mentioned evils.

2. To the home it is an enemy—proving itself to be a disturber and destroyer of its peace, prosperity and happiness; taking from it the earnings of the husband; depriving the dependent wife and children of essential food, clothing, and education; bringing into it profanity, abuse and violence; setting at naught the vows of the marriage altar; breaking up the family and sundering the children from the parents, and thus destroying one of the most beneficent institutions of our Creator, and removing the sure foundation of good government, national prosperity and welfare.

3. To the community it is equally an enemy—producing vice, demoralization and wickedness; its places of sale being resorts of gaming, lewdness and debauchery, and the hiding-place of those who prey upon society; counteracting the efficacy of religious effort, and of all means of intellectual elevation, moral purity, social happiness, and the eternal good of mankind, without rendering any counteracting or compensating benefits; being in its influence and effect evil and only evil, and that continually.

4. To the State it is equally an enemy—legislative inquiries, judicial investigations, and official reports of all penal, reformatory and dependent institutions showing that the manufacture and sale of such beverages is the promoting cause of intemperance, crime, and pauperism, and of demands upon public and private charity, imposing the larger part of taxation, paralyzing thrift, industry, manufactures and commercial life, which, but for it, would be unnecessary; disturbing the peace of streets and highways; filling prisons and poorhouses; corrupting politics, legislation, and the execution of the laws; shortening lives; diminishing health, industry and productive power of manufactures and art; and is manifestly unjust as well as injurious to the community upon which it is imposed, and is contrary to all just views of civil liberty, as well as a violation of the fundamental maxim of our common law, to use your own property or liberty so as to not injure others.

5. It is neither right nor politic for the State to afford legal protection to any traffic or any system which tends to waste the resources, to corrupt the social habits, and to destroy the health and lives of the people; that the importation, manufacture, and sale of intoxicating beverages is proven to be inimical to the true interests of the individual home, community and State, and destructive to the order and welfare of society, and ought, therefore, to be classed among crimes to be prohibited.

6. In this time of profound peace at home and abroad, the entire separation of the General Government from the drink-traffic, and its prohibition in the District of Columbia, Territories, and in all places and ways over which, under the Constitution, Congress has control and power, is a political issue of the first importance to the peace and prosperity of the Nation. There can be no stable peace and protection to personal liberty, life, or property, until secured by national or State Constitutional provisions, enforced by adequate laws.

7. All legitimate industries require deliverance from the taxation and loss which the liquor traffic imposes upon them; and financial and other legislation could not accomplish so much to increase production and cause a demand for labor, and, as a result, for the comforts of living, as the suppression of this traffic would bring to thousands of homes as one of its blessings.

8. The administration of the government and the execution of the laws are through political parties; and we arraign the Republican party, which has been in continuous power in the Nation for twenty years, as being false to duty, as false to loudly proclaimed principles of equal justice to all and special favors to none, and of protection to the weak and dependent, insensible to the mischief which the trade in liquor has constantly inflicted upon industry, trade, commerce, and the social happiness of the people; that 5,652 distilleries, 3,830 breweries and 175,266 places for the sale of these poisonous liquors, involving an annual waste of one million five hundred thousand dollars, and the sacrifice of one hundred thousand lives, have under its legislation grown up and been fostered as a legitimate source of revenue; that during its history, six Territories have been organized and five States been admitted to the Union, with constitutions provided and approved by Congress, but the prohibition of this debasing and destructive traffic has not been provided, nor even the people given at the time of admission, power to forbid it in any one of them. Its history further shows, that not in a single instance has an original prohibitory law been passed by any State that was controlled by it, while in four States, so governed, the laws found on its advent to power have been repealed. At its national convention in 1872, it declared, as part of its party faith, that "it disapproves of the resort to unconstitutional laws for the purpose of removing evils, by interference with rights not surrendered by the people to either the State or national Government," which, the author of this plank says, was adopted by the platform committee with the full and implicit understanding that its purpose was the discountenancing of all

so-called temperance, prohibitory and Sunday laws.

9. We arraign, also, the Democratic party as unfaithful and unworthy of reliance on this question; for, although not clothed with power, but occupying the relation of an opposition party during twenty years past, strong in numbers and organization, it has allied itself with liquor traffickers, and become, in all the States of the Union, their special political defenders, and in its national convention in 1876, as an article of its political faith, declared against prohibition and just laws in restraint of the trade in drink, by saying it was opposed to what it was pleased to call "all sumptuary laws." The National party has been dumb on this question.

10. Drink traffickers, having the history and experience of all ages, climes, and conditions of men, declaring their business destructive of all good—finding no support in the Bible, morals or reason—appeal to misapplied law for their justification, and intrench themselves behind the evil elements of political party for defense, party tactics and party inertia become battling forces, protecting this evil.

11. In view of the foregoing facts and history, we cordially invite all voters without regard to former party affiliations, to unite with us in the use of the ballot for the abolition of the drinking system, under the authority of our national and State governments. We also demand as a right, that women, having the privileges of citizens in other respects, be clothed with the ballot for their protection, and as a rightful means for the proper settlement of the liquor question.

12. To remove the apprehension of some who allege that a loss of public revenue would follow the suppression of the direct trade, we confidently point to the experience of governments abroad and at home, which shows that thrift and revenue from the consumption of legitimate manufactures and commerce have so largely followed the abolition of drink as to fully supply all loss of liquor taxes.

13. We recognize the good providence of Almighty God, who has preserved and prospered us as a Nation; and, asking for His Spirit to guide us to ultimate success, we all look for it, relying upon His omnipotent arm.

Democratic Platform.

The Democrats of the United States; in convention assembled, declare:

1. We pledge ourselves anew to the Constitutional doctrines and traditions of the Democratic party, as illustrated by the teachings and examples of a long line of Democratic statesmen and patriots, and embodied in the platform of the last national convention of the party.

2. Opposition to centralization, and to that dangerous spirit of encroachment which tends to consolidate the powers of all the departments in one, and thus to create, whatever the form of government, a real despotism; no sumptuary laws; separation of the church and State for the good of each; common schools fostered and protected.

3. Home rule; honest money, consisting of gold and silver, and paper convertible into coin on demand; the strict maintenance of the public faith, State and national; and a tariff for revenue only; the subordination of the military to the civil power; and a general and thorough reform of the civil service.

4. The right to a free ballot is a right preservative of all rights; and must and shall be maintained in every part of the United States.

5. The existing administration is the representative of conspiracy only; and its claim of right to surround the ballot-boxes with troops and deputy marshals, to intimidate and obstruct the elections, and the unprecedented use of the veto to maintain its corrupt and despotic power, insults the people and imperils their institutions. We execrate the course of this administration in making places in the civil service a reward for political crime; and demand a reform, by statute, which shall make it forever impossible for a defeated candidate to bribe his way to the seat of a usurper by billeting villains upon the people.

6. The great fraud of 1876-7, by which, upon a false count of the electoral votes of two States, the candidate defeated at the polls was declared to be President, and for the first time in American history, the will of the people was set aside under a threat of military violence, struck a deadly blow to our system of representative government. The Democratic party, to preserve the country from the horrors of a civil war, submitted for the time, in the firm and patriotic belief that the people would punish the crime in 1880. This issue precedes and dwarfs every other. It imposes a more sacred duty upon the people of the Union than ever addressed the consciences of a nation of freemen.

7. The resolution of Samuel J. Tilden not again to be a candidate for the exalted place to which he was elected by a majority of his countrymen, and from which he was excluded by the leaders of the Republican party, is received by the Democrats of the United States with deep sensibility; and they declare their confidence in his wisdom, patriotism and integrity unshaken by the assaults of the common enemy; and they further assure him that he is followed into the retirement he has chosen for himself by the sympathy and respect of his fellow-citizens, who regard him as one who, by elevating the standard of the public morality, and adorning and purifying the public service, merits the lasting gratitude of his country and his party.

8. Free ships and a living chance for American commerce upon the seas; and on the land, no discrimination in favor of transportation lines, corporations, or monopolies.

9. Amendments of the Burlingame treaty, no more Chinese immigration, except for travel, education, and foreign commerce, and, therein, carefully guarded.

10. Public money and public credit for public purposes solely, and public land for actual settlers.

11. The Democratic party is the friend of labor and the laboring man, and pledges itself to protect him alike against the cormorants and the commune.

12. We congratulate the country upon the honesty and thrift of a Democratic Congress, which has reduced the public expenditure $10,-000,000 a year; upon a continuation of prosperity at home and national honor abroad; and, above all, upon the promise of such a change in the administration of the Government as shall insure a genuine and lasting reform in every department of the public service.

PLATFORMS OF 1884.

The campaign of 1884 was a very spirited one. The National (Greenback Labor) party was in the field before the close of May. Its national convention met in Indianapolis, May 28, and nominated Gen. Benjamin F. Butler for President, and this became the central movement of the reform forces outside of the Prohibition party. The union of the reformers in support of the Butler movement was called the People's Party. The Republicans held their national convention in Chicago, beginning June 6. The national convention of the Democratic party met in Chicago, July 11. The Prohibitionists assembled in Pittsburgh in national convention, July 23.

Greenback-Labor Platform.

We, the National party of the United States, in national convention assembled, this 29th day of May, A. D. 1884, declare:

1. That we hold the late decision of the Supreme Court on the legal tender question to be a full vindication of the theory which our party has always advocated on the right and authority of Congress over the issue of legal tender notes, and we hereby pledge ourselves to uphold said decision, and to defend the Constitution against alterations or amendments intended to deprive the people of any rights or privileges conferred

by that instrument. We demand the issue of such money in sufficient quantities to supply the actual demand of trade and commerce, in accordance with the increase of population and the development of our industries. We demand the substitution of greenbacks for national bank notes and the prompt payment of the public debt. We want that money which saved our country in time of war and which has given it prosperity and happiness in peace. We condemn the retirement of the fractional currency and the small denominations of greenbacks and demand their restoration. We demand the issue of the hoards of money now locked up in the United States Treasury, by applying them to the payment of the public debt now due.

2. We denounce as dangerous to our republican institutions, those methods and policies of the Democratic and Republican parties which have sanctioned or permitted the establishment of land, railroad, money and other gigantic corporate monopolies; and we demand such governmental action as may be necessary to take from such monopolies the powers they have so corruptly and unjustly usurped, and restore them to the people, to whom they belong.

3. The public lands being the natural inheritance of the people, we denounce that policy which has granted to corporations vast tracts of land, and we demand that immediate and vigorous measures be taken to reclaim from such corporations, for the people's use and benefit, all such land grants as have been forfeited by reason of non-fulfillment of contract, or that may have been wrongfully acquired by corrupt legislation, and that such reclaimed lands and other public domain be henceforth held as a sacred trust, to be granted only to actual settlers in limited quantities; and we also demand that the alien ownership of land, individual or corporate, shall be prohibited.

4. We demand Congressional regulation of inter-state commerce. We denounce "pooling," stock watering and discrimination in rates and charges, and demand that Congress shall correct these abuses, even if necessary, by the construction of national railroads. We also demand the establishment of a Government postal telegraph system.

5. All private property, all forms of money and obligations to pay money should bear their just proportion of the public taxes. We demand a graduated income tax.

6. We demand the amelioration of the condition of labor by enforcing the sanitary laws in industrial establishments by the abolition of the convict labor system, by a rigid inspection of mines and factories, by a reduction of the hours of labor in industrial establishments, by fostering educational institutions and by abolishing child labor.

7. We condemn all importations of contracted labor, made with a view of reducing to starvation wages the workingmen of this country and demand laws for its prevention.

8. We insist upon a Constitutional amendment reducing the terms of United States Senators.

9. We demand such rules for the government of Congress as shall place all representatives of the people upon an equal footing and take away from committees a veto power greater than that of the President.

10. The question as to the amount of duties to be levied upon various articles of import has been agitated and quarreled over and has divided communities for nearly a hundred years. It is not now and never will be settled unless by the abolition of indirect taxation. It is a convenient issue—always raised when people are excited over abuses in their midst. While we favor a wise revision of the tariff laws, with a view to raising a revenue from luxuries rather than necessaries, we insist that as an economic question its importance is insignificant as compared with financial issues; for whereras we have suffered our worst panics under low and also under high tariffs, we have never suffered from a panic nor seen our factories and workshops closed while the volume of money in circulation was adequate to the needs of commerce. Give our farmers and manufacturers money as cheap as you now give it to our bankers, and they can pay high wages to labor and compete with all the world.

11. For the purpose of testing the sense of the people upon the subject, we are in favor of submitting to a vote of the people an amendment to the Constitution in favor of suffrage, regardless of sex, and also on the subject of liquor traffic.

12. All disabled soldiers of the late war should be equitably pensioned, and we denounce the policy of keeping a small army of office-holders whose only business is to prevent, on technical grounds, deserving soldiers from obtaining justice from the Government they helped to save.

13. As our name indicates, we are a national party, knowing no East, no West, no North, no South. Having no sectional prejudices, we can properly place in nomination for the high offices of State, as candidates, men from any section of the Union.

14. We appeal to all people who believe in our principles to aid us by voice, pen and votes.

Republican Platform.

The Republicans of the United States in national convention assembled, renew their allegiance to the principles upon which they have triumphed in six successive Presidential elections, and congratulate the American people on the attainment of so many results in legislation and administration by which the Republican party has, after saving the Union, done so much to render its institutions just, equal and beneficent, the safeguard of liberty and the embodiment of the best thought and highest purpose of our citizens. The Republican party has gained its strength by quick and faithful response to the demands of the people for the freedom and equality of all men; for a united Nation, assuring the rights of all citizens; for the elevation of labor, for an honest currency, for purity in legislation and for integrity and accountability in all departments of the Government; and it accepts anew the duty of leading in the work of progress and reform. We lament the death of President Garfield, whose sound statesmanship, long conspicuous in Congress, gave promise of strong and successful administration, a promise fully realized during the short period of his office as President of the United States. His distinguished services in war and peace have endeared him to the hearts of the American people. In the administration of President Arthur we recognize a wise, conservative and patriotic policy, under which the country has been blessed with remarkable prosperity, and we believe his eminent services are entitled to and will receive the hearty approval of every citizen.

It is the first duty of a good government to protect the rights and promote the interests of its own people. The largest diversity of industry is most productive of general prosperity and of the comfort and independence of the people. We therefore demand that the imposition of duties on foreign imports shall be made not "for revenue only," but that in raising the requisite revenues for the Government such duties shall be so levied as to afford security to our diversified industries and protection to the rights and wages of the laborer, to the end that active and intelligent labor as well as capital may have its just award and the laboring man his full share in the national prosperity, against the so-called economic system of the Democratic party which would degrade our labor to the foreign standard, we enter our earnest protest. The Democratic party has failed completely to relieve the people of the unnecessary taxation by a wise reduction of the surplus. The Republican party pledges itself to correct the inequalities of the tariff and to reduce the surplus, not by a vicious and indiscriminate process of horizontal reduction, but by such methods as will relieve the tax-payer without injuring the laborer or great productive interests of the country.

We recognize the importance of sheep husbandry in the United States, the serious depression which it is now experiencing and the danger threatening its future prosperity, and we therefore respect the demands of the representatives of this important agricultural interest for a readjustment of duty upon foreign wool, in order that such industry shall have full and adequate protection. We have always recommended the best money known to the civilized world, and we urge that efforts should be made to unite all commercial nations in the establishment of an international standard, which shall fix for all the relative value of gold and silver coinage. The regulations of commerce with foreign nations and between the States is one of the most important prerogatives of the General Government. The Republican party distinctly announces its purpose to support such legislation as will fully and efficiently carry out the Constitutional power of Congress over interstate commerce. The principle of the public regulation of railway corporations is a wise and salutary one for the protection of all classes of the people and favor legislation that shall prevent unjust discrimination and excessive charges for transportation, and that shall secure to the people and the railways alike the fair and equal protection of the laws. We favor the establishment of a national bureau of labor; the enforcement of the eight hour law; a wise and judicious system of general education by adequate appropriations from the national revenue wherever the same is needed. We believe that everywhere the protection to citizens of American birth must be secured to citizens by American adoption, and we favor the settlement of national differences by international arbitration. The Republican party having its birth in the hatred of slave labor, and a desire that all men may be truly free and equal, is unutterably opposed to place workingmen in competition with any form of servile labor, whether at home or abroad. In this spirit we denounce the importation of contract labor whether from Europe or Asia, as an offense against the spirit of American institutions. We pledge ourselves to sustain the present law restricting Chinese immigration and to provide such further legislation as is necessary to carry out its purposes.

The reform of the civil service so conspicuously begun under Republican administration, should be completed by the further extension of the reformed system already established by law, to all the grades of the service to which it is applicable. The spirit and purpose of the reform should be observed in all executive appointments, and all laws at variance with the object of existing reformed legislation should be repealed, to the end that damage to free institutions which lurks in the power of official patronage may be wisely and effectively avoided. The public lands are a heritage of the people of the United States, and should be reserved as far as possible for small holdings by actual settlers. We are opposed to the acquisition of large tracts of these lands by corporations or individuals, especially where such holdings are in the hands

of non-resident aliens, and we will endeavor to obtain such legislation as will tend to correct this evil.

We demand of Congress the speedy forfeiture of all land grants which have lapsed by reason of non-compliance with the act of incorporation; in all cases where there has been no attempt in good faith to perform the condition of such grants.

The grateful thanks of the American people are due to the Union soldiers and sailors of the late war, and the Republican party stands pledged to suitable pensions for all who were disabled, and for the widows and orphans of those who died in the war. The Republican party also pledges itself to the repeal of the limitation contained in the arrears act of 1879, so that all invalid soldiers shall share alike and their pensions begin with the date of disability or discharge, and not with date of application.

The Republican party favors a policy which shall keep us from entangling alliances with foreign nations, and which gives us the right to expect foreign nations shall refrain from meddling in American affairs. The policy which seeks peace and trade with all powers, but especially with those of the Western hemisphere.

We demand the restoration of our navy to its old-time strength and efficiency, that it may in any high sea protect the rights of American citizens and the interest of American commerce, and we call upon Congress to remove the burdens under which American shipping has been depressed, so that it may again be true that we have a commerce which leaves no sea unexplored and a navy which takes no law from superior force.

Resolved, That appointments by the President to offices in the Territories should be made from the bona fide citizens and residents of the Territories wherein they are to serve.

Resolved, That it is the duty of Congress to enact such laws as shall promptly and effectually suppress the system of polygamy within our territory and divorce the political from the ecclesiastical power of the so-called Mormon church, and that the law so enacted should be rigidly enforced by the civil authorities, if possible, and by the military if need be.

The people of the United States in their organized capacity constitute a Nation and not a mere confederacy of States. The National Government is supreme within the sphere of its national duty, but the States have reserved rights which should be faithfully maintained. Each should be guarded with jealous care, so that the harmony of our system of Government may be preserved and the Union kept inviolate. The perpetuity of our institutions rests upon the maintenance of a free ballot and an honest count and correct returns.

We denounce the fraud and violence practiced by the Democracy in the Southern States, by which the will of the voter is defeated, as dangerous to the preservation of free institutions; and we solemnly arraign the Democratic party as being the guilty recipient of the fruits of such fraud and violence. We extend to Republicans of the South, regardless of their former party affiliations, our cordial sympathy, and pledge to them our most earnest efforts to promote the passage of such legislation as will secure to every citizen of whatever race and color, the full and complete recognition, possession and exercise of all civil and political rights.

Democratic Platform.

The Democratic party of the Union, through its representatives in the national convention assembled, recognizes that, as the Nation grows older, new issues are born of time and progress, and the old issues perish, but the fundamental principles of the Democracy, approved by the united voice of the people, remain, and will ever remain, as the best and only security for the continuance of free government. The preservation of personal rights, the equality of all citizens before the law, the reserved rights of the States and the supremacy of the Federal Government within the limits of the Constitution will ever form the true basis of our liberties, and can never be surrendered without destroying that balance of rights and power which enables a continent to be developed in peace and social order, to be maintained by means of local self-government. But it is indispensable for the practical application and enforcement of these fundamental principles that the Government should not always be controlled by one political party. Frequent change of administration is as necessary as the constant recurrence to the popular will. Otherwise abuses grow, and the Government, instead of being carried on for the general welfare, becomes the instrumentality for imposing heavy burdens on the many who are governed for the benefit of the few who govern. Public servants thus become arbitrary rulers. This is now the condition of the country, hence a change is demanded. The Republican party, so far as principle is concerned, is a reminiscence. In practice, it is an organization for enriching those who control its machinery. The frauds and jobbery which have been brought to light in every department of the Government are sufficient to have called for reform within the Republican party, yet those in authority, made reckless by the long possession of power, have succumbed to its corrupting influence, and have placed in nomination a ticket against which the independent portion of the party are in open revolt.

Therefore, a change is demanded. Such a change was alike necessary in 1876, but the will of the people was then defeated by a fraud which can never be forgotten or condoned. Again, in 1880, the change demanded by the people was defeated by the lavish use of money contributed by unscrupulous contractors and shameless jobbers, who had bargained for unlawful profits or for high office. The Republican party, during its legal, its stolen, and its bought tenure of power, has steadily decayed in moral character and political capacity. Its platform promises are now a list of its past failures. It demands the restoration of our navy. It has squandered hundreds of millions to create a navy that does not exist. It calls upon Congress to remove the burdens under which American shipping has been depressed. It imposed and has continued these burdens. It professes the policy of reserving the public lands for small holdings by actual settlers. It has given away the people's heritage, till now a few railroads and non-resident aliens, individual and corporate, possess a larger area than that of all our farms between the seas. It professes a preference for free institutions. It organized and tried to legalize a control of State elections by Federal troops. It professes a desire to elevate labor; it has subjected the American workingmen to the competition of convict and imported contract labor. It professes gratitude to all who were disabled or died in the war, leaving widows and orphans; it left to a Democratic House of Representatives the first one to equalize both bounties and pensions. It proffers a pledge to correct the irregularities of our tariff; it created and has continued them. Its own tariff commission confessed the need of more than 20 per cent. reduction; its Congress gave a reduction of less than 4 per cent. It professes the protection of American manufacturers; it has subjected them to an increasing flood of manufactured goods and a hopeless competition with manufacturing nations, not one of which taxes raw materials. It professes to protect all American industries; it has impoverished many to subsidize a few. It professes the protection of American labor; it has depleted the returns of American agriculture, an industry followed by half our people. It professes the equality of all men before the law, attempting to fix the status of colored citizens. The acts of its Congress were overset by the decisions of its courts. It "accepts anew the duty of leading in the work of progress and reform." Its caught criminals are permitted to escape through contrived delays or actual connivance in the prosecution. Honeycombed with corruption, outbreaking exposures no longer shock its moral sense. Its honest members, its independent journals no longer maintain a successful contest for authority in its councils or a veto upon its bad nominations. That a change is necessary is proven by an existing surplus of more than $100,000,000, which has yearly been collected from a suffering people. Unnecessary taxation is unjust taxation. We denounce the Republican party for having failed to relieve the people from crushing war taxes, which have paralyzed business, crippled industry and deprived labor of employment and of just reward. The Democracy pledges itself to purify the administration from corruption, to restore economy, to revive respect for the law, and to reduce taxation to the lowest limit consistent with due regard to the preservation of the faith of the Nation to its creditors and pensioners. Knowing full well, however, that legislation affecting the occupations of the people should be cautious and conservative in method, not in advance of public opinion, but responsive to its demands, the Democratic party is pledged to revise the tariff in a spirit of fairness to all interests.

But in making a reduction in taxes it is not proposed to injure any of the domestic industries, but rather to promote their healthy growth. From the foundation of this Government taxes collected at the custom-house have been the chief source of Federal revenue. Such they must continue. Moreover, many industries have come to rely upon legislation for a successful continuance, so that any change of law must be at every step regardful of the labor and capital thus involved. The process of reform must be subject in the execution to the plain dictates of justice. All taxation shall be limited to the requirements of an economical government. The necessary reduction in taxation can and must be effected without depriving American labor of the ability to compete successfully with foreign labor, and without imposing lower rates of duty than will be ample to cover any increased cost of production, which may exist in consequence of the higher rate of wages prevailing in this country. Sufficient revenue to pay all the expenses of the Federal Government economically administered, including pensions, interest and principal of the public debt, can be got under our present system of taxation, from custom-house taxes on fewer imported articles, bearing heaviest on articles of luxury and bearing lightest on the articles of necessity. We therefore denounce the abuse of existing tariff, and, subject to the preceding limitations, we demand that Federal taxation shall be exclusively for public purposes, and shall not exceed the needs of the Government economically administered. The system of direct taxation known as the "internal revenue" is a war tax, and so long as the tax continues all the money derived therefrom should be sacredly devoted to the relief of the people from the remaining burdens of the war, and be made a fund to defray the expenses of the care and comfort of worthy soldiers disabled in the line of duty in the wars of the Republic, and for the payment of such pensions as Congress may, from time to time, grant to such soldiers, a like fund for the sailors having been already provided, and any surplus should be paid into the Treasury.

We favor an American continental policy, based upon more intimate commercial and political relations with the fifteen sister republics of North, Central and South America, but an entangling alliance with none.

We believe in honest money, the gold and silver coinage of the Constitution, and a circulating medium convertible into such money without loss.

Asserting the equality of all men before the law, we hold that it is the duty of the Government, in its dealings with the people, to mete out equal and exact justice to all citizens of whatever nativity, race, color or persuasion, religious or political. We believe in a free ballot and a fair count, and we recall to the memory of the people the noble struggle of the Democrats in the 45th and 46th Congresses, by which a reluctant Republican opposition was compelled to assent to legislation making everywhere illegal the presence of troops at the polls, as conclusive proof that a Democratic administration will preserve liberty with order. The selection of Federal officers for the Territories should be restricted to citizens previously residents therein.

We oppose sumptuary laws which vex the citizens and interfere with individual liberty. We favor honest civil service reform and the compensation of all United States officers by fixed salaries; the separation of church and State, and the diffusion of free education by the common schools, so that every child in the land may be taught the rights and duties of citizenship.

While we favor all legislation which will tend to the equitable distribution of property, the prevention of monopoly and to the strict enforcement of individual rights against corporate abuses, we hold that the welfare of society depends upon a scrupulous regard for the rights of property as defined by law.

We believe that labor is the best rewarded where it is freest and most enlightened. It should therefore be fostered and cherished. We favor the repeal of all laws restricting the free action of labor, and the enactment of laws by which labor organizations may be incorporated, and of all such legislation as will tend to enlighten the people as to the true relations of capital and labor.

We believe that the public lands ought, as far as possible, to be kept as homesteads for actual settlers; that all unearned lands heretofore improvidently granted to railroad corporations by the action of the Republican party, should be restored to the public domains, and that no more grant of lands shall be made to corporations or be allowed to fall into the ownership of alien absentees.

We are opposed to all propositions which upon any pretext would convert the General Government into a machine for collecting taxes to be distributed among the States or citizens thereof.

In reaffirming the declaration of the Democratic platform of 1856, that "the liberal principles embodied by Jefferson in the Declaration of Independence, and sanctioned by the Constitution, which makes ours the land of liberty and the asylum of the oppressed of every nation, have ever been the cardinal principles of the Democratic faith," we nevertheless do not sanction the importation of foreign labor, or the admission of servile races, unfitted by habits, training, religion or kindred for absorption into the great body of our people, or for the citizenship which our laws confer. American civilization demands that against the immigration or importation of Mongolians to these shores our gates shall be closed.

The Democratic party insists that it is the duty of this Government to protect with equal fidelity and vigilance the rights of its citizens, native and naturalized, at home and abroad, and to the end that this protection may be assured, United States papers of naturalization, issued by courts of competent jurisdiction, must be respected by the executive and legislative departments of our own Government, and by all foreign powers. It is an imperative duty of this Government to efficiently protect all the rights of persons and property of every American citizen in foreign lands, and demand and enforce full reparation for any invasion thereof. An American citizen is only responsible to his own Government for any act done in his own country, or under her flag, and is only to be tried therefor on her own soil and according to her laws; and no power exists in this Government to expatriate an American citizen to be tried in any foreign land for any such act. This country has never had a well defined and executed foreign policy save under a Democratic administration; that policy has ever been, in regard to foreign nations, so long as they do not act detrimental to the interest of the country or hurtful to our citizens, to let them alone; that as the result of this policy we recall the acquisition of Louisiana, Florida, California, and of the adjacent Mexican territory by purchase alone, and contrast these grand acquisitions of Democratic statesmanship with the purchase of Alaska, the sole fruit of a Republican administration of nearly a quarter of a century.

The Federal Government should care for and improve the Mississippi River and other great waterways of the Republic, so as to secure for the interior States easy and cheap transportation to the tide water.

Under a long period of Democratic rule and policy our merchant marine was fast overtaking and on the point of outstripping that of Great Britain. Under twenty years of Republican rule and policy our commerce has been left to British bottoms, and almost has the American flag been swept off the high seas. Instead of the Republican party's British policy, we demand for the people of the United States an American policy. Under Democratic rule and policy our merchants and sailors flying the stars and stripes in every port, successfully searched out a market for the varied products of American industry. Under a quarter of a century of Republican rule and policy, despite our manifest advantage over all other nations in high-paid labor, favorable climates, and teeming soils; despite the freedom of trade among all these United States; despite their population by the foremost races of men and annual immigration; despite our freedom here from the inherited burdens of life and industry in the Old World monarchies, their costly war navies, their vast tax-consuming, non-producing standing armies; despite twenty years of peace, that Republican rule and policy have managed to surrender to Great Britain, along with our commerce, the control of the markets of the world. Instead of the Republican party's British policy we demand in behalf of the American Democracy an American policy. Instead of the Republican party's discredit scheme and false pretenses of friendship for American labor, expressed by imposing taxes, we demand in behalf of the Democracy, freedom for American labor by reducing taxes, to the end that these United States may compete with unhindered powers for the primacy among nations in all the arts of peace and fruits of liberty.

With profound regret we have been apprised by the venerable statesman through whose person was struck that blow at the vital principle of Republicans (acquiescence in the will of the majority), that he cannot permit us again to place in his hands the leadership of the Democratic hosts, and for the reason that the achievement of reform in the administration of the Federal Government is an undertaking too heavy for his age and failing strength. Rejoicing that his life has been prolonged until the judgment of our fellow-countrymen is united in the wish that that wrong were righted in his person, for the Democracy of the United States, we offer to him in his withdrawal from public life not only our respectful sympathy and esteem, but also that best homage of freemen, the pledge of our devotion to the principles and the cause, now inseparable in the history of the Republic from the labors and the name of Samuel J. Tilden.

With this statement of the hopes, principles and purposes of the Democratic party, the great issue of reform and change of administration is submitted to the people in calm confidence that the popular voice will pronounce in favor of new men and new and more favorable conditions for the growth of industry, the extension of trade, the employment and due reward of labor and capital and the general welfare of the whole country.

Prohibition Party Platform.

1. The Prohibition party in national convention assembled, acknowledge Almighty God as the rightful sovereign of all men, from whom the just powers of government are derived, and to whose laws human enactments should conform as an absolute condition of peace, prosperity and happiness.

2. That the importation, manufacture, supply and sale of alcoholic beverages, created and maintained by the laws of the National and State Governments, during the entire history of such laws, is everywhere shown to be the promoting cause of intemperance, with resulting crime and pauperism, making large demands upon public and private charity, imposing large and unjust taxation for the support of penal and sheltering institutions, upon thrift, industry, manufactures and commerce; endangering the public peace; desecrating the Sabbath; corrupting our politics, legislation and administration of the laws; shortening lives, impairing health and diminishing productive industry; causing education to be neglected and despised; nullifying the teachings of the Bible, the church and the school, the standards and guides of our fathers and their children in the founding and growth of our widely extended country, and which, imperiling the perpetuity of our civil and religious liberties, are baleful fruits by which we know that these laws are contrary to God's laws and contravene our happiness. We, therefore, call upon our fellow-citizens to aid in the repeal of these laws and in the legal suppression of this baneful liquor traffic.

3. During the twenty-four years in which the Republican party has controlled the General Government and many of the States, no effort has been made to change this policy. Territories have been created, governments for them established, States admitted to the Union, and in no instance in either case has this traffic been forbidden or the people been permitted to prohibit it; that there are now over 200,000 distilleries, breweries, wholesale and retail dealers in their products, holding certificates and claiming the authority of the Government for the continuation of the business so destructive to the moral and material welfare of the people, together with the fact that they have turned a deaf ear to

remonstrance and petition for the correction of this abuse of civil government, is conclusive that the Republican party is insensible to or impotent for the redress of these wrongs, and should no longer be entrusted with the powers and responsibilities of government; that although this party in its late national convention was silent on the liquor question, not so its candidates, Messrs. Blaine and Logan. Within the past year Mr. Blaine has recommended that the revenue derived from the liquor traffic be distributed among the States; and Senator Logan has by bill proposed to devote these revenues to the support of the public schools. Thus both virtually recommend the perpetuation of the traffic, and that the States and their citizens become partners in the liquor crime.

4. That the Democratic party has in its national deliverances of party policy arrayed itself on the side of the drink makers and sellers by declaring against the policy of prohibition under the false name of "sumptuary laws;" that when in power in any of the States it has refused remedial legislation, and that in Congress it has obstructed the creation of a commission of inquiry into the effects of this traffic, proving that it should not be entrusted with power and place.

5. That there can be no greater peril to the Nation than the existing competition of the Republican and Democratic parties for the liquor vote. Experience shows that any party not openly opposed to the traffic will engage in this competition; will court the favor of the criminal classes; will barter the public morals, the purity of the ballot and every trust and object of good government for party success. Patriots and good citizens should, therefore, immediately withdraw from all connection with these parties.

6. That we favor reforms in the abolition of all sinecures with useless offices and officers, and in elections by the people instead of appointments by the President; that as competency, honesty and sobriety are essential qualifications for office, we oppose removals except when absolutely necessary to secure effectiveness in vital issues; that the collection of revenues from alcoholic liquor and tobacco should be abolished, since the vices of men are not proper subjects of taxation; that revenue from customs duties should be levied for the support of the Government, economically administered, and in such manner as will foster American industries and labor; that the public lands should be held for homes for the people, and not bestowed as gifts to corporations, or sold in large tracts for speculation upon the needs of actual settlers; that grateful care and support should be given to our soldiers and sailors disabled in the service of their country, and to their dependent widows and orphans; that we repudiate as un-American and contrary to and subversive of the principles

of the Declaration of Independence, that any persons or people should be excluded from residence or citizenship who may desire the benefits which our institutions confer upon the oppressed of all nations; that while these are important reforms and are demanded for purity of administration and the welfare of the people, their importance sinks into insignificance when compared with the drink traffic, which now annually wastes $800,000,000 of the wealth created by toil and thrift; dragging down thousands of families from comfort to poverty; filling jails, penitentiaries, insane asylums, hospitals and institutions for dependency; impairing the health and destroying the lives of thousands; lowering intellectual vigor, and dulling the cunning hand of the artisan, causing bankruptcy, insolvency and loss in trade, and by its corrupting power endangering the perpetuity of free institutions; that Congress should exercise its undoubted power by prohibiting the manufacture and sale of intoxicating beverages in the District of Columbia, the Territories of the United States, and all places over which the Government has exclusive jurisdiction; that hereafter no State should be admitted to the Union until its constitution shall expressly and forever prohibit polygamy and the manufacture and sale of intoxicating beverages, and that Congress shall submit to the States an amendment to the Constitution forever prohibiting the importation, exportation, manufacture and sale of alcoholic drinks.

7. We earnestly call the attention of the mechanic, the miner and manufacturer to the investigation of the baneful effects upon labor and industry of the needless liquor business. It will be found the robber who lessens wages and profits, foments discontent and strikes, and the destroyer of family welfare. Labor and all legitimate industries demand deliverance from the taxation and loss which this traffic imposes; and no tariff or other legislation can so healthily stimulate production, or increase the demand for capital and labor, or insure so much of comfort and content to the laborer, mechanic and capitalist, as would the suppression of this traffic.

8. That the activity and co-operation of the women of America for the promotion of temperance has, in all the history of the past, been a strength and encouragement which we gratefully acknowledge and record. In the later and present phase of the movement for the prohibition of the traffic, the purity of purpose and method, the earnestness, zeal, intelligence and devotion of the mothers and daughters of the Women's Christian Temperance Union have been eminently blessed of God. Kansas and Iowa have been given them as "sheaves" of rejoicing, and the education and arousing of the public mind, and the now prevailing demands for the Constitutional amendment are largely the fruit of their prayers and labors. Sharing in the efforts that shall bring the question of the abolition of this traffic to the polls, they shall join in the grand "Praise God from Whom All Blessings Flow," when by law victory shall be achieved.

9. That believing in the civil and political equality of the sexes, and that the ballot in the hands of woman is her right for protection, and would prove a powerful ally for the abolition of the liquor traffic, the execution of law, the promotion of reform in civil affairs, and the removal of corruption in public life, we enunciate the principle and relegate the practical outworking of this reform to the discretion of the Prohibition party in the several States, according to the condition of public sentiment in those States.

10. That we gratefully acknowledge the presence of the Divine Spirit guiding the counsels and granting the success which has been vouchsafed in the progress of the temperance reform, and we earnestly ask the voters of the United States to make the principles of the above declaration dominant in the Government of the Nation.

PLATFORMS OF 1888.

No less than eight parties were in the field in 1888. The Industrial Reform party met in convention at Washington, February 22. The Equal Rights party held their first national convention in Des Moines, May 15. The following day, May 16, the Union Labor party and the United Labor party each met in convention in Cincinnati. On May 30 the Prohibitionists opened their convention at Indianapolis. The Democratic convention met in St. Louis June 5, and the 19th of the same month the Republicans met in convention at Chicago. The eighth national party convention of the year was held in Washington by the American party, August 15.

Democratic Platform.

The Democratic Party of the United States, in national convention assembled, renews the pledge of its fidelity to Democratic faith, and reaffirms the platform adopted by its representatives in the convention of 1884, and endorses the views expressed by President Cleveland in his last annual message to Congress, as the correct interpretation of that platform upon the question of tariff reduction; and also endorses the efforts of our Democratic representatives in Congress to secure a reduction of excessive taxation.

Chief among its principles of party faith are the maintenance of an indissoluble union of free and indestructible States, now about to enter upon its second century of unexampled progress and renown; devotion to a plan of government regulated by a written Constitution, strictly specifying every granted power and expressly reserving to the States or people the entire ungranted residue of power; the encouragement of a jealous popular vigilance, directed to all who have been chosen for brief terms to enact and execute the laws and are charged with the duty of preserving peace, insuring equality and establishing justice.

The Democratic party welcomes an exacting scrutiny of the administration of the executive power which, four years ago, was committed to its trust in the selection of Grover Cleveland, President of the United States, and it challenges the most searching inquiry concerning its fidelity and devotion to the pledges which then invited the suffrages of the people. During a most critical period of our financial affairs, resulting from over-taxation, the anomalous condition of our currency, and a public debt unmatured, it has, by the adoption of a wise and conservative course, not only averted disaster but greatly promoted the prosperity of the people.

It has reversed the unwise and improvident policy of the Republican party touching the public domain, and has reclaimed from corporations and syndicates, alien and domestic, and restored to the people, nearly one hundred millions of acres of valuable land to be sacredly held as homesteads for our citizens.

While carefully guarding the interests of the taxpayers and conforming strictly to the principles of justice and equity, it has paid out more for pensions and bounties to the soldiers and sailors of the Republic than was ever paid before during an equal period.

By intelligent management and a judicious and economical expenditure of the public money, it has set on foot the reconstruction of the American navy upon a system which forbids the recurrence of scandal and insures successful results.

It has adopted and consistently pursued a firm and prudent foreign policy, preserving peace with all nations, while scrupulously maintaining all the rights and interests of our own Government and people, at home and abroad. The exclusion from our shores of Chinese laborers has been effectually secured under the provisions of a treaty, the operation of which has been postponed by the action of a Republican majority in the Senate.

Honest reform in the civil service has been inaugurated and maintained by President Cleveland, and he has brought the public service to the highest standard of efficiency, not only by rule and precept, but by the example of his own untiring and unselfish administration of public affairs.

In every branch and department of the Government under Democratic control the rights and the welfare of all the people have been guarded and defended; every public interest has been protected, and the equality of all our citizens before the law, without regard to race or color, has been steadfastly maintained.

Upon its record thus exhibited and upon the pledge of a continuance to the people of the benefits of good government, the National Democracy invoke a renewal of popular trust by the re-election of a Chief Magistrate who is faithful, able and prudent.

They invoke an addition to that trust by the transfer also to the Democracy of the entire legislative power.

The Republican party, controlling the Senate and resisting in both Houses a reformation of unjust and unequal tax laws, which have outlasted the necessities of war and are now undermining the abundance of a long peace, deny to the people equality before the law and the fairness and the justness which are their right. Thus the cry of American labor for a better share in the rewards of industry is stifled with false pretenses; enterprise is fettered and bound down to home markets; capital is discouraged with doubt, and unequal, unjust laws can neither be properly amended nor repealed.

The Democratic party will continue, with all the power confided to it, the struggles to reform these laws in accordance with the pledges of its last platform, endorsed at the ballot-box by the suffrages of the people.

Of all the industrious freemen of our land an immense majority, including every tiller of the soil, gain no advantage from the tax laws, but the price of nearly everything they buy is increased by the favoritism of an unequal system of tax legislation.

All unnecessary taxation is unjust taxation.

It is repugnant to the creed of Democracy that by such taxation the cost of the necessaries of life should be unjustifiably increased to all our people.

Judged by Democratic principles, the interests of the people are betrayed when by unnecessary taxation trusts and combinations are permitted and fostered, which, while unduly enriching the few that combine, rob the body of our citizens by depriving them as purchasers of the benefits of natural competition. Every Democratic rule of governmental action is violated when, through unnecessary taxation, a vast sum of money, far beyond the needs of an economical administration, is drawn from the people and the channels of trade and accumulated as a demoralizing surplus in the National Treasury.

The money now lying idle in the Federal Treasury resulting from superfluous taxation, amounts to more than $125,000,000, and the surplus collected is reaching the sum of more than $60,000,000 annually.

Debauched by this immense temptation, the remedy of the Republican party is to meet and exhaust by extravagant appropriations and expenditures, whether constitutional or not, the accumulations of extravagant taxation.

The Democratic policy is to enforce frugality in public expense and abolish unnecessary taxation.

Our established domestic industries should not and need not be endangered by a reduction and correction of the burdens of taxation. On the contrary, a fair and careful revision of our tax laws, with due allowance for the difference between the wages of American and foreign labor must promote and encourage every branch of such industries and enterprises by giving them assurance of an extended market and steady and continuous operation.

In the interest of American labor, which should in no event be neglected, the revision of our tax laws contemplated by the Democratic party would promote the advantage of such labor by cheapening the cost of the necessaries of life in the home of every workingman, and at the same time secure to him steady and remunerative employment.

Upon this question of tariff reform, so closely concerning every phase of our national life, and upon every question involved in the problem of good government, the Democratic party submits its principles and professions to the intelligent suffrages of the American people.

Resolved, That this convention hereby endorses and recommends the early passage of the bill for the reduction of the revenue now pending in the House of Representatives.

Resolved, That a just and liberal policy should be pursued in reference to the Territories; that right of self-government is inherent in the people and guaranteed under the Constitution; that the Territories of Washington, Dakota, Montana and New Mexico, are by virtue of population and development, entitled to admission into the Union as States, and we unqualifiedly condemn the course of the Republican party in refusing statehood and self-government to their people.

Resolved, That we express our cordial sympathy with the struggling people of all nations in their efforts to secure for themselves the inestimable blessings of self-government and civil and religious liberty, and we especially declare our sympathy with the efforts of those noble patriots who, led by Gladstone and Parnell, have conducted their grand and peaceful contest for Home Rule in Ireland.

Republican Platform.

The Republicans of the United States, assembled by their delegates in national convention, pause on the threshold of their proceedings to honor the memory of their first great leader, the immortal champion of liberty and the rights of the people—Abraham Lincoln; and to cover also with wreaths of imperishable remembrance and gratitude the heroic names of our later leaders who have more recently been called away from our councils—Grant, Garfield, Arthur, Logan and Conkling. May their memories be faithfully cherished.

We also recall with our greetings and with prayer for his recovery, the name of one of our living heroes, whose memory will be treasured in the history both of Republicans and of the Republic—the name of that noble soldier and favorite child of victory, Philip H. Sheridan.

In the spirit of those great leaders and of our own devotion to human liberty, and with that hostility to all forms of despotism and oppression which is the fundamental idea of the Republican party, we send fraternal congratulations to our fellow-Americans of Brazil upon their great act of emancipation, which completes the abolition of slavery throughout the two American continents.

We earnestly hope that we may soon congratulate our fellow-citizens of Irish birth upon the peaceful recovery of Home Rule for Ireland.

We reaffirm our unswerving devotion to the national Constitution and the indissoluble union of the States; to the autonomy reserved to the States under the Constitution; to the personal rights and liberties of citizens in all the States and Territories in the Union, and especially to the supreme and sovereign right of every lawful citizen, rich or poor, native or foreign-born, white or black, to cast one free ballot in public elections, and to have that ballot duly counted. We hold the free and honest popular ballot, and the just and equal representation of all the people, to be the foundation of our republican government, and demand effective legislation to secure the integrity and purity of elections, which are the foundations of public authority. We charge that the present administration and the Democratic majority in Congress owe their existence to the suppression of the ballot by a criminal nullification of the Constitution and laws of the United States.

We are uncompromisingly in favor of the American system of Protection; we protest against its destruction as proposed by the President and his party. They serve the interests of Europe; we will support the interest of America We accept the issue and confidently appeal to the people for their judgment. The protective system must be maintained. Its abandonmen has always been followed by general disaster to all interests, except those of the usurer and the sheriff. We denounce the Mills bill as destructive to the general business, the labor and the farming interests of the country, and we heartily endorse the consistent and patriotic action of the Republican representatives in Congress in opposing its passage.

We condemn the proposition of the Democratic party to place wool on the free list, and we insist that the duties thereon shall be adjusted and maintained so as to furnish full and adequate protection to that industry throughout the United States.

The Republican party would effect all needed reduction of the national revenue by repealing the taxes upon tobacco which are an annoyance and burden to agriculture, and the tax upon spirits used in the arts and for mechanical purposes, and by such revision of the tariff laws as will tend to check imports of such articles as are produced by our people, the production of which gives employment to our labor, and release from import duties those articles of foreign production (except luxuries) the like of which cannot be produced at home. If there shall still remain a larger revenue than is requisite for the wants of the Government, we favor the entire repeal of internal taxes rather than the surrender of any part of our protective system at the joint behest of the whiskey trusts and the agents of foreign manufacturers.

We declare our hostility to the introduction into this country of foreign contract labor and of Chinese labor, alien to our civilization and Constitution, and we demand the rigid enforcement of the existing laws against it, and favor such immediate legislation as will exclude such labor from our shores.

We declare our opposition to all combinations of capital, organized in trusts or otherwise, to control arbitrarily the condition of trade among our citizens, and we recommend to Congress and the State Legislatures, in their respective jurisdictions, such legislation as will prevent the execution of all schemes to oppress the people by undue charges on their supplies, or by unjust rates for the transportation of their products to market. We approve the legislation by Congress to prevent any unjust burdens and unfair discriminations between the States.

We reaffirm the policy of appropriating the public lands of the United States to be homesteads for American citizens and settlers—not aliens—which the Republican party established in 1862 against the persistent opposition of the Democrats in Congress, and which has brought our great Western domain into such magnificent development. The restoration of unearned railroad land grants to the public domain for the use of settlers, which was begun under the administration of President Arthur, should be continued. We deny that the Democratic party has ever restored one acre to the people, but declare that by the joint action of Republicans and Democrats in Congress about 50,000,000 acres of unearned lands originally granted for the construction of railroads have been restored to the public domain in pursuance of the conditions inserted by the Republican party in the original grants. We charge the Democratic administration with failure to execute the laws securing to settlers titles to their homesteads, and with using appropriations made for that purpose to harass innocent settlers with spies and prosecutions under the false pretense of exposing frauds and vindicating the law.

The government by Congress of the Territories is based upon necessity, only to the end that they may become States in the Union. Therefore, whenever the conditions of population, material resources, public intelligence and morality are such as to insure a stable local government therein, the people of such Territories should be permitted as a right inherent in them to form for themselves Constitutions and State Governments and be admitted into the Union. Pending the preparation for Statehood, all officers thereof should be selected from the bona fide residents and citizens of the Territory wherein they are to serve. South Dakota should of right be immediately admitted as a State in the Union, under the constitution framed and adopted by her people, and we heartily endorse the act of the Republican Senate in twice passing bills for her admission. The refusal of the Democratic House of Representatives, for partisan purposes, to favorably consider these bills, is a willful violation of the sacred American principle of local self-government, and merits the condemnation of all just men. The pending bills in the Senate to enable the people of Washington, North Dakota and Montana Territories to form constitutions and establish State governments, should be passed without unnecessary delay. The Republican party pledges itself to do all in its power to facilitate the admission of the Territories of New Mexico, Wyoming, Idaho and Arizona to the enjoyment of self-government as States, such of them as are now qualified as soon as possible and the others as soon as they may become so.

The political power of the Mormon Church in the Territories, as exercised in the past, is a menace to free institutions, a danger no longer to be suffered. Therefore we pledge the Republican party to appropriate legislation asserting the sovereignty of the Nation in all Territories where the same is questioned, and in furtherance of that end to place upon the statute books legislation stringent enough to divorce the political from the ecclesiastical power, and thus stamp out the attendant wickedness of polygamy.

The Republican party is in favor of the use of both gold and silver as money, and condemns the policy of the Democratic administration in its efforts to demonetize silver.

We demand the reduction of letter postage to one cent per ounce.

In a Republic like ours, where the citizen is the sovereign and the official the servant, where no power is exercised except by the will of the people, it is important that the sovereign—the people—should possess intelligence. The free school is the promoter of that intelligence which is to preserve us as a free Nation; therefore the State, or Nation, or both combined, should support free institutions of learning sufficient to afford to every child growing in the land the opportunity of a good common school education.

We earnestly recommend that prompt action be taken by Congress on the enactment of such legislation as will best secure the rehabilitation of our American merchant marine, and we protest against the passage by Congress of a free-ship bill, as calculated to work injustice to labor by lessening the wages of those engaged in preparing materials, as well as those directly employed in our shipyards. We demand appropriation for the early rebuilding of our navy, for the construction of coast fortifications and modern ordnances and other approved modern means of defense for the protection of our defenseless harbors and cities; for the payment of just pensions to our soldiers; for necessary works of national importance in the improvement of harbors and the channels of internal, coastwise and foreign commerce; for the encouragement of the shipping interests of the Atlantic, Gulf and Pacific States, as well as for the payment of the maturing public debt. This policy will give employment to our labor, activity to our various industries, increase the security of our country, promote trade, open new and direct markets for our produce and cheapen the cost of transportation. We affirm this to be far better for our country than the Democratic policy of loaning the Government's money, without interest, to "pet banks."

The conduct of affairs by the present administration has been distinguished by its inefficiency and cowardice. Having withdrawn from the Senate all pending treaties effected by Republican administrations for the removal of foreign burdens and restrictions upon our commerce, and for its extension into better markets, it has neither effected nor proposed any others in their stead. Professing adherence to the Monroe Doctrine, it has seen, with idle complacency, the extension of foreign influence in Central America and of foreign trade every-

where among our neighbors. It has refused to charter, sanction or encourage any American organization for constructing the Nicaragua Canal, a work of vital importance to the maintenance of the Monroe Doctrine, and of our national influence in Central and South America, and necessary for the development of trade with our Pacific territory, with South America and with the islands and farther coasts of the Pacific Ocean.

We arraign the present Democratic Administration for its weak and unpatriotic treatment of the fisheries question, and its pusillanimous surrender of the essential privileges to which our fishing vessels are entitled in Canadian ports under the treaty of 1818, the reciprocal maritime legislation of 1830 and the comity of nations, and which Canadian fishing vessels receive in the ports of the United States. We condemn the policy of the present administration and the Democratic majority in Congress toward our fisheries as unfriendly and conspicuously unpatriotic, and as tending to destroy a valuable national industry and an indispensable source of defense against a foreign enemy.

The name American applies alike to all citizens of the Republic, and imposes upon all alike the same obligation of obedience to the laws. At the same time that citizenship is and must be the panoply and safeguard of him who wears it, and protect him, whether high or low, rich or poor, in all his civil rights. It should and must afford him protection at home and follow and protect him abroad, in whatever land he may be on a lawful errand.

The men who abandoned the Republican party in 1884 and continue to adhere to the Democratic party, have deserted not only the cause of honest government, of sound finance, of freedom, of purity of the ballot, but especially have deserted the cause of reform in the civil service. We will not fail to keep our pledges because they have broken theirs, or because their candidate has broken his. We therefore repeat our declaration of 1884, to-wit: "The reform of the civil service, auspiciously begun under the Republican administration, should be completed by the further extension of the reform systems already established by law to all the grades of service to which it is applicable. The spirit and purpose of the reform should be observed in all executive appointments, and all laws at variance with the object of existing reform legislation should be repealed, to the end that the dangers to free institutions, which lurk in the power of official patronage, may be wisely and effectively avoided."

The gratitude of the Nation to the defenders of the Union cannot be measured by laws. The legislation of Congress should conform to the pledges made by a loyal people, and be so enlarged and extended as to provide against the possibility that any man who honorably wore the Federal uniform shall become an inmate of an almshouse or dependent upon private charity. In the presence of an overflowing Treasury it would be a public scandal to do less for those whose valorous service preserved the Government. We denounce the hostile spirit shown by President Cleveland in his numerous vetoes of measures for pension relief, and the action of the Democratic Representatives in refusing even a consideration of general pension legislation.

In support of the principles herewith enunciated we invite the co-operation of patriotic men of all parties, and especially of all workingmen, whose prosperity is seriously threatened by the free trade policy of the present administration.

Prohibition Platform.

The Prohibition party, in national convention assembled, acknowledging Almighty God as the source of all power in government, do hereby declare:

1. That the manufacture, importation, exportation, transportation and sale of alcoholic beverages should be made public crimes and prohibited as such.

2. That such prohibition must be secured through amendments to our National and State Constitutions, enforced by adequate laws adequately supported by administrative authority; and to this end the organization of the Prohibition party is imperatively demanded in State and Nation.

3. That any form of license, taxation or regulation of the liquor traffic is contrary to good government; that any party which supports regulation, license or taxation enters into alliance with such traffic and becomes the actual foe of the State's welfare, and that we arraign the Republican and Democratic parties for their persistent attitude in favor of the license iniquity, whereby they oppose the demand of the people for prohibition, and, through open complicity with the liquor crime, defeat the enforcement of law.

4. For the immediate abolition of the internal revenue system, whereby our National Government is deriving support from our greatest national vice.

5. That an adequate public revenue being necessary, it may properly be raised by import duties, but import duties should be so reduced that no surplus shall be accumulated in the Treasury, and that the burdens of taxation shall be removed from foods, clothing and other comforts and necessaries of life and imposed on such articles of import as will give protection both to the manufacturing employer and producing laborer against the competition of the world.

6. That the right of suffrage rests on no mere circumstances of race, color, sex or nationality;

and that where from any cause it has been withheld from citizens who are of suitable age and mentally and morally qualified for the exercise of an intelligent ballot, it should be restored by the people through the Legislatures of the several States on such educational basis as they may deem wise.

7. That civil service appointments for all civil offices, chiefly clerical in their duties, should be based upon moral, intellectual and physical qualifications and not upon party service or party necessity.

8. For the abolition of polygamy and the establishment of uniform laws governing marriage and divorce.

9. For prohibiting all combinations of capital to control and to increase the cost of products for popular consumption.

10. For the preservation and defense of the Sabbath as a civil institution, without oppressing any who religiously observe the same on other than the first day of the week.

11. That arbitration is the Christian, wise and economical method of settling national differences, and the same method should by judicious legislation be applied to the settlement of disputes between large bodies of employes and their employers; that the abolition of the saloon would remove the burdens moral, physical, pecuniary and social, which now oppress labor and rob it of its earnings, and would prove to be a wise and successful way of promoting labor reform, and we invite labor and capital to unite with us for the accomplishment thereof; that monopoly in land is a wrong to the people, and the public lands should be reserved to actual settlers; and that men and women should receive equal wages for equal work.

12. That our immigration laws should be so enforced as to prevent the introduction into our country of all convicts, inmates of other dependent institutions, and others physically incapacitated for self-support, and that no person should have the ballot in any State who is not a citizen of the United States.

13. Recognizing and declaring that prohibition of the liquor traffic has become the dominant issue in national politics, we invite to full party fellowship all those who, on this one dominant issue, are with us agreed, in the full belief that this party can and will remove sectional differences, promote national unity and insure the best welfare of our entire land.

Union Labor Platform.

1. While we believe that the proper solution of the financial system will greatly relieve those now in danger of losing their homes by mortgage foreclosure, and enable all industrious persons to secure a home as the highest result of civilization, we oppose land monopoly in every

form, demand the forfeiture of unearned grants, the limitation of land ownership, and such other legislation as will stop speculation in land and holding it unused from those whose necessities require it. We believe the earth was made for the people and not to enable an idle aristocracy to subsist through rents upon the toil of the industrious, and that "corners" in land are as bad as "corners" in food, and that those who are not residents or citizens should not be allowed to own land in the United States. A homestead should be exempt to a limited extent from execution or taxation.

2. The means of communication and transportation should be owned by the people, as is the United States postal system.

3. The establishing of a national monetary system in the interest of the producers instead of the speculators and usurers, by which the circulating medium in necessary quantity and full legal tender should be issued directly to the people without the intervention of banks, or loaned to citizens upon land security at a low rate of interest. To relieve them from extortions of usury and enable them to control the money supply, postal savings banks should be established. While we have free coinage of gold we should have free coinage of silver. We demand the immediate application of all the idle money in the United States Treasury to the payment of the bonded debt, and condemn the further issue of interest bearing bonds either by the National Government or by States, Territories, or by municipalities.

4. Arbitration should take the place of strikes and other injurious methods of settling labor disputes. The letting of convict labor to contractors should be prohibited, the contract system be abolished in public works, the hours of labor in industrial establishments be reduced commensurate with the increased production by labor-saving machinery, employes be protected from bodily injury, equal pay given for equal work for both sexes, and labor, agricultural and co-operative associations be fostered and encouraged by law. The foundation of a republic is in the intelligence of its citizens, and children who are drawn into workshops, mines and factories, are deprived of the education which should be secured to all by proper legislation.

5. We demand the passage of a service pension bill to pension every honorably discharged soldier and sailor of the United States.

6. A graduated income tax is the most equitable system of taxation, placing the burden of government upon those who are best able to pay, instead of laying it upon the farmers and exempting millionaire bondholders and corporations.

7. We demand a Constitutional amendment making United States Senators elective by a direct vote of the people.

8. We demand a strict enforcement of laws prohibiting the importation of subjects of foreign countries under contracts.

9. We demand the passage and enforcement of such legislation as will absolutely exclude the Chinese from the United States.

10. The right to vote is inherent in citizenship, irrespective of sex, and is properly within the province of State legislation.

11. The paramount issues to be solved in the interest of humanity are the abolition of usury, monopoly and trusts; and we denounce the Democratic and Republican parties for creating and perpetuating these monstrous evils.

United Labor Platform.

We, the delegates of the United Labor party of the United States, in national convention assembled, hold that the corruptions of government and the impoverishment of the masses result from neglect of the self-evident truths proclaimed by the founders of this Republic, that all men are created equal and endowed with inalienable rights. We aim at the abolition of the system which compels men to pay their fellow-creatures for the use of the common bounties of nature and permits monopolizers to deprive labor of natural opportunities for employment.

We see access to farming land denied to labor except on payment of exorbitant rent or the acceptance of mortgage burdens, and labor, thus forbidden to employ itself, driven into the cities. We see the wage workers of the cities subjected to this unnatural competition and forced to pay an exorbitant share of their scanty earnings for cramped and unhealthy lodgings. We see the same intense competition condemning the great majority of business and professional men to a bitter and often unavailing struggle to avoid bankruptcy, and that while the price of all that labor produces ever falls the price of land ever rises.

We trace these evils to a fundamental wrong the making of the land on which all must live the exclusive property of but a portion of the community. To this denial of natural rights are due want of employment, low wages, business depressions, that intense competition which makes it so difficult for the majority of men to get a comfortable living, and that wrongful distribution of wealth which is producing the millionaire on one side and the tramp on the other.

To give all men an interest in the land of their country; to enable all to share in the benefits of social growth and improvement; to prevent the shutting out of labor from employment by the monopolization of natural opportunities; to do away with the one-sided competition which cuts down wages to starvation rates; to restore life to business and prevent periodical depressions; to do away with that monstrous injustice which deprives producers of the fruits of their toil while idlers grow rich; to prevent the conflicts which are arraying class against class, and which are fraught with menacing dangers to society, we propose so to change the existing system of taxation that no one shall be taxed on the wealth he produces, nor any one suffered to appropriate wealth he does not produce by taking to himself the increasing values which the growth of society adds to the land.

What we propose is not the disturbing of any man in his holding or title, but, by taxation of land according to its value and not according to its area, to devote to common use and benefit those values which arise, not from the exertion of the individual, but from the growth of society, and to abolish the taxes on industry and its products. This increased taxation of land values must, while relieving the working farmer and small homestead owner of the undue burdens now imposed upon them, make it unprofitable to hold land for speculation, and thus throw open abundant opportunities for the employment of labor and the building up of homes.

We would do away with the present unjust and wasteful system of finance, which piles up hundreds of millions of dollars in treasury vaults while we are paying interest on an enormous debt; and we would establish in its stead a monetary system in which a legal tender circulating medium should be issued by the Government without the intervention of banks.

We wish to abolish the present unjust and wasteful system of ownership of railroads and telegraphs by private corporations—a system which, while failing to supply adequately public needs, impoverishes the farmer, oppresses the manufacturer, hampers the merchant, impedes travel and communication, and builds up enormous fortunes and corrupting monopolies that are becoming more powerful than the Government itself. For this system we would substitute Government ownership and control for the benefit of the whole people instead of private property.

While declaring the foregoing to be the fundamental principles and aims of the United Labor party, and while conscious that no reform can give effectual and permanent relief to labor that does not involve the legal recognition of equal rights to natural opportunities, we, nevertheless, as measures of relief from some of the evil effects of ignoring those rights, favor such legislation as may tend to reduce the hours of labor, to prevent the employment of children of tender years, to avoid the competition of convict labor with honest industry, to secure the sanitary inspection of tenements, factories and mines, and to put an end to the abuse of the conspiracy laws.

We desire also to simplify the procedure of our courts and diminish the expense of legal proceedings that the poor therein may be placed on an equality with the rich, and the long delays which now result in scandalous miscarriages of justice may be prevented.

Since the ballot is the only means by which, in our Republic, the redress of political and social grievances is to be sought, we especially and emphatically declare for the adoption of what is known as the Australian system of voting, in order that the effectual secrecy of the ballot and the relief of candidates for public office from the heavy expense now imposed upon them may prevent bribery and intimidation, do away with practical discriminations in favor of the rich and unscrupulous, and lessen the pernicious influence of money in politics.

We denounce the Democratic and Republican parties as hopelessly and shamelessly corrupt, and by reason of their affiliation with monopolies, equally unworthy of the suffrages of those who do not live upon public plunder; we therefore require of those who would act with us that they sever all connection with both.

In support of these aims we solicit the co-operation of all patriotic citizens who, sick of the degradation of politics, desire, by constitutional methods, to establish justice, to preserve liberty, to extend the spirit of fraternity and to elevate humanity.

American Platform.

Believing that the time has arrived when a due regard for the present and future prosperity of our country makes it imperative that the people of the United States of America should take full and entire control of their Government, to the exclusion of revolutionary and incendiary foreigners now seeking our shores from every quarter of the world, and recognizing that the first and most important duty of an American citizen is to maintain this Government in all attainable purity and strength, we make the following declaration of principles:

Resolved, That all law-abiding citizens of the United States of America, whether native or foreign born, are political equals (except as provided by the Constitution), and all are entitled to and should receive the full protection of the laws.

WHEREAS, There are seventeen States in this Union wherein persons are allowed to vote at all elections without being citizens of the United States; and whereas such a system tends to place the management of the Government into the hands of those who owe no allegiance to our political institutions: Therefore,

Resolved, That the Constitution of the United States should be so amended as to prohibit the Federal and State Governments from conferring upon any person the right to vote unless such person be a citizen of the United States.

Resolved, That we are in favor of fostering and encouraging American industries of every class and kind; that the issue of " protection " versus "free trade " is a fraud and a snare. The best " protection " is that which protects the labor and life-blood of the Republic from the degrading competition with and contamination by imported foreigners; and the most dangerous " free trade " is that in paupers, criminals, communists and anarchists, in which the balance has always been against the United States.

WHEREAS, One of the greatest evils of unrestricted foreign immigration is the reduction of the wages of American workingmen and American workingwomen to the level of the underfed and underpaid laborer of foreign countries: Therefore,

Resolved, That we demand that no immigrant shall be admitted into the United States without a passport obtained from the American consul at the port from which he sails; that no passport shall be issued to any pauper, criminal or insane person, or to any person who, in the judgment of the consul, is not likely to become a desirable citizen of the United States, and that for each immigrant passport there shall be collected by the consul issuing the same the sum of $100, to be by him paid into the Treasury of the United States.

Resolved, That all persons not in sympathy with our Government should be prohibited from immigration to these United States.

Resolved, That the naturalization laws of the United States should be unconditionally repealed.

Resolved, That the soil of America should belong to Americans; that no alien non-resident should be permitted to own real estate in the United States, and that the realty possessions of the resident alien should be limited in value and area.

Resolved, That we favor educating the boys and girls of American citizens as mechanics and artisans, thus fitting them for the places now filled by foreigners, who supply the greater part of our skilled labor, and thereby almost entirely control the great industries of our country, save, perhaps, that of agriculture alone; and that our boys and girls may be taught trades, we demand the establishment and maintenance of free technical schools.

Resolved, That universal education is a necessity of our Government, and that an American free school system should be maintained and preserved as the safeguard of American liberty.

Resolved, That no language except the English shall be taught in the common schools supported at the public expense.

WHEREAS, Unemployed population is the greatest evil that can befall any nation, and in this country it cannot be eliminated by any European methods, such as extra police and standing armies: Therefore,

Resolved, That the surplus in the Treasury should be devoted to the material improvement of our coast and frontier defenses and the construction of an American navy in American workshops by American labor.

Resolved, That we demand the enactment of a law which shall require all persons having charge in any way in any department, bureau or division of the Government, to forthwith dismiss from the public service all persons employed in or about any such department, bureau or division in any way or manner who are not citizens of the United States by nativity, or by having fully completed their naturalization papers by due process of law; that no person shall be appointed to or hold office or place in the service of the United States, who is not a citizen of the United States, either by having fully completed his naturalization and taken out his final papers by due form and process of law, or who is not a citizen of the United States by nativity.

Resolved, That after the year 1898 it shall be required of every voter, before he exercises the right of suffrage, to be able to read the written or printed Constitution of the United States in the English language and to write his own name upon the register, to show that he is fitted to share the administration of the Republic.

Resolved, That we recognize the right of labor to organize for its protection, and by all lawful and peaceful means to secure to itself the greatest reward for its thrift and industry, and we believe in governmental arbitration in the settlement of industrial differences.

Resolved, That we are in favor of such legislation by Congress as will re-establish the American marine.

Resolved, That no flag shall float over any public building—municipal, state or national—in the United States, except the stars and stripes.

Resolved, That we reassert the American principles of absolute freedom of religious worship and belief; the permanent separation of church and State; and we oppose the appropriation of public money or property to any church or institution administered by a church. We maintain that all church property should be subject to taxation.

Resolved, That the Presidential term shall be extended to six years, and the President shall be ineligible for re-election.

Resolved, That the American party declares that it recognizes no North, no South, no East, no West, in these United States, but one people, pledged to our liberty and our independence.

Equal Rights Platform.

Resolved, That while we do not espouse the cause of woman's rights or man's rights distinctively and separately as such, we judge it best in the present formative state of public opinion, and as a proper balancing in the present, in view of the past, to put a woman's name at the head of the ticket.

Resolved, That history having demonstrated the fact that women in all ages have proven capable, in isolated instances, of leading armies, conquering cities and ruling nations, and believing that we have such a one among us to-day, a woman with scope of vision, intellectual vigor and executive ability equal to the task; one possessing, moreover, from a long residence at the Capital and extensive travel, a thorough acquaintance with the state, conditions of our country, and with the magnates of its chosen masculine rulers; and who, comprehending the abuse of our times with quick intuitions, grasps the remedy; a woman who has stormed the redoubts of legal practice and prejudice, and fought her right of way to stand and plead the people's cause before the bar of our highest courts; upon whose benign brow is set the signet of an infinite womanly sympathy, blended with favor.

Resolved, That we place her name at the head of the Equal Rights ticket, believing Belva A. Lockwood its most fitting exponent and leader.

Believing that the disfranchisement of women has much to do with the growing influence of crime in the Nation, we, the women of America, by their representatives here assembled, do pledge ourselves that if our party and candidates come into power, equal rights shall be meted out to all citizens, without regard to sex or color—a fair ballot and an honest count.

We shall ask Congress to pass an enabling act giving the women of this Nation the right to vote in all election precincts of the United States, as women are citizens, amenable to the laws and liable to taxation.

That the settlement of estates shall be the same as in the courts of joint property, and in the case of the death of the wife, her heirs shall receive the same consideration as those of the husband without consulting his interests. In case of the death of the husband the wife shall be administrator and guardian of her children without any process of law.

We pledge ourselves to the cause of temperance, and are in favor of arbitration by international commission instead of the sword, although under the circumstances of the late war our Union soldiers and sailors were inspired by the purest patriotism and principles of right. And we will demand of Congress to pension them each and every one if they need help.

That we urge measures to be taken to stop the immigration of the scum of Europe and Asia to our shores, and that we protect our workingmen from cheap foreign labor by protecting our home markets and manufactures.

That land owned by foreign landlords and wealthy corporations be heavily taxed to support the Government, and put sugar and lumber on the free list; and abolish taxes on whisky and tobacco, as it makes the Government a partner in their excessive use—the evil of the century.

That in our candidates, Belva A. Lockwood and Albert H. Love, of Philadelphia, we have every confidence in their ability, integrity and firmness in carrying out these grand and glorious principles.

Industrial Reform Platform.

WHEREAS, It is possible to secure many needed reforms under a correct financial and industrial system: Therefore,

Resolved, By the Industrial party, in national convention assembled at the City of Washington, D. C., on the 22d day of February, 1888:

1. That the Government shall provide full legal tender money sufficient in volume to meet the requirements of the people.

2. That the Secretary of the Treasury shall immediately redeem all public interest-bearing bonds.

3. That all banks of issue shall be abolished.

4. That the privilege of voting is inherent in citizenship, and the right to vote should be accorded to women.

THE FIRST PEOPLE'S PARTY.

On May 19, 1891, there assembled at Cincinnati over 1,400 representatives of reform organizations in accordance with a call for a National Reform Conference. This meeting adopted a platform which gave birth to a new political organization, the "People's Party of the United States of America." Following in this line a great labor conference was held in St. Louis, beginning February 22, 1892. Its platform is known as that of the "Confederated Industrial Organizations."

People's Party Platform.

1. That in view of the great social, industrial, and economical revolution now dawning upon the civilized world, and the new and living issues confronting the American people, we believe that the time has arrived for a crystallization of the political reform forces of our country and the formation of what should be known as the "People's Party of the United States of America."

2. That we most heartily endorse the demands of the platforms as adopted at St. Louis, Mo., in 1880; Ocala, Fla., in 1890, and Omaha, Neb., in 1891 by industrial organizations there represented, summarized as follows:

A—The right to make and issue money is a sovereign power to be maintained by the people for the common benefit; hence we demand the abolition of national banks as banks of issue, and as a substitute for national bank notes we demand that legal tender Treasury notes be issued, in sufficient volume to transact the business of the country on a cash basis, without damage or special advantage to any class or calling, such notes to be legal tender in the payment of all debts, public and private, and such notes when demanded by the people shall be loaned to them at not more than two per cent. per annum upon non-perishable products, as indicated in the sub-treasury plan, and also upon real estate with proper limitation upon the quantity of land and the amount of money.

B—We demand the free and unlimited coinage of silver.

C—We demand the passage of laws prohibiting alien ownership of land, and that Congress take prompt action to devise some plan to obtain all lands now owned by alien and foreign syndicates, and that all lands held by railroads and other corporations in excess of such as is actually used and needed by them be reclaimed by the Government and held for actual settlers only.

D—Believing the doctrine of equal rights to all and special privilege to none, we demand that taxation—national, State or municipal—shall not be used to build up one interest or class at the expense of another.

E—We demand that all revenues—national, State or county—shall be limited to the necessary expenses of the Government, economically and honestly administered.

F—We demand a just and equitable system of graduated tax on incomes.

G—We demand the most rigid, honest and just national control and supervision of the means of public communication and transportation, and if this control and supervision does not remove the abuses now existing, we demand the Government ownership of such means of communication and transportation.

H We demand the election of President, Vice-President and United States Senators by a direct vote of the people.

3. That we urge united action of all progressive organizations attending the conference called for February 22, 1892, by six of the leading reform organizations.

4. That a national central committee be appointed by this conference, to be composed of a chairman, to be elected by this body, and of three members from each State represented, to be named by each State delegation.

5. That this central committee shall represent this body, attend the national conference on February 22, 1892, and if possible unite with that and all other reform organizations there assembled. If no satisfactory arrangement can be effected, this committee shall call a national convention not later than June 1, 1892, for the purpose of nominating candidates for President and Vice-President.

6. That the members of the central committee for each State where there is no independent political organization, conduct an active system of political agitation in their respective States.

Resolved, That the question of universal suffrage be recommended to the favorable consideration of the various States and Territories.

Resolved, That while the party in power in 1889 pledged the faith of the Nation to pay a debt in coin that had been contracted on a depreciated currency basis and payable in currency, thus adding nearly one billion dollars to the burdens of the people, which meant gold for the bondholder and depreciated currency for the soldier, and holding that the men who imperiled their lives to save the life of a nation should have been paid in money as good as that paid to the bondholder, we demand the issue of legal tender Treasury notes in sufficient amount to make the pay of the soldiers equal to par with coin, or such other legislation as shall do equal and exact justice to the Union soldiers of this country.

Resolved, That as eight hours constitutes a legal day's work for Government employes in mechanical departments, we believe this principle should be further extended so as to apply to all corporations employing labor in the different States of the Union.

Resolved, That this conference condemns in unmeasured terms the action of the directors of the World's Columbian Exposition, on May 19, in refusing the minimum rate of wages asked for by the labor organizations of Chicago.

Resolved, That the Attorney-General submit the act of March 2, 1889, providing for the opening of Oklahoma to homestead settlement, to the Supreme Court of the United States at the earliest possible moment, that the unhappy settlers of that afflicted Territory may understand the law and Constitutional meaning of said act, and thus put a stop to so much litigation and expense.

Confederated Industrial Platform.

This, the first great labor conference of the United States and of the world, representing all divisions of urban and rural organized industry, assembled in national congress, invoking upon its action the blessing and protection of Almighty God, puts forth to and for the producers of the Nation this declaration of union and independence. The conditions which surround us best justify our co-operation. We meet in the midst of a Nation brought to the verge of moral, political and material ruin. Corruption dominates the ballot-box, the Legislatures, the Congress, and touches even the ermine of the bench. The people are demoralized. Many of the States have been compelled to isolate the voters at the polling places in order to prevent universal intimidation or bribery. The newspapers are subsidized or muzzled, public opinion silenced, business prostrated, our homes covered with mortgages, labor impoverished and the land concentrating in the hands of capitalists. The urban workmen are denied the right of organization for self-protection; imported pauperized labor beats down their wages; a hireling standing army, unrecognized by our laws, is established to shoot them down, and they are rapidly degenerating to European conditions.

The fruits of the toils of millions are boldly stolen to build up colossal fortunes unprecedented in the history of the world, while their possessors despise the Republic and endanger liberty. From the same prolific womb of governmental injustice breed the two great classes—paupers and millionaires. The national power to create money is appropriated to enrich bondholders; silver, which has been accepted as coin since the dawn of history, has been demonetized to add to the purchasing power of gold by decreasing the value of all forms of property, as well as human labor, and the supply of currency is purposely abridged to fatten usurers, bankrupt enterprise and enslave industry. A vast conspiracy against mankind has been organized on two continents, and is taking possession of the world. If not met and overthrown at once it forebodes terrible social convulsions, the destruction of civilization or the establishment of an absolute despotism.

In this human crisis of human affairs intelligent working people and producers of the United States have come together in the name of peace, order and society to defend liberty, prosperity and justice.

We declare our union and independence. We assert our purpose to support the political organization which represents our principles.

We charge that the controlling influence dominating the old political parties has allowed the existing dreadful conditions to develop without serious effort to restrain or prevent them. They have agreed together to ignore in the coming campaign every issue but one. They propose to drown the outcries of a plundered people with the uproar of a sham battle over the tariff, so that corporations, national banks, rings, trusts, "watered stock," the demonetization of silver and the oppression of usurers may all be lost sight of. They propose to sacrifice our homes and children upon the altar of Mammon; to destroy the hopes of the multitude in order to secure corruption funds from the great lords of plunder.

We assert that a political organization, representing the political principles herein stated is necessary to redress the grievances of which we complain.

Assembled on the anniversary of the birth of the illustrious man who led the first great revolution on this continent against oppression, filled with the sentiments which actuated that grand generation, we seek to restore the government of the Republic to the hands of the " plain people " with whom it originated. Our doors are opened to all points of the compass. We ask all honest men to join with and help us.

In order to restrain the extortions of aggregate capital, to drive the money-changers out of the temple, to form a perfect union, establish justice, insure domestic tranquillity, provide for the common defense, promote the general welfare, and secure the blessings of liberty for ourselves and our posterity, we do ordain and establish the following platform of principles:

1. We declare the union of the labor forces of the United States this day accomplished permanent and perpetual. May its spirit enter into all hearts for the salvation of the Republic and the uplifting of mankind.

2. Wealth belongs to him who created it. Every dollar taken from industry without an equivalent is robbery. If any one will not work, neither shall he eat. The interests of rural and urban labor are the same, their enemies are identical.

3. We demand a national currency safe, sound and flexible, issued by the General Government only, a full legal tender for all debts, public and private; and that without the use of banking corporations a just, equitable and efficient means of distribution direct to the people at a tax not to exceed two per cent., be provided, as set forth in the sub-treasury plan of the Farmers' Alliance, or some better system; also, by payments in discharge of its obligations for public improvements.

4. We demand free and unlimited coinage of silver.

5. We demand that the amount of circulating medium be speedily increased to not less than $50 per capita.

6. We demand a graduated income tax.

7. We believe that the money of the country should be kept as much as possible in the hands of the people, and hence we demand all national and State revenue shall be limited to the necessary expenses of the Government, economically and honestly administered.

8. We demand that postal savings banks be established by the Government for the safe deposit of the earnings of the people and to facilitate exchange.

9. The land, including all the natural resources of wealth, is the heritage of all the people, and should not be monopolized for speculative purposes, and alien ownership of land should be prohibited. All land now held by railroads and other corporations in excess of their actual needs, and all lands now owned by aliens, should be reclaimed by the Government and held for actual settlers only.

10. Transportation being a means of exchange and a public necessity, the Government should own and operate the railroads in the interest of the people.

11. The telegraph and the telephone, like the post office system, being a necessity for transmission of news, should be owned and operated by the Government in the interest of the people.

PLATFORMS OF 1892.

The Republican national convention this year assembled in Minneapolis, June 7; the Democrats met in Chicago, June 21; the Prohibitionists held their national convention in Cincinnati, June 29; and the People's party's first convention to nominate a Presidential ticket met in Omaha, July 14. All these adopted platforms, and an additional platform was adopted by the grand council of the Independent People's Labor party at a meeting held in Cleveland, June 24, at which the Republican Presidential ticket was endorsed. For the first time in its history in the United States, the Socialist Labor party placed a Presidential ticket in the field, at a convention which met in New York, August 28. The platform of 1889 was reaffirmed.

Republican Platform.

The representatives of the Republicans of the United States, assembled in general convention on the shores of the Mississippi River, the everlasting bond of an indestructible Republic whose most glorious chapter of history is the record of the Republican party, congratulating their countrymen on the majestic march of the Nation under the banners inscribed with the principles of our platform of 1888, vindicated by victory at the polls and prosperity in our fields, workshops and mines, make the following declaration of principles:

We reaffirm the American doctrine of protection. We call attention to its growth abroad.

We maintain that the prosperous condition of our country is largely due to the wise revenue legislation of the Republican Congress. We believe that all articles which cannot be produced in the United States, except luxuries, should be admitted free of duty; and that on all imports coming into competition with the products of American labor there should be duties levied equal to the difference between wages abroad and at home. We assert that the prices of manufactured articles of general consumption have been reduced under the operation of the tariff act of 1890. We denounce the efforts of the Democratic majority of the House to destroy our tariff laws by piecemeal, as manifested by their attacks on wool, lead and lead ore, and we ask the people for their judgment thereon.

We point to the success of the Republican policy of reciprocity, under which our export trade has vastly increased and new and enlarged markets have been opened for the products of our farms and workshops. We remind the people of the bitter opposition of the Democratic party to this practical business measure, and claim that, executed by a Republican administration, our present laws will eventually give us control of the trade of the world.

The American people from tradition and interest favor bimetallism, and the Republican party demands the use of both gold and silver as standard money, such restrictions to be determined by contemplation of values of the two metals, so that the purchasing and debt paying power of the dollar, whether of silver, gold or paper, shall be equal at all times.

The interests of the producers of the country, its farmers and its workingmen, demand that every dollar—paper or gold—issued by the Government, shall be as good as any other. We commend the wise and patriotic steps already taken by our Government to secure an international parity of value between gold and silver for use as money throughout the world.

We demand that every citizen of the United States shall be allowed to cast one free and unrestricted ballot in all public elections, and that such ballot shall be counted and returned as cast; that such laws shall be enacted and enforced as will secure to every citizen, be he rich or poor, native or foreign born, white or black, this sovereign right, guaranteed by the Constitution, the free and honest popular ballot, the just and equal representation of all the people, as well as the just and equal protection under the laws as the foundation of our republican institutions, and the party will never relax its efforts until the integrity of the ballot and the purity of elections shall be fully guaranteed and protected in every State.

We denounce the continued inhuman outrages perpetrated on American citizens for political reasons in certain Southern States of the Union.

We favor the extension of our foreign commerce ; the restoration of our mercantile marine by home-built ships, and the construction of a navy for the protection of our national interests and the honor of our flag ; the maintenance of the most friendly relations with all foreign powers, entangling alliances with none, and the protection of the rights of our fishermen. We reaffirm our approval of the Monroe doctrine and believe in the achievement of the manifest destiny of the Republic in its broadest sense. We favor the enactment of more stringent laws and regulations for the restriction of criminal, pauper and contract immigration.

We favor efficient legislation by Congress to protect the life and limbs of employes of railroad companies engaged in carrying inter-state commerce, and recommend legislation by the respective States that will protect employes engaged in inter-state commerce, in mining and in manufacturing.

The Republican party has always been the champion of the oppressed, and recognizes the dignity of manhood, irrespective of faith, color or nationality. It sympathizes with the cause of home-rule in Ireland, and protests against the persecution of the Jews in Russia. The ultimate reliance of free, popular government is the intelligence of the people and the maintenance of freedom among men.

We declare anew our devotion to liberty of thought and conscience, of speech and of the press, and approve all agencies and instrumentalities which contribute to the education of the children of the land ; but while insisting upon the fullest measure of religious liberty, we are opposed to any union of church and state.

We reaffirm our opposition declared in the Republican platform of 1888, to all combinations of capital organized to control arbitrarily the condition of trade among our citizens. We heartily endorse the action taken on this issue, and ask for such further legislation as may be required to remedy any defects in existing laws and to render their enforcement more complete and effective.

We approve the policy of extending to towns and rural communities the advantages of the free delivery service now enjoyed by the large cities of the country, and reaffirm the declaration contained in the Republican platform of 1888, pledging the reduction of letter postage to one cent at the earliest possible moment.

We commend the spirit and evidence of reform in the civil service and the wise and consistent enforcement by the Republican party of the laws relating to the same.

The construction of the Nicaragua canal is of the highest importance to the American people, both as a measure of national defense and to build up and maintain American commerce, and it should be controlled by the United States Government.

We favor the admission of the remaining Territories at the earliest possible moment, having due regard to the interests of the people of the Territories and for the United States. All the federal office-holders appointed in the Territories should be selected from the residents thereof, and the right of self-government should be accorded as far as possible.

We favor the cession, subject to the homestead laws, of the arid public lands to the States and Territories in which they lie, under such Congressional restrictions as to disposition, reclamation and occupancy by settlers as will secure the maximum benefits for the people.

The World's Columbian Exposition is a great national undertaking, and Congress should promptly enact such reasonable legislation in aid thereof as will ensure a discharge of the expenses and obligations incident thereto, and the attainment of results commensurate with the dignity and progress of the Nation.

We sympathize with all wise and legitimate efforts to lessen and prevent the evils of intemperance and promote morality.

Ever mindful of the services and sacrifices of the men who saved the life of the Nation, we pledge anew to the veteran soldiers of the Republic a watchful care and recognition of their just claims upon a grateful people.

We commend the able, patriotic, and thoroughly American administration of President Harrison. Under it the country has enjoyed remarkable prosperity, and the dignity and honor of the Nation, at home and abroad, have been faithfully maintained, and we offer the record of pledges kept as a guarantee of faithful performance in the future.

Democratic Platform.

1. The representatives of the Democratic party of the United States in national convention assembled, do reaffirm their allegiance to the principles of the party, as formulated by Jefferson and exemplified by the long and illustrious line of his successors in Democratic leadership from Madison to Cleveland; we believe the public welfare demands that these principles be applied to the conduct of the Federal Government through the accession to power of the party that advocates them; and we solemnly declare that the need of a return to these fundamental principles of a free popular government, based on home rule and individual liberty, was never more urgent than now when the tendency to centralize all power at the Federal Capital has become a menace to the reserved rights of the States that strikes at the very roots of our Government

under the Constitution as framed by the fathers of the Republic.

2. We warn the people of our common country, zealous for the preservation of their free institutions, that the policy of Federal control of elections to which the Republican party has committed itself is fraught with the greatest dangers, scarcely less momentous than would result from a revolution practically establishing monarchy on the ruins of the Republic. It strikes at the North as well as the South, and injures the colored citizen even more than the white. It means a horde of deputy marshals at every polling place armed with Federal power, returning boards appointed and controlled by Federal authority, the outrage of electoral rights of the people in the several States, the subjugation of the colored people to the control of the party in power, and the reviving of race antagonisms now happily abated, of the utmost peril to the safety and happiness of all; a measure deliberately and justly described by a leading Republican Senator as the "most infamous bill that ever crossed the threshold of the Senate." Such a policy, if sanctioned by law, would mean the dominance of a self-perpetuating oligarchy of office-holders, and the party first intrusted with its machinery could be dislodged from power only by an appeal to the reserved right of the people to resist oppression, which is inherent in all self-governing communities. Two years ago this revolutionary policy was emphatically condemned by the people at the polls; but in contempt of that verdict the Republican party has definitely declared, in its latest authoritative utterance, that its success in the coming elections will mean the enactment of the Force Bill, and the usurpation of despotic control over elections in all the States. Believing that the preservation of Republican Government in the United States is dependent upon the defeat of this policy of legalized force and fraud, we invite the support of all citizens who desire to see the Constitution maintained in its integrity with the laws pursuant thereto which have given our country a hundred years of unexampled prosperity; and we pledge the Democratic party, if it be entrusted with power, not only to the defeat of the Force Bill, but also to relentless opposition to the Republican policy of profligate expenditure which, in the short space of two years, has squandered an enormous surplus, and emptied an overflowing treasury, after piling new burdens of taxation upon the already overtaxed labor of the country.

3. We denounce the Republican protection as a fraud, a robbery of the great majority of the American people for the benefit of the few. We declare it to be a fundamental principle of the Democratic party that the Federal Government has no Constitutional power to impose and collect tariff duties, except for the purposes of revenue only, and we demand that the collection of such taxes shall be limited to the necessities of the Government when honestly and economically administered.

We denounce the McKinley tariff law enacted by the Fifty-first Congress as the culminating atrocity of class legislation; we endorse the efforts made by the Democrats of the present Congress to modify its most oppressive features in the direction of free raw materials and cheaper manufactured goods that enter into general consumption, and we promise its repeal as one of the beneficent results that will follow the action of the people in entrusting power to the Democratic party. Since the McKinley tariff went into operation there have been ten reductions of the wages of laboring men to one increase. We deny that there has been any increase of prosperity to the country since that tariff went into operation, and we point to the dullness and distress, the wages, reductions and strikes in the iron trade as the best possible evidence that no such prosperity has resulted from the McKinley act.

We call the attention of thoughtful Americans to the fact that, after thirty years of restrictive taxes against the importation of foreign wealth in exchange for our agricultural surplus, the homes and farms of the country have become burdened with a real estate mortgage debt of over $2,500,000,000, exclusive of all other forms of indebtedness; that in one of the chief agricultural States of the West there appears a real estate mortgage debt averaging $165 per capita of the total population, and that similar conditions and tendencies are shown to exist in the other agricultural exporting States. We denounce a policy which fosters no industry so much as it does that of the sheriff.

4. Trade interchange on the basis of reciprocal advantage to the countries participating is a time-honored doctrine of the Democratic faith; but we denounce the sham reciprocity which juggles with the people's desires for enlarged foreign markets and freer exchanges, by pretending to establish closer trade relations for a country whose articles of export are almost exclusively agricultural products with other countries that are also agricultural, while erecting a customhouse barrier of prohibitive tariff taxes against the richest countries of the world, that stand ready to take our entire surplus of products and to exchange therefor commodities which are necessaries and comforts of life among our own people.

5. We recognize in the trusts and combinations, which are designed to enable capital to secure more than its just share of the joint product of capital and labor, a natural consequence of the prohibitive taxes which prevent the free

competition which is the life of honest trade, but we believe their worst evils can be abated by law, and we demand the rigid enforcement of the laws made to prevent and control them, together with such further legislation in restraint of their abuses as experience may show to be necessary.

6. The Republican party, while professing a policy of reserving the public lands for small holding by actual settlers, has given away the people's heritage, till now a few railroads and non-resident aliens, individual and corporate, possess a larger area than that of all our farms between the two seas. The last Democratic administration reversed the improvident and unwise policy of the Republican party touching the public domain, and reclaimed from corporations and syndicates, alien and domestic, and restored to the people nearly 100,000,000 acres of valuable land, to be sacredly held as homesteads for our citizens, and we pledge ourselves to continue this policy until every acre of land so unlawfully held shall be reclaimed and restored to the people.

7. We denounce the Republican legislation known as the Sherman act of 1890 as a cowardly makeshift, fraught with possibilities of danger in the future which should make all of its supporters, as well as its author, anxious for its speedy repeal. We hold to the use of both gold and silver as the standard money of the country, and to the coinage of both gold and silver without discrimination against either metal or charge for mintage, but the dollar unit of coinage of both metals must be of equal intrinsic and exchangeable value, or be adjusted through international agreement or by such safeguards of legislation as shall ensure the maintenance of the parity of the two metals and the equal power of every dollar at all times in the markets and in the payment of debts; and we demand that all paper currency shall be kept at par with and redeemable in such coin. We insist upon this policy as especially necessary for the protection of the farmers and laboring classes, the first and most defenseless victims of unstable money and a fluctuating currency.

8. We recommend that the prohibitory 10 per cent. tax on State bank issues be repealed.

9. Public office is a public trust. We reaffirm the declaration of the Democratic National Convention of 1876 for the reform of the civil service, and we call for the honest enforcement of all laws regulating the same. The nomination of a President, as in the recent Republican convention, by delegations composed largely of his appointees, holding office at his pleasure, is a scandalous satire upon free popular institutions and a startling illustration of the methods by which a President may gratify his ambition. We denounce a policy under which Federal office-holders usurp control of party conventions in the States, and we pledge the Democratic party to the reform of these and all other abuses which threaten individual liberty and local self-government.

10. The Democratic party is the only party that has ever given the country a foreign policy consistent and vigorous, compelling respect abroad and inspiring confidence at home. While avoiding entangling alliances, it has aimed to cultivate friendly relations with other nations, and especially with our American neighbors on the American continent, whose destiny is closely linked with our own, and we view with alarm the tendency to a policy of irritation and bluster which is liable at any time to confront us with the alternative of humiliation or war. We favor the maintenance of a navy strong enough for all purposes of national defense and to properly maintain the honor and dignity of the country abroad.

11. This country has always been the refuge of the oppressed from every land —exiles for conscience' sake—and in the spirit of the founders of our Government we condemn the oppression practiced by the Russian government upon its Lutheran and Jewish subjects, and we call upon our national Government, in the interests of justice and humanity by all just and proper means, to use its prompt and best efforts to bring about a cessation of these cruel persecutions in the dominions of the Czar, and to secure to the oppressed equal rights. We tender our profound and earnest sympathy to those lovers of freedom who are struggling for home rule and the great cause of local self-government in Ireland.

12. We heartily approve of all legitimate efforts to prevent the United States from being used as a dumping ground for the known criminals and professional paupers of Europe; and we demand the rigid enforcement of the laws against Chinese immigration or the importation of foreign workmen under contract to degrade American labor and lessen its wages; but we condemn and denounce any and all attempts to restrict the immigration of the industrious and worthy of foreign lands.

13. This convention hereby renews the expression of appreciation of the patriotism of the soldiers and sailors of the Union in the war for its preservation, and we favor just and liberal pensions for all disabled Union soldiers, their widows and dependents; but we demand that the work of the pension office shall be done industriously, impartially and honestly. We denounce the present administration of that office as incompetent, corrupt, disgraceful and dishonest.

14. The Federal Government should care for and improve the Mississippi River and other great waterways of the Republic, so as to secure for the interior States easy and cheap transpor-

tation to the tidewater. When any waterway of the Republic is of sufficient importance to demand the aid of the Government such aid should be extended for a definite plan of continuous work until permanent improvement is secured.

15. For purposes of national defense and the promotion of commerce between the States, we recognize the early construction of the Nicaragua Canal and its protection against foreign control as of great importance to the United States.

16. Recognizing the World's Columbian Exposition as a national undertaking of vast importance, in which the General Government has invited the co-operation of all the powers of the world, and appreciating the acceptance by many of such powers of the invitation extended, and the broadest liberal efforts being made by them to contribute to the grandeur of the undertaking, we are of the opinion that Congress should make such necessary financial provisions as shall be requisite to the maintenance of the national honor and public faith.

17. Popular education being the only safe basis of popular suffrage, we recommend to the several States most liberal appropriations for the public schools. Free common schools are the nursery of good government, and they have always received the fostering care of the Democratic party, which favors every means of increasing intelligence. Freedom of education being an essential of civil and religious liberty, as well as a necessity for the development of intelligence, must not be interfered with under any pretext whatever. We are opposed to State interference with parental rights and rights of conscience in the education of children as an infringement of the fundamental Democratic doctrine that the largest individual liberty consistent with the rights of others ensures the highest type of American citizenship and the best government.

18. We approve the action of the present House of Representatives in passing bills for the admission into the Union as States of the Territories of New Mexico and Arizona, and we favor the early admission of all the Territories having necessary population and resources to admit them to statehood, and, while they remain Territories, we hold that the officials appointed to administer the government of any Territory, together with the Districts of Columbia and Alaska, should be bona fide residents of the Territory or District in which their duties are to be performed. The Democratic party believes in home rule and the control of their own affairs by the people of the vicinage.

19. We favor legislation by Congress and State legislatures to protect the lives and limbs of railway employes and those of other hazardous transportation companies, and denounce the in-activity of the Republican party, and particularly the Republican Senate, for causing the defeat of measures beneficial and protective to this class of wage-workers.

20. We are in favor of the enactment by the States of laws for abolishing the notorious sweating system, for abolishing contract convict labor, and for prohibiting the employment in factories of children under 15 years of age.

21. We are opposed to all sumptuary laws as an interference with the individual rights of the citizen.

22. Upon this statement of principles and policies, the Democratic party asks the intelligent judgment of the American people. It asks a change of Administration and a change of party in order that there may be a change of system and a change of methods, thus assuring the maintenance unimpaired of institutions under which the Republic has grown great and powerful.

Independent People's Labor Platform.

Resolved, That we heartily indorse the administration of President Harrison, from the fact that he has done all in his power for the Union soldiers of the late war of the rebellion in advising in his message to Congress to pension the Union soldiers of the late war of the rebellion.

Resolved, That we highly commend President Harrison for his good judgment in selecting such an able and competent person for the position of Secretary of the Treasury of the United States as Hon. Charles Foster of Ohio, who has always proved himself to be a friend of the laboring classes.

Resolved, That we heartily indorse the McKinley bill, believing it to be in the interest of the laboring and producing element of this country as well as the whole people.

Resolved, That we heartily indorse protection to American labor, believing that free trade is detrimental to the laboring and producing elements of this country.

Resolved, That we do condemn the acts of Grover Cleveland while President of the United States in favoring the return of the rebel battle flags.

Resolved, That we do condemn the act of Grover Cleveland while President of the United States, in the veto of the dependent pension bill, from the fact that the Union army of the late war of the rebellion was mostly composed of laboring men, and are deserving of a pension which has been granted to them under the administration of President Harrison.

Resolved, That we are proud of our indorsement of Benjamin Harrison and Morton in 1888 at our grand council meeting held in Detroit, Michigan, because President Harrison has given the people of this country a pure and clean administration.

Resolved, That we, as representatives of the Independent People's Labor party, looking forward in the interest of the laboring and producing elements of this country, cannot support a party that will nominate a man for President of the United States who proclaims that free trade is in the interest of the laboring and producing elements of this country.

Resolved, That we cannot support free trade if for no other reason than that England favors it, because we believe that England never favors anything which is in the interest of America.

Prohibition Platform.

The Prohibition party, in national convention assembled, acknowledging Almighty God as the source of all true government and His law as the standard to which business enactments must conform to secure the blessings of peace and prosperity, presents the following declaration of principles:

The liquor traffic is a foe to civilization, the arch-enemy of popular government and a public nuisance. It is the citadel of the forces that corrupt politics, promote poverty and crime, degrade the Nation's home life, thwart the will of the people, and deliver our country into the hands of rapacious class interests. All laws that under the guise of regulation legalize and protect this traffic, or make the Government share in its ill-gotten gains, are vicious in principle and powerless of a remedy. We declare anew for the entire suppression of the manufacture, sale, importation, exportation and transportation of alcoholic liquors as a beverage, by federal and State legislation, and the full powers of government should be exerted to secure this result. No party that fails to recognize the nature of this issue in American politics is deserving of the support of the people.

No citizen should be denied the right to vote on account of sex, and equal labor should receive equal wages without regard to sex.

The money of the country should be issued by the General Government only and in sufficient quantity to meet the demands of business and give full opportunity for the employment of labor. To this end an increase in the volume of money is demanded. No individual or corporation should be allowed to make any profit through its issue. It should be made a legal tender for the payment of all debts, public and private. Its volume should be fixed at a definite sum per capita and made to increase with population.

Tariff should be levied only as a defense against foreign governments which levy tariff upon or bar out our products from their markets, revenue being incidental. The residue of means

necessary to an economical administration of the Government should be raised by levying the burden on what the people possess instead of upon what we consume.

Railroads, telegraphs, and other public corporations should be controlled by the Government in the interest of the people, and no higher charges allowed than necessary to give fair interest on the capital actually invested.

Foreign immigration has become a burden upon industry, one of the factors in depressing wages and causing discontent; therefore our immigration laws should be revised and strictly enforced. The time of residence for naturalization should be extended and no naturalized person should be allowed to vote until one year after he becomes a citizen. No resident aliens should be allowed to acquire land in this country, and we favor the limitation of individual and corporate ownership of land —all unearned grants to railroads, companies or other corporations should be reclaimed. Years of inaction and treachery on the part of the Republican and Democratic parties have resulted in the present reign of mob law, and we demand that every citizen be protected in the right of trial by Constitutional tribunals. All men should be protected by law in their right to one day of rest in seven.

Arbitration is the wisest and most economical and humane method of settling national differences.

Speculation in margins, the cornering of grain, money and products and the formation of pools, trusts and combinations for the arbitrary advancement of prices should be suppressed.

We arraign the Republican and Democratic parties as false to the standards reared by their founders and faithless to the principles of the illustrious leaders of the past, to whom they do homage with the lips, as recreant to "the higher law," which is as inflexible in political affairs as in personal life, and as no longer embodying the aspirations of the American people or inviting the confidence of enlightened, progressive patriotism. Their protest against the admission of "moral issues" into politics is a confession of their own moral degeneracy. The declaration of an eminent authority that municipal misrule is "the one conspicuous failure of American politics" follows as a natural consequence of such degeneracy, and is true alike of cities under Republican and Democratic control. Each accuses the other of extravagance in Congressional appropriations, and both are alike guilty. Each protests when out of power against infractions of the civil service laws, and each when in power violates those laws in letter and in spirit. Each professes fealty to the toiling masses, but both covertly truckle to the money power in the administration of public affairs. Even the tariff issue, as represented in the Democratic Mills bill and the Republican McKinley bill, is no longer treated by them as an issue between great and divergent principles of government, but is a mere catering to different sectional and class interests.

The attempt in many States to wrest the Australian ballot system from its true purpose, and to so deform it as to render it extremely difficult for new parties to exercise the rights of suffrage, is an outrage upon popular government. The competition of both these parties for the vote of the slums, and their assiduous courting of the liquor power and subserviency to the money power, has resulted in placing those powers in position of practical arbiters of the destinies of the Nation. We renew our protests against these personal tendencies, and invite all citizens to join us in the upbuilding of a party that has shown in five national campaigns that it prefers temporary defeat to an abandonment of the claims of justice, sobriety, personal rights and the protection of American homes. We pledge that the Prohibition party, if elected to power, will ever grant just pensions to disabled veterans of the Union army and navy, their widows and orphans.

We stand unequivocally for the American public school, and opposed to any appropriation of public moneys for sectarian schools. We believe that only by united support of such common schools taught in the English language can we hope to become and remain a homogeneous and harmonious people.

People's Party Platform.

Assembled upon the 116th anniversary of the Declaration of Independence, the People's party of America, invoking upon their action the blessing of Almighty God, puts forth in the name and on behalf of the people of this country the following preamble and platform:

The conditions which surround us best justify our co-operation. We meet in the midst of a Nation brought to the verge of moral, political and material ruin. Corruption dominates the ballot-box, the legislatures, the Congress, and touches even the ermine of the bench. The people are demoralized; most of the States have been compelled to isolate the voters at the polling places to prevent universal intimidation or bribery. The newspapers are largely subsidized or muzzled, public opinion silenced, business prostrated, our homes covered with mortgages, labor impoverished and the land concentrating in the hands of the capitalists. The urban workmen are denied the right of organization for self-protection, imported pauperized labor beats down their wages, a hireling standing army, unrecognized by our laws, is established to shoot them down, and they are rapidly degenerating into European conditions. The fruits of the toil of millions are boldly stolen to build up colossal fortunes for a

few, unprecedented in the history of mankind, and the possessors of these in turn despise the Republic and endanger liberty. From the same prolific womb of governmental injustice we breed the two classes—tramps and millionaires. The national power to create money is appropriated to enrich bondholders. A vast public debt, payable in legal tender currency, has been funded into gold bearing bonds, thereby adding millions to the burdens of the people. Silver, which has been accepted as coin since the dawn of history, has been demonetized to add to the purchasing power of gold, by decreasing the value of all forms of property as well as human labor, and the supply of currency is purposely abridged to fatten usurers, bankrupt enterprise and enslave industry. A vast conspiracy against mankind has been organized on two continents, and it is rapidly taking possession of the world. If not met and overthrown at once it forbodes terrible social convulsions, the destruction of civilization or the establishment of an absolute despotism. We have witnessed for more than a quarter of a century the struggles of the two great political parties for power and plunder, while grievous wrongs have been inflicted upon the suffering people. We charge that the controlling influences dominating both these parties have permitted the existing dreadful conditions to develop without serious effort to prevent or restrain them. Neither do they now promise us any substantial reform. They have agreed together to ignore, in the coming campaign, every issue but one. They propose to drown the outcries of a plundered people with the uproar of a battle over the tariff, so that capitalists, corporations, national banks, rings, trusts, watered stock, the demonetization of silver and the oppressions of usurers may all be lost sight of. They propose to sacrifice our homes, lives and children on the altar of Mammon; to destroy the multitude in order to secure corruption funds from the millionaires.

Assembled on the anniversary of the birthday of the Nation and filled with the spirit of the grand generation who established our independence, we seek to restore the Government of the Republic to the hands of "the plain people," with whose class it originated. We assert our purposes to be identical with the purposes of the national Constitution, to form a more perfect union, establish justice, insure domestic tranquility, provide for the common defense, promote the general welfare and secure the blessings of liberty for ourselves and our posterity.

We declare that this Republic can endure only as a free government while built upon the love of the whole people for each other and for the Nation; that it cannot be pinned together by bayonets; that the civil war is over, and that every passion and resentment which grew out of it must die with it, and that we must be in fact as we are in name, one united brotherhood of free men. Our country finds itself confronted by conditions for which there is no precedent in the history of the world; our annual agricultural productions amount to billions of dollars in value, which must within a few weeks or months be exchanged for billions of dollars of commodities consumed in their production; the existing currency supply is wholly inadequate to make this exchange; the results are falling of prices, the formation of combines and rings, the impoverishment of the producing class. We pledge ourselves that if given power we will labor to correct these evils by wise and reasonable legislation in accordance with the terms of our platform.

We believe that the powers of government—in other words of the people—should be expanded (as in the case of the postal service) as rapidly and as far as the good sense of an intelligent people and the teachings of experience shall justify, to the end that oppression, injustice and poverty shall eventually cease in the land.

While our sympathies as a party of reform are naturally upon the side of every proposition which will tend to make men intelligent, virtuous and temperate, we nevertheless regard these questions—important as they are—as secondary to the great issues now pressing for solution, and upon which not only our individual prosperity but the very existence of free institutions depend; and we ask all men to first help us to determine whether we are to have a Republic to administer, we differ as to the conditions upon which it is to be administered; believing that the forces of reform this day organized will never cease to move forward until every wrong is remedied, and equal rights and equal privileges securely established for all the men and women of this country. We declare, therefore,

First—That the union of the labor forces of the United States this day consummated shall be permanent and perpetual; may its spirit enter into all hearts for the salvation of the Republic and the uplifting of mankind.

Second—Wealth belongs to him who creates it, and every dollar taken from industry without an equivalent is robbery. "If any will not work, neither shall he eat." The interests of rural and civic labor are the same; their enemies are identical.

Third—We believe that the time has come when the railroad corporations will either own the people or the people must own the railroads, and should the Government enter upon the work of owning and managing any or all railroads, we should favor an amendment to the Constitution by which all persons engaged in the Government service shall be placed under a civil service

regulation of the most rigid character, so as to prevent an increase of the power of the national administration by the use of such additional Government employes.

We demand a national currency, safe, sound and flexible, issued by the general Government only, a full legal tender for all debts, public and private, and that without the use of banking corporations, a just, equitable and efficient means of distribution direct to the people, at a tax not to exceed 2 per cent. per annum to be provided as set forth in the sub-treasury plan of the Farmers' Alliance, or a better system; also by payments in discharge of its obligations for public improvements.

1. We demand free and unlimited coinage of silver and gold at the present legal ratio of 16 to 1.

2. We demand that the amount of circulating medium be speedily increased to not less than $50 per capita.

3. We demand a graduated income tax.

4. We believe that the money of the country should be kept as much as possible in the hands of the people, and hence we demand that all State and national revenues shall be limited to the necessary expenses of the Government, economically and honestly administered.

5. We demand that postal savings banks be established by the Government for the safe deposit of the earnings of the people and to facilitate exchange.

Transportation being a means of exchange and a public necessity, the Government should own and operate the railroads in the interest of the people.

The telegraph and telephone, like the post-office system, being a necessity for the transmission of news, should be owned and operated by the Government in the interest of the people.

The land, including all the natural sources of wealth, is the heritage of the people, and should not be monopolized for speculative purposes, and alien ownership of land should be prohibited. All land now held by railroads and other corporations in excess of their actual needs, and all lands now owned by aliens should be reclaimed by the Government and held for actual settlers only.

The following supplementary resolutions were adopted:

WHEREAS, Other questions have been presented for our consideration, we hereby submit the following, not as a part of the platform of the People's Party, but as resolutions expressive of the convention:

Resolved, That we demand a free ballot and a fair count in all elections, and pledge ourselves to secure it to every legal voter without federal intervention through the adoption by the States of the unperverted Australian or secret ballot system.

Resolved, That the revenue derived from a graduated income tax should be applied to the reduction of the burden of taxation, now levied upon the domestic industries of this country.

Resolved, That we pledge our support to fair and liberal pensions to ex-Union soldiers and sailors.

Resolved, That we condemn the fallacy of protecting American labor under the present system, which opens our ports to the pauper and criminal classes of the world and crowds out our wage earners; and we denounce the present ineffective laws against contract labor, and demand the further restriction of undesirable immigration.

Resolved, That we cordially sympathize with the efforts of organized workmen to shorten the hours of labor, and demand a rigid enforcement of the existing eight hour law on government work, and ask that a penalty clause be added to to the said law.

Resolved, That we regard the maintenance of a large standing army of mercenaries, known as the Pinkerton system, as a menace to our liberties, and we demand its abolition ; and we condemn the recent invasion of the Territory of Wyoming by the hired assassins of plutocracy, assisted by Federal officers.

Resolved, That we commend to the thoughtful consideration of the people and the reform press the legislative system known as the initiative and referendum.

Resolved, That we favor a Constitutional provision limiting the office of President and Vice-President to one term, and providing for the election of Senators of the United States by a direct vote of the people.

Resolved, That we oppose any subsidy or national aid to any private corporation for any purpose.

Socialist Labor Platform.

(Adopted in 1889, Reaffirmed in 1892.)

The Socialist Labor party of the United States, in convention assembled, reasserts the inalienable right of all men to life, liberty, and the pursuit of happiness.

With the founders of the American Republic we hold that the purpose of government is to secure every citizen in the enjoyment of this right; but in the light of our social conditions we hold, furthermore, that no such right can be exercised under a system of economic inequality, essentially destructive of life, of liberty, and of happiness.

With the founders of this Republic we hold that the true theory of politics is that the machinery of government must be owned and controlled by the whole people; but in the light of our industrial development we hold, further-

more, that the true theory of economics is that the machinery of production must likewise belong to the people in common.

To the obvious fact that our despotic system of economics is the direct opposite of our Democratic system of politics, can plainly be traced the existence of a privileged class, the corruption of government by that class, the alienation of public property, public franchises and public functions to that class, and the abject dependence of the mightiest of nations upon that class.

Again, through the perversion of Democracy to the ends of plutocracy, labor is robbed of the wealth which it alone produces, is denied the means of self-employment, and by compulsory idleness in wage slavery, is even deprived of the necessaries of life.

Human power and natural forces are thus wasted that the plutocracy may rule.

Ignorance and misery, with all their concomitant evils, are perpetuated that the people may be kept in bondage.

Science and inventions are diverted from their humane purpose to the enslavement of women and children.

Against such a system the Socialist Labor party once more enters its protest. Once more it reiterates its fundamental declaration, that private property, in the natural source of production and in the instruments of labor, is the obvious cause of all economic sevitude and political dependence; and,

WHEREAS, The time is fast coming when, in the natural course of social evolution, this system, through the destructive action of its failures and crises on the one hand and the constructive tendencies of its trusts and other capitalistic combinations on the other hand, shall have worked out its own downfall: Therefore, be it

Resolved, That we call upon the people to organize with a view to the substitution of the cooperative commonwealth for the present state of planless production, industrial war and social disorder; a commonwealth in which every worker shall have the free exercise and full benefit of his faculties, multiplied by all the modern factors of civilization.

We call upon them to unite with us in a mighty effort to gain by all practicable means the political power.

In the meantime, and with a view to immediate improvement in the condition of labor, we present the following "demands :"

SOCIAL DEMANDS.

1. Reduction in the hours of labor in proportion to the progress of production.

2. The United States shall obtain possession of the railroads, canals, telegraphs and telephones and all other means of public transportation and communication.

3. The municipalities to obtain possession of the local railroads, ferries, water works, gas works, electric plants, and all industries requiring municipal franchises.

4. The public lands to be declared inalienable. Revocation of all land grants to corporations or individuals the conditions of which have not been complied with.

5. Legal incorporation by the States of local trade unions, which have no national organization.

6. The United States to have the exclusive right to issue money.

7. Congressional legislation providing for the scientific management of forests and waterways and prohibiting the waste of the natural resources of the country.

8. Inventions to be free to all, the inventors to be remunerated by the Nation.

9. Progressive income tax and tax on inheritances; the smaller incomes to be exempt.

10. School education of all children under 14 years of age to be compulsory, gratuitous and accessible to all by public assistance in meals, clothing, books, etc., where necessary.

11. Repeal of all pauper, tramp, conspiracy and sumptuary laws. Unabridged right of combination.

12. Official statistics concerning the condition of labor. Prohibition of the employment of children of school age, and of the employment of female labor in occupations detrimental to health or morality. Abolition of the convict labor contract system.

13. All wages to be paid in lawful money of the United States. Equalization of women's wages with those of men where equal services are performed.

14. Laws for the protection of life and limb in all occupations, and an efficient employers' liability law.

POLITICAL DEMANDS.

1. The people to have the right to propose laws and to vote upon all measures of importance according to the referendum principle.

2. Abolition of the Presidency, Vice-Presidency and Senate of the United States. An executive board to be established, whose members are to be elected, and may at any time be recalled by the House of Representatives as the only legislative body. The States and municipalities to adopt corresponding amendments to their constitutions and statutes.

3. Municipal self-government.

4. Direct vote and secret ballots in all elections. Universal and equal right of suffrage without regard to color, creed or sex. Election days to be legal holidays. The principle of minority representation to be introduced.

5. All public officers to be subject to recall by their respective constituencies.

9. Uniform civil and criminal law throughout the United States. Administration of justice to be free of charge. Abolition of capital punishment.

PLATFORMS OF 1896.

The first national nominating convention of 1896 was that of the Prohibition party, which met at Pittsburgh, May 27, and adopted a "single plank" platform. The "broad gauge" Prohibitionists, who had insisted that their party should declare for other measures besides that of prohibition of the liquor traffic, at once withdrew, and on the 29th of the same month organized the National party. On the 17th of June the Republican convention assembled in St. Louis; the Socialist Labor party met in convention in New York, July 4; the Democratic convention met in Chicago July 7; the People's party and the Silver party met in St. Louis July 22. September 2, representatives of those Democrats who opposed the Chicago platform and candidates met in convention in Indianapolis. All these parties adopted platforms and nominated candidates for President and Vice-President.

Prohibition Platform.

The Prohibition party in national convention assembled declares its firm conviction that the manufacture, exportation, importation and sale of alcoholic beverages has produced such commercial, industrial, social and political wrongs and is now so threatening the perpetuity of all our social and political institutions that the suppression of the same by a national party organized therefor is the greatest object to be accomplished by the voters of our country, and is of such importance as that it, of right, ought to control the political action of all our patriotic citizens until such suppression is accomplished. The urgency of this cause demands the union, without further delay, of all citizens who desire the prohibition of the liquor traffic. Therefore, be it resolved that we favor the legal prohibition, by State and national legislation, of the exportation, inter-state transportation and sale of alcoholic beverages; that we declare our purpose to organize and unite all the friends of prohibition into one party, and in order to accomplish this end we deem it but right to leave every Prohibitionist the freedom of his own convictions upon all other political questions, and trust our Representatives to legislate upon other political questions as the changes occasioned by prohibition and the welfare of the whole people shall demand.

National Platform.

The National party, recognizing God as the author of all just power in government, presents the following declaration of principles, which it pledges itself to enact into effective legislation when given the power to do so:

1. The suppression of the manufacture and sale, importation, exportation and transportation of intoxicating liquors for beverage purposes. We utterly reject all plans for regulating or compromising with this traffic, whether such plans be called local option, taxation, license or public control. The sale of liquors for medicinal and other legitimate uses should be conducted by the State, without profit, and with such regulations as will prevent fraud or evasion.

2. No citizen should be denied the right to vote on account of sex.

3. All money should be issued by the General Government only, and without the intervention of any private citizen, corporation or banking institution. It should be based upon the wealth, stability and integrity of the Nation. It should be a full legal tender for all debts, public and private, and should be of sufficient volume to meet the demands of the legitimate business interests of the country. For the purpose of honestly liquidating our outstanding coin obligations, we favor the free and unlimited coinage of both silver and gold, at the ratio 16 to 1, without consulting any other nation.

4. Land is the common heritage of the people and should be preserved from monopoly and speculation. All unearned grants of land, subject to forfeiture, should be reclaimed by the Government, and no portion of the public domain should hereafter be granted except to actual settlers, continuous use being essential to tenure.

5. Railroads, telegraphs and other natural monopolies should be owned and operated by the Government, giving to the people the benefit of service at actual cost.

6. The national Constitution should be so amended as to allow the national revenues to be raised by equitable adjustment of taxation on the properties and incomes of the people, and import duties should be levied as a means of securing equitable commercial relations with other nations.

7. The contract convict labor system, through which speculators are enriched at the expense of the State, should be abolished.

8. All citizens should be protected by law in their right to one day of rest in seven, without oppressing any who conscientiously observe any other than the first day of the week.

9. The American public schools, taught in the English language, should be maintained, and no public funds should be appropriated for sectarian institutions.

10. The President, Vice-President and United States Senators should be elected by direct vote of the people.

11. Ex-soldiers and sailors of the United States army and navy, their widows and minor children, should receive liberal pensions, graded on disability and term of service, not merely as a debt of gratitude, but for service rendered in the preservation of the Union.

12. Our immigration laws should be so revised as to exclude paupers and criminals. None but citizens of the United States should be allowed to vote in any State, and naturalized citizens should not vote until one year after naturalization papers have been issued.

13. The initiative and referendum and proportional representation, should be adopted.

14. Having herein presented our principles and purposes, we invite the co-operation and support of all citizens who are with us substantially agreed.

Republican Platform.

The Republicans of the United States, assembled by their representatives in national convention, appealing for the popular and historical justification of their claims to the matchless achievements of thirty years of Republican rule, earnestly and confidently address themselves to the awakened intelligence, experience and conscience of their countrymen in the following declaration of facts and principles:

For the first time since the civil war the American people have witnessed the calamitous consequences of full and unrestricted Democratic control of the Government. It has been a record of unparalleled incapacity, dishonor and disaster. In administrative management it has ruthlessly sacrificed indispensable revenue, entailed an unceasing deficit, eked out ordinary expenses with borrowed money, piled up the public debt by $262,000,000 in time of peace, forced an adverse balance of trade, kept a perpetual menace hanging over the redemption fund, pawned American credit to alien syndicates, and reversed all the measures and results of successful Republican rule. In the broad effect of its policy it has precipitated panic, blighted industry and trade with prolonged depression, closed factories, reduced work and wages, halted enterprise and crippled American production, while stimulating foreign production for the American market. Every consideration for public safety and individual interest demands that the Government shall be rescued from the hands of those who have shown themselves incapable to conduct it without disaster at home and dishonor abroad, and shall be restored to the party which for thirty years administered it with unequaled success and prosperity, and in this connection we heartily endorse the wisdom, patriotism, and the success of the administration of President Harrison.

We renew and emphasize our allegiance to the policy of protection as the bulwark of American industrial independence and the foundation of American development and prosperity. This true American policy taxes foreign products and encourages home industry; it puts the burden of revenue on foreign goods; it secures the American market for the American producer; it upholds the American standard of wages for the American workingman; it puts the factory by the side of the farm and makes the American farmer less dependent on foreign demand and price; it diffuses general thrift and founds the strength of all on the strength of each. In its reasonable application it is just, fair and impartial, equally opposed to foreign control and domestic monopoly, to sectional discrimination and individual favoritism. We denounce the present Democratic tariff as sectional, injurious to the public credit and destructive to business enterprise. We demand such an equitable tariff on foreign imports which come into competition with American products as will not only furnish adequate revenue for the necessary expenses of the Government, but will protect American labor from degradation to the wage level of other lands. We are not pledged to any particular schedules. The question of rates is a practical question, to be governed by the conditions of the times and of production; the ruling and uncompromising principle is the protection and development of American labor and industry. The country demands a right settlement, and then it wants rest.

We believe the repeal of the reciprocity arrangements negotiated by the last Republican administration was a national calamity, and we demand their renewal and extension on such terms as will equalize our trade with other nations, remove the restrictions which now obstruct the sale of American products in the ports of other countries and secure enlarged markets for the products of our farms, forests and factories. Protection and reciprocity are twin measures of Republican policy and go hand in hand. Democratic rule has recklessly struck down both and both must be re-established. Protection for what we produce; free admission for the necessaries of life which we do not produce; reciprocal agreements of mutual interests which gain open markets for us in return for our open markets to others. Protection builds up domestic industry and trade and secures our own market for ourselves; reciprocity builds up foreign trade and finds an outlet for out surplus.

We condemn the present administration for not keeping faith with the sugar producers of this country. The Republican party favors such protection as will lead to the production on American soil of all the sugar which the American people use, and for which they pay other countries more than $100,000,000 annually.

To all our products—to those of the mine and the field, as well as to those of the shop and the factory—to hemp, to wool, the product of the great industry of sheep husbandry, as well as to the finished woolens of the mill—we promise the most ample protection.

We favor restoring the early American policy of discriminating duties for the upbuilding of our merchant marine and the protection of our shipping in the foreign carrying trade, so that American ships—the product of American labor employed in American shipyards, sailing under the stars and stripes and manned, officered and owned by Americans—may regain the carrying of our foreign commerce.

The Republican party is unreservedly for sound money. It caused the enactment of the law providing for the resumption of specie payments in 1879; since then every dollar has been as good as gold. We are unalterably opposed to every measure calculated to debase our currency or impair the credit of our country. We are therefore opposed to the free coinage of silver except by international agreement with the leading commercial nations of the world, which we pledge ourselves to promote, and until such agreement can be obtained, the existing gold standard must be preserved. All our silver and paper currency must be maintained at parity with gold, and we favor all measures designed to maintain inviolably the obligations of the United States, and all our money, whether coin or paper, at the present standard, the standard of the most enlightened nations of the earth.

The veterans of the Union army deserve and should receive fair treatment and generous recognition. Whenever practicable they should be given the preference in the matter of employment, and they are entitled to the enactment of such laws as are best calculated to secure the fulfillment of the pledges made to them in the dark days of the country's peril. We denounce the practice in the Pension Bureau, so recklessly and unjustly carried on by the present administration, of reducing pensions and arbitrarily dropping names from the rolls, as deserving the severest condemnation of the American people.

Our foreign policy should be at all times firm, vigorous and dignified, and all our interests in the Western Hemisphere carefully watched and guarded. The Hawaiian Islands should be controlled by the United States, and no foreign power should be permitted to interfere with them; the Nicaraguan Canal should be built, owned and operated by the United States, and by the purchase of the Danish Islands we should secure a proper and much needed naval station in the West Indies.

The massacres in Armenia have aroused the deep sympathy and just indignation of the American people, and we believe that the United States should exercise all the influence it can properly exert to bring these atrocities to an end. In Turkey, American residents have been exposed to the gravest dangers, and American property destroyed. There and everywhere American citizens and American property must be absolutely protected at all hazards and at any cost.

We reassert the Monroe doctrine in its full extent, and we reaffirm the right of the United States to give the doctrine effect by responding to the appeals of any American state for friendly intervention, in case of European encroachment. We have not interfered and shall not interfere with the existing possessions of any European power in this hemisphere, but those possessions must not, on any pretext, be extended. We hopefully look forward to the eventual withdrawal of the European powers from this hemisphere, and to the ultimate union of all English-speaking parts of the continent by the free consent of its inhabitants.

From the hour of achieving their own independence the people of the United States have regarded with sympathy the struggles of other American people to free themselves from European domination. We watch with deep and abiding interest the heroic battle of the Cuban patriots against cruelty and oppression, and our best hopes go out for the full success of their determined contest for liberty. The government of Spain having lost control of Cuba and being unable to protect the property or lives of resident American citizens, or to comply with its treaty obligations, we believe the Government of the United States should actively use its influence and good offices to restore peace and give independence to the island.

The peace and security of the Republic and the maintenance of its rightful influence among the nations of the earth, demand a naval power commensurate with its position and responsibility. We, therefore, favor the continued enlargement of the navy, and a complete system of harbor and seacoast defenses.

For the protection of the quality of our American citizenship and of the wages of our workmen against the fatal competition of low-priced labor, we demand that the immigration laws be thoroughly enforced and so extended as to exclude from entrance to the United States those who can neither read nor write.

The civil service law was placed on the statute book by the Republican party, which has always sustained it, and we renew our repeated declarations that it shall be thoroughly and honestly enforced and extended wherever practicable.

We demand that every citizen of the United States shall be allowed to cast one free and unrestricted ballot, and that such ballot shall be counted and returned as cast.

We proclaim our unqualified condemnation of the uncivilized and barbarous practice, well known as lynching or killing of human beings, suspected or charged with crime, without process of law.

We favor the creation of a national board of arbitration to settle and adjust differences which may arise between employer and employes engaged in interstate commerce.

We believe in the immediate return to the free homestead policy of the Republican party; and urge the passage by Congress of the satisfactory free homestead measure which has already passed the House and is now pending in the Senate.

We favor the admission of the remaining Territories at the earliest practicable date, having due regard to the interests of the people of the Territories and of the United States. All federal officers appointed for the Territories should be elected from bona fide residents thereof, and the right of self-government should be accorded so far as practicable.

We believe the citizens of Alaska should have representation in the Congress of the United States, to the end that needful legislation may be intelligently enacted.

We sympathize with all wise and legitimate efforts to lessen and prevent the evils of intemperance, and promote morality.

The Republican party is mindful of the rights and interests of women. Protection of American industries includes equal opportunities, equal pay for equal work, and protection to the home. We favor the admission of women to wider spheres of usefulness, and welcome their co-operation in rescuing the country from Democratic and Populist mismanagement and misrule.

Such are the principles and policies of the Republican party. By these principles we will abide, and these policies we will put into execution. We ask for them the considerate judgment of the American people. Confident alike in the history of our great party and in the justice of our cause, we present our platform and our candidates in the full assurance that the election will bring victory to the Republican party and prosperity to the people of the United States.

Socialist Labor Platform.

The Socialist Labor party of the United States, in convention assembled, reasserts the inalienable rights of all men to life, liberty and the pursuit of happiness.

With the founders of the American Republic we hold that the purpose of government is to secure every citizen in the enjoyment of this right; but in the light of our social conditions we hold, furthermore, that no such right can be exercised under a system of economic inequality, essentially destructive of life, of liberty and of happiness.

With the founders of this Republic we hold that the true theory of politics is that the machinery of government must be owned and controlled by the whole people; but in the light of our industrial development we hold, furthermore, that the true theory of economics is that the machinery of production must likewise belong to the people in common.

To the obvious fact that our despotic system of economics is the direct opposite of our democratic system of politics, can plainly be traced the existence of a privileged class, the corruption of government by that class, the alienation of public property, public franchises and public functions to that class, and the abject dependence of the mightiest of nations upon that class.

Again, through the perversion of Democracy to the ends of plutocracy, labor is robbed of the wealth which it alone produces, is denied the means of self-employment, and, by compulsory idleness in wage slavery, is even deprived of the necessaries of life.

Human power and natural forces are thus wasted, that the plutocracy may rule.

Ignorance and misery with all their concomitant evils, are perpetuated, that the people may be kept in bondage.

Science and invention are diverted from their humane purpose to the enslavement of women and children.

Against such a system the Socialist Labor party once more enters its protest. Once more it reiterates its fundamental declaration that private property in the natural sources of production and in the instruments of labor is the obvious cause of all economic servitude and political dependence.

The time is fast coming when, in the natural course of social evolution, this system, through the destructive action of its failures and crises on the one hand, and the constructive tendencies of its trusts and other capitalistic combinations on the other hand, shall have worked out its own downfall.

We, therefore, call upon the wage workers of the United States, and upon all other honest citizens, to organize under the banner of the Socialist Labor party into a class-conscious body, aware of its rights and determined to conquer them by taking possession of the public powers; so that, held together by an indomitable spirit of solidarity under the most trying conditions of the present class struggle, we may put a summary end to that barbarous struggle by the abolition of classes, the restoration of the land and of all the means of production, transportation and distribution to the people as a collective body, and the substitution of the Co-operative Commonwealth for the present state of planless production, industrial war and social disorder; a commonwealth in which every worker shall have the free exercise and full benefit of his faculties, multiplied by all the modern factors of civilization.

RESOLUTIONS.

With a view to immediate improvement in the condition of labor we present the following demands:

1. Reduction of the hours of labor in proportion to the progress of production.

2. The United States shall obtain possession of the railroads, canals, telegraphs, telephones and all other means of public transportation and communication; the employes to operate the same co-operatively under control of the Federal Government and to elect their own superior officers, but no employe shall be discharged for political reasons.

3. The municipalities shall obtain possession of the local railroads, ferries, water works, gas works, electric plants and all industries requiring municipal franchises; the employes to operate the same co-operatively under control of the municipal administration and to elect their own superior officers, but no employes shall be discharged for political reasons.

4. The public lands declared inalienable. Revocation of all land grants to corporations or individuals, the conditions of which have not been complied with.

5. The United States have the exclusive right to issue money.

6. Congressional legislation providing for the scientific management of forests and waterways and prohibiting the waste of the natural resources of the country.

7. Inventions to be free to all; the inventors to be remunerated by the Nation.

8. Progressive income tax and tax on inheritances; the smaller incomes to be exempt.

9. School education of all children under fourteen years of age to be compulsory, gratuitous and accessible to all by public assistance in meals, clothing, books, etc., where necessary.

10. Repeal of all pauper, tramp, conspiracy and sumptuary laws. Unabridged right of combination.

11. Prohibition of the employment of children of school age and the employment of female labor in occupations detrimental to health or morality. Abolition of the convict labor contract system.

12. Employment of the unemployed by the public authorities (county, city, state and Nation).

13. All wages to be paid in lawful money of the United States. Equalization of woman's wages with those of men, where equal service is performed.

14. Laws for the protection of life and limb in all occupations, and an efficient employers' liability law.

15. The people have the right to propose laws and to vote upon all measures of importance according to the referendum principle.

16. Abolition of the veto power of the Executive (National, State and municipal) wherever it exists.

17. Abolition of the United States Senate and all upper legislative chambers.

18. Municipal self-government.

19. Direct vote and secret ballots in all elections. Universal and equal right of suffrage without regard to color, creed or sex. Election days to be legal holidays. The principle of proportional representation to be introduced.

20. All public officers to be subject to recall by their respective constituencies.

21. Uniform civil and criminal law throughout the United States. Administration of justice to be free of charge. Abolition of capital punishment.

Democratic Platform—(Chicago).

We, the Democrats of the United States, in National Convention assembled, do reaffirm our allegiance to those great essential principles of justice and liberty upon which our institutions are founded, and which the Democratic party has advocated from Jefferson's time to our own—freedom of speech, freedom of the press, freedom of conscience, the preservation of personal rights, the equality of all citizens before the law, and the faithful observance of Constitutional limitations.

During all these years the Democratic party has resisted the tendency of selfish interests to the centralization of governmental power, and steadfastly maintained the integrity of the dual scheme of government established by the founders of this Republic of republics. Under its guidings and teachings the great principle of local self-government has found its best expression in the maintenance of the rights of the States and in its assertion of the necessity of confining the General Government to the exercise of the powers granted by the Constitution of the United States.

The Constitution of the United States guarantees to every citizen the rights of civil and religious liberty. The Democratic party has always been the exponent of political liberty and religious freedom, and it renews its obligations and reaffirms its devotion to these fundamental principles of the Constitution.

Recognizing that the money question is paramount to all others at this time, we invite attention to the fact that the Federal Constitution named silver and gold together as the money metals of the United States, and that the first coinage law passed by Congress under the Constitution made the silver dollar the monetary unit and admitted gold to free coinage at a ratio based upon the silver-dollar unit.

We declare that the act of 1873, demonetizing silver without the knowledge or approval of the American people, has resulted in the appreciation of gold and a corresponding fall in the prices of commodities produced by the people; a heavy increase in the burden of taxation and of all debts, public and private; the enrichment of the money-lending class at home and abroad; the prostration of industry and impoverishment of the people.

We are unalterably opposed to monometallism which has locked fast the prosperity of an industrial people in the paralysis of hard times. Gold monometallism is a British policy, and its adoption has brought other nations into financial servitude to London. It is not only un-American, but anti-American, and it can be fastened on the United States only by the stifling of that spirit and love of liberty which proclaimed our political independence in 1776 and won it in the War of the Revolution.

We demand the free and unlimited coinage of both silver and gold at the present legal ratio of 16 to 1 without waiting for the aid or consent of any other nation. We demand that the standard silver dollar shall be a full legal tender, equally with gold, for all debts, public and private, and we favor such legislation as will prevent for the future the demonetization of any kind of legal tender money by private contract.

We are opposed to the policy and practice of surrendering to the holders of the obligations of the United States the option reserved by law to the Government of redeeming such obligations in either silver coin or gold coin.

We are opposed to the issuing of interest-bearing bonds of the United States in time of peace, and condemn the trafficking with banking syndicates, which, in exchange for bonds and at an enormous profit to themselves, supply the Federal Treasury with gold to maintain the policy of gold monometallism.

Congress alone has the power to coin and issue money, and President Jackson declared that this power could not be delegated to corporations or individuals. We therefore denounce the issuance of notes intended to circulate as money by National banks as in derogation of the Constitution, and we demand that all paper which is made a legal tender for public and private debts or which is receivable for dues to the United States shall be issued by the Government of the

United States and shall be redeemable in coin.

We hold that tariff duties should be levied for purposes of revenue, such duties to be so adjusted as to operate equally throughout the country and not discriminate between class or section, and that taxation should be limited by the needs of the Government honestly and economically administered. We denounce as disturbing to business the Republican threat to restore the McKinley law, which has twice been condemned by the people in national elections, and which, enacted under the false plea of protection to home industry, proved a prolific breeder of trusts and monopolies, enriched the few at the expense of the many, restricted trade and deprived the producers of the great American staples of access to their natural markets.

Until the money question is settled we are opposed to any agitation for further changes in our tariff laws, except such as are necessary to meet the deficit in revenue caused by the adverse decision of the Supreme Court on the income tax. But for this decision by the Supreme Court, there would be no deficit in the revenue under the law passed by a Democratic Congress in strict pursuance of the uniform decisions of that court for nearly 100 years, that court having in that decision sustained Constitutional objections to its enactment, which had previously been overruled by the ablest judges who have ever sat on that bench. We declare that it is the duty of Congress to use all the Constitutional power which remains after that decision or which may come from its reversal by the court as it may hereafter be constituted, so that the burdens of taxation may be equally and impartially laid, to the end that wealth may bear its due proportion of the expense of the Government.

We hold that the most efficient way of protecting American labor is to prevent the importation of foreign pauper labor to compete with it in the home market, and that the value of the home market to our American farmers and artisans is greatly reduced by a vicious monetary system which depresses the prices of their products below the cost of production, and thus deprives them of the means of purchasing the products of our home manufactories; and as labor creates the wealth of the country, we demand the passage of such laws as may be necessary to protect it in all its rights.

We are in favor of the arbitration of differences between employers engaged in inter-state commerce and their employes, and recommend such legislation as is necessary to carry out this principle.

The absorption of wealth by the few, the consolidation of our leading railroad systems and the formation of trusts and pools require a stricter control by the Federal Government of those arteries of commerce. We demand the enlargement of the powers of the Inter-State Commerce Commission and such restriction and guarantees in the control of railroads as will protect the people from robbery and oppression.

We denounce the profligate waste of the money wrung from the people by oppressive taxation and the lavish appropriations of recent Republican Congresses, which have kept taxes high, while the labor that pays them is unemployed and the products of the people's toil are depressed in price till they no longer repay the cost of production. We demand a return to that simplicity and economy which befits a Democratic Government, and a reduction in the number of useless offices the salaries of which drain the substance of the people.

We denounce arbitrary interference by federal authorities in local affairs as a violation of the Constitution of the United States and a crime against free institutions, and we especially object to government by injunction as a new and highly dangerous form of oppression by which federal judges, in contempt of the laws of the States and rights of citizens, become at once legislators, judges, and executioners; and we approve the bill passed at the last session of the United States Senate, and now pending in the House of Representatives, relative to contempts in federal courts and providing for trials by jury in certain cases of contempt.

No discrimination should be indulged in by the Government of the United States in favor of any of its debtors. We approve of the refusal of the Fifty-third Congress to pass the Pacific Railroad Funding bill, and denounce the effort of the present Republican Congress to enact a similar measure.

Recognizing the just claims of deserving Union soldiers, we heartily indorse the rule of the present Commissioner of Pensions, that no names shall be arbitrarily dropped from the pension roll; and the fact of enlistment and service should be deemed conclusive evidence against disease and disability before enlistment.

We favor the admission of the Territories of New Mexico, Arizona and Oklahoma, into the Union as States, and we favor the early admission of all the Territories having the necessary population and resources to entitle them to Statehood, and, while they remain Territories, we hold that the officials appointed to administer the government of any Territory, together with the District of Columbia and Alaska, should be bona fide residents of the Territory or District in which their duties are to be performed. The Democratic party believes in home rule, and that all public lands of the United States should be appropriated to the establishment of free homes for American citizens.

We recommend that the Territory of Alaska be granted a delegate in Congress, and that the general land and timber laws of the United States be extended to said Territory.

The Monroe doctrine, as originally declared, and as interpreted by succeeding Presidents, is a permanent part of the foreign policy of the United States, and must at all times be maintained.

We extend our sympathy to the people of Cuba in their heroic struggle for liberty and independence.

We are opposed to life tenure in the public service, except as provided in the Constitution. We favor appointments based on merit, fixed terms of office, and such an administration of the civil service laws as will afford equal opportunities to all citizens of ascertained fitness.

We declare it to be the unwritten law of this Republic, established by custom and usage of 100 years and sanctioned by the examples of the greatest and wisest of those who founded and have maintained our Government, that no man should be eligible for a third term of the Presidential office.

The Federal Government should care for and improve the Mississippi River and other great waterways of the Republic, so as to secure for the interior States easy and cheap transportation to tide water. When any waterway of the Republic is of sufficient importance to demand aid of the Government, such aid should be extended upon a definite plan of continuous work until permanent improvement is secured.

Confiding in the justice of our cause and the necessity of its success at the polls, we submit the foregoing declaration of principles and purposes to the considerate judgment of the American people. We invite the support of all citizens who approve them and who desire to have them made effective through legislation, for the relief of the people and the restoration of the country's prosperity.

Silver Platform.

The National Silver party in convention assembled makes this the declaration of its principles:

First—The paramount issue at this time in the United States is indisputably the money question. It is between the gold standard, gold bonds and bank currency on the one side, and the bimetallic standard, no bonds and Government currency on the other.

On this issue we declare ourselves to be in favor of a distinctively American system. We are unalterably opposed to the single gold standard, and demand immediate return to the constitutional standard of gold and silver, by restoration by this government, independently of any foreign power, of the unrestricted coinage of both gold and silver into standard money, at the ratio of 16 to 1, and upon terms of exact equality, as they existed prior to 1873; the silver coin to be full legal tender equally with gold for all debts and dues, public and private, and we favor such legislation as will prevent for the future the demonetization of any kind of legal tender money by private contract.

We hold that the power to control and regulate paper currency is inseparable from the power to coin money; and hence that all currency intended to circulate as money should be issued and its volume controlled by the General Government only, and should be legal tender.

We are unalterably opposed to the issue by the United States of interest-bearing bonds in time of peace, and we denounce as a blunder worse than a crime the present Treasury policy, concurred in by a Republican House, of plunging the country in debt by hundreds of millions in the vain attempt to maintain the gold standard by borrowing gold, and we demand the payment of all coin obligations of the United States, as provided by existing laws, in either gold or silver coin, at the option of the Government, and not at the option of the creditor.

The demonetization of silver in 1873 enormously increased the demand for gold, enhancing its purchasing power and lowering all prices measured by that standard. And since that unjust and indefensible act, the prices of American products have fallen upon an average, nearly 50 per cent., carrying down with them proportionately the money value of all other forms of property.

Such fall of prices has destroyed the profits of legitimate industry, injuring the producer for the benefit of the non-producer, increasing the burden of the debtor, swelling the gains of the creditor, paralyzing the productive energies of the American people, relegating to idleness vast numbers of willing workers, sending the shadows of despair into the home of the honest toiler, filling the land with tramps and paupers, and building up colossal fortunes at the money centers.

In the effort to maintain the gold standard, the country has within the last two years in a time of peace and plenty been loaded down with $262,000,000 of additional interest-bearing debt under such circumstances as to allow a syndicate of native and foreign bankers to realize a net profit of millions on a single deal. It stands confessed that the gold standard can only be upheld by so depleting our paper currency as to force the prices of our products below the European and even below the Asiatic level, to enable us to sell in foreign markets, thus aggravating the very evils of which our people so bitterly complain, degrading American labor and striking at the foundations of our civilization itself.

The advocates of the gold standard persistently claim that the cause of our distress is overproduction—that we have produced so much that it has made us poor—which implies that the true remedy is to close the factory, abandon the farm and throw the multitude of people out of employment. A doctrine that leaves us unnerved and disheartened and absolutely without hope for the future. We affirm it to be unquestioned that there can be no such economic paradox as overproduction and at the same time tens of thousands of our fellow-citizens remaining half clad and half fed and who are piteously clamoring for the common necessities of life.

Over and above all other questions of policy, we are in favor of restoring to the people of the United States the time-honored money of the Constitution, gold and silver, not one, but both, the money of Washington, and Hamilton, and Jefferson, and Monroe, and Jackson, and Lincoln, to the end that the American people may receive honest pay for an honest product; that the American debtor may pay his just obligations in an honest standard and not in a standard that has appreciated 100 per cent. above all the great staples of our country; and to the end, further, that silver standard countries may be deprived of the unjust advantage they now enjoy in the difference in exchange between gold and silver, an advantage which tariff legislation alone cannot overcome.

We, therefore, confidently appeal to the people of the United States to leave in abeyance for the moment all other questions, however important, and even momentous, they may appear, to sunder, if need be, all former party ties and affiliations, and unite in one supreme effort to free themselves and their children from the domination of the money power, a power more destructive than any which has ever been fastened upon the civilized men of any race or any age. And upon the consummation of our desires and efforts, we invoke the gracious favor of Divine Providence.

Inasmuch as the patriotic majority of the Chicago convention embodied in the financial plank of its platform the principle enunciated in the platform of the American bimetallic party, promulgated at Washington, D. C., January 22, 1896, and herein reiterated, which is not only paramount, but the only real issue in the pending campaign, therefore recognizing that their nominees embody these patriotic principles, we recommend that this convention nominate Wm. J. Bryan of Nebraska for President and Arthur Sewall of Maine for Vice-President.

People's Party Platform.

The People's Party, assembled in national convention, reaffirms its allegiance to the principles declared by the founders of the Republic and also to the fundamental principles of just government as enunciated in the platform of the party in 1892. We recognize that through the connivance of the present and preceding administrations the country has reached a crisis in its national life, as predicted in our declarations four years ago, and that prompt and patriotic action is the supreme duty of the hour. We realize that while we have political independence, our financial and industrial independence is yet to be attained by restoring to our country the constitutional control and exercise of the functions necessary to a people's government, which functions have been basely surrendered by our public servants to corporate monopolies. The influence of European money changers has been more potent in shaping legislation than the voice of the American people. Executive power and patronage have been used to corrupt our legislatures and defeat the will of the people, and plutocracy has thereby been enthroned upon the ruins of the Democracy. To restore the government intended by the fathers and for the welfare and prosperity of this and future generations, we demand the establishment of an economic and financial system which shall make us masters of our own affairs, independent of European control, by the adoption of the following declaration of principles:

We demand a national money, safe and sound, issued by the General Government only, without the intervention of banks of issue, to be a full legal tender for all debts, public and private; a just, equitable and efficient means of distribution direct to the people, and through the lawful disbursements of the Government.

We demand the free and unrestricted coinage of silver and gold at the present legal ratio of 16 to 1 by the United States without waiting for the consent of foreign nations.

We demand that the volume of circulating medium be speedily increased to an amount sufficient to meet the demands of the business and population of this country, and to restore the just level of prices of labor and production.

We denounce the sale of bonds and the increase of the public interest-bearing debt made by the present administration as unnecessary and without authority of law, and demand that no more bonds be issued except by specific act of Congress.

We demand such legislation as will prevent the demonetization of the lawful money of the United States by private contract.

We demand that the Government in payment of its obligations shall use its option as to the kind of lawful money in which they are to be paid, and we denounce the present and preceding administrations for surrendering this option to the holders of Government obligations.

We demand a graduated income tax to the end that aggregated wealth shall bear its just proportion of taxation, and we regard the recent decision of the Supreme Court relative to the income tax law as a misinterpretation of the Constitution and an invasion of the rightful powers of Congress over the subject of taxation.

We demand that postal savings banks be established by the Government for the safe deposit of the savings of the people and to facilitate exchange.

Transportation being a means of exchange and a public necessity, the Government should own and operate the railroads in the interest of the people and on a non-partisan basis, to the end that all may be accorded the same treatment in transportation, and that the tyranny and political power now exercised by the great railroad corporations, which result in the impairment, if not the destruction, of the political rights and personal liberties of the citizen, may be destroyed. Such ownership is to be accomplished gradually in a manner consistent with sound public policy. The interest of the United States in the public highways, built with public moneys and the proceeds of extensive grants of land to the Pacific railroads should never be alienated, mortgaged or sold, but guarded and protected for the general welfare as provided by the laws organizing such railroads. The foreclosure of existing liens of the United States on these railroads should follow default in payment thereof by the debtor companies, and at the foreclosure sales of said roads the Government shall purchase the same if it becomes necessary to protect its interest therein, or if they can be purchased at reasonable price, and the Government shall operate said railways as public highways for the benefit of the whole people and not in the interest of the few, under suitable provisions for protection of life and property, giving to all transportation interests, equal privileges and equal rates for fares and freights.

We denounce the present infamous schemes for refunding these debts, and demand that the laws now applicable thereto be executed and administered according to their true intent and spirit.

The telegraph, like the post office system, being a necessity for the transmission of news, should be owned and operated by the Government in the interest of the people.

A true policy demands that the national and State legislation shall be such as will ultimately enable every prudent and industrious citizen to secure a home, and, therefore, the land should not be monopolized for speculative purposes. The lands now occupied by railroads and other corporations in excess of their actual needs should, by lawful means, be reclaimed by the Government and held for actual settlers only,

and private land monopoly, as well as alien ownership, should be prohibited.

We condemn the frauds by which the land grants to the Pacific railroad companies have, through the connivance of the Interior Department, robbed multitudes of actual and bona fide settlers of their homes and miners of their claims, and we demand legislation by Congress which will enforce the exemption of mineral lands from such grants after as well as before patent.

We demand that bona fide settlers on all public lands be granted free homes as provided in the National Homestead law, and that no exception be made in the case of Indian reservations when opened for settlement, and that all lands not now patented come under this demand.

We favor a system of direct legislation through the initiative and referendum under proper constitutional safeguards.

We demand the election of President, Vice-President and United States Senators by the direct vote of the people.

We tender to the patriotic people of Cuba our deepest sympathy in their heroic struggle for political freedom and independence, and we believe the time has come when the United States, the great Republic of the world, should recognize that Cuba is, and of right ought to be, a free and independent state.

We favor home rule in the Territories and the District of Columbia, and the early admission of the Territories as States.

All public salaries should be made to correspond to the price of labor and its products.

In times of great industrial depression idle labor should be employed on public works as far as practicable.

Arbitrary course of the courts in assuming to imprison citizens for indirect contempt and ruling by injunction, should be prevented by proper legislation.

We favor just pensions for our disabled Union soldiers.

Believing that the elective franchise and untrammeled ballot are essential to a government of, for and by the people, the People's Party condemns the wholesale system of disfranchisement adopted in some of the States as unrepublican and undemocratic, and we declare it to be the duty of the several State Legislatures to take such action as will secure a full, free and fair ballot and an honest count.

While the foregoing propositions constitute the platform upon which our party stands, and for the vindication of which its organization will be maintained, we recognize that the great and pressing issue of the pending campaign upon which the present Presidential election will turn, is the financial question, and upon this great and specific issue between the parties we cordially invite the aid and co-operation of all organizations and citizens agreeing with us upon this vital question.

National Democratic Platform.

This convention has assembled to uphold the principles upon which depend the honor and welfare of the American people, in order that Democrats throughout the Union may unite their patriotic efforts to avert disaster from their country and ruin from their party.

The Democratic party is pledged to equal and exact justice to all men of every creed and condition; to the largest freedom of the individual consistent with good government; to the preservation of the Federal Government in its constitutional vigor, and the support of the States in all their just rights; to economy in the public expenditures; to the maintenance of the public faith and sound money; and it is opposed to paternalism and all class legislation.

The declarations of the Chicago convention attack individual freedom, the right of private contract, the independence of the judiciary, and the authority of the President to enforce Federal laws. They advocate a reckless attempt to increase the price of silver by legislation, to the debasement of our monetary standard, and threaten unlimited issues of paper money by the government. They abandon for Republican allies the Democratic cause of tariff reform, to court the favor of protectionists to their fiscal heresy.

In view of these and other grave departures from Democratic principles we cannot support the candidate of that convention, nor be bound by its acts. The Democratic party has survived many defeats, but could not survive a victory won in behalf of the doctrine and policy proclaimed in its name at Chicago.

The conditions which, however, make possible such utterances from a national convention are the direct result of class legislation by the Republican party. It still proclaims, as it has for years, the power and duty of the Goverment to raise and maintain prices by law, and it proposes no remedy for existing evils except oppressive and unjust taxation.

The National Democracy here reconvened, therefore renews its declaration of faith in Democratic principles, especially as applicable to the conditions of the times.

Taxation tariff, excise or direct, is rightfully imposed only for public purposes and not for private gain. Its amount is justly measured by public expenditures, which should be limited by scrupulous economy. The sum derived by the Treasury from the tariff and excise levies is affected by the state of trade and volume of consumption. The amount required by the Treasury is determined by the appropriations made by Congress. The demand of the Republican party for an increase in tax has its pretext in the deficiency of revenue, which has its causes in the stagnation of trade and reduced consumption, due entirely to the loss of confidence that has followed the Populist threat of free coinage and depreciation of our money and the Republican practice of extravagant appropriations beyond the needs of good government. We arraign and condemn the Populistic conventions of Chicago and St. Louis for their co-operation with the Republican party, increasing these conditions which are pleaded in justification of a heavy increase of burdens of the people and a further resort to protection. We therefore denounce protection and its ally, free coinage of silver, as schemes for the personal profit of a few at the expense of the many, and oppose the two parties which stand for these schemes as hostile to the people of the Republic, whose food and shelter, comfort and property, are attacked by higher taxes and depreciated money. In fine, we reaffirm the historic Democratic doctrine of tariff for revenue only.

We demand that henceforth modern and liberal policies toward American shipping shall take the place of our imitation of the restricted statutes of the eighteenth century, which were abandoned by every maritime power but the United States, and which, to the nation's humiliation, have driven American capital and enterprise to the use of alien flags and alien crews, have made the stars and stripes an almost unknown emblem in foreign waters, and have virtually extinguished the race of American seamen. We oppose the pretense that discriminating duties will promote shipping. That scheme is an invitation to commercial warfare upon the United States, un-American in the light of our great commercial treaties, offering no gain whatever to American shipping, while greatly increasing ocean freights on our agricultural and manufactured products.

The experience of mankind has shown that by reason of their natural qualities gold is the necessary money of the large affairs of commerce and business, while silver is conveniently adapted to minor transactions, and the most beneficial use of both together can be insured only by the adoption of the former as a standard of monetary measure and the maintenance of silver at a parity with gold by its limited coinage under such safeguards of law. Thus the largest possible enjoyment of both metals is gained, with a value universally accepted throughout the world, which constitutes the only practical currency assuring the most stable standard and especially the best and safest money for all who earn a livelihood by labor or the produce of husbandry. They cannot suffer when paid in the best money known to man, but are the peculiar and most defenseless victims of a debased and fluctuating currency, which offers continued profits to the money changers at their cost.

Realizing these truths, demonstrated by long public inconvenience and loss, the Democratic party in the interests of the masses and of equal justice to all, practically established, by the legislation of 1834 and 1853, the gold standard of monetary measurement, and likewise entirely divorced the Government from banking and currency issues. To this long established Democratic policy we adhere, and insist upon the maintenance of the gold standard and of the parity therewith of every dollar issued by the Government, and are firmly opposed to the free and unlimited coinage of silver and to the compulsory purchase of silver bullion. But we denounce also the further maintenance of the present costly patchwork scheme of national paper currency as a constant source of injury and peril.

We assert the necessity of such intelligent currency reform as will confine the Government to its legitimate functions; completely separated from the banking business, and afford to all sections of our country a uniform, safe, and elastic bank currency under Government supervision, measured in volume by the needs of business.

The fidelity, patriotism, and courage with which President Cleveland has fulfilled his great public trust, the high character of his administration, its wisdom and energy in the maintenance of order and the enforcement of laws; its equal regard for the rights of every class and section, its firm and dignified conduct of foreign affairs, and its sturdy persistence in upholding the credit and the honor of the Nation, are fully recognized by the Democratic party, and will secure to him a place in history beside the fathers of the Republic. We also commend the administration for the great progress made in the reform of the public service, and we endorse its effort to extend the merit system still further. We demand that no backward step be taken, but that the reform be supported and advanced until the undemocratic spoils system of appointments shall be eradicated.

We demand strict economy in the appropriations and in the administration of the Government.

We favor arbitration for the settlement of international disputes.

We favor a liberal policy of pensions to deserving soldiers and sailors of the United States.

The Supreme Court of the United States was wisely established by the framers of our Constitution as one of the three co-ordinate branches of the Government. Its independence and authority to interpret the law of the land without fear or favor must be maintained. We condemn all efforts to degrade that tribunal, or impair the confidence and respect which it has deservedly held.

The Democratic party ever has maintained, and ever will maintain the supremacy of law, the independence of its judicial administration, the inviolability of contract, and the obligations of all good citizens to resist every illegal trust, combination, and attempt against the just rights of property and the good order of society, in which are bound up the peace and happiness of our people.

Believing these principles to be essential to the well being of the Republic, we submit them to the consideration of the American people.

PRESIDENTIAL CANDIDATES AND ELECTORAL AND POPULAR VOTES.

FOR PRESIDENT.	Party.	Electoral Vote.	Popular Vote.	Year.	FOR VICE PRESIDENT.	Party.	Electoral Vote.
George Washington		69		1789			
John Adams		34					
John Jay		9					
R. H. Harrison		6					
John Rutledge		6					
John Hancock		4					
George Clinton		3					
Samuel Huntingdon		2					
John Milton		2					
James Armstrong		1					
Benjamin Lincoln		1					
Edward Telfair		1					
Votes not cast		4					
George Washington	Fed.	132		1792			
John Adams	Fed.	77					
George Clinton	Rep.	50					
Thomas Jefferson	Rep.	4					
Aaron Burr	Rep.	1					
Votes not cast		3					
John Adams	Fed.	71		1796			
Thomas Jefferson	Rep.	68					
Thomas Pinckney	Fed.	59					
Aaron Burr	Rep.	30					
Samuel Adams	Rep.	15					
Oliver Ellsworth	Ind.	11					
Geo. Clinton	Rep.	7					
John Jay	Fed.	5					
James Iredell	Fed.	3					
George Washington	Fed.	2					
John Henry	Fed.	2					
S. Johnson	Fed.	2					
Charles C. Pinckney	Fed.	1					
Thomas Jefferson	Rep.	73		1800			
Aaron Burr	Rep.	73					
John Adams	Fed.	65					
Charles C. Pinckey	Fed.	64					
John Jay	Fed.	1					
Thomas Jefferson	Rep.	162		1804	George Clinton	Rep.	162
Charles C. Pinckney	Fed.	14			Rufus King	Fed.	14
James Madison	Rep.	122		1808	George Clinton	Rep.	113
Charles C. Pinckney	Fed	47			Rufus King	Fed.	47
George Clinton	Rep.	6			John Langdon		9
					James Madison	Rep.	3
					James Monroe	Rep.	3
					Votes not cast		1
James Madison	Rep.	128		1812	Elbridge Gerry	Rep.	131
DeWitt Clinton	Fed.	89			Jared Ingersoll	Fed.	86
					Votes not cast		1

PRESIDENTIAL CANDIDATES AND ELECTORAL AND POPULAR VOTES—Continued.

FOR PRESIDENT.	Party.	Electoral Vote.	Popular Vote.	Year.	FOR VICE PRESIDENT.	Party.	Electoral Vote.
James Monroe	Rep.	183		1816	Daniel D. Tompkins	Rep.	183
Rufus King	Fed.	34			John E. Howard	Fed.	22
					James Ross		5
					John Marshall		4
					Robert G. Harper		3
					Votes not cast		1
James Monroe	Rep.	231		1820	Daniel D. Tompkins	Rep.	218
John Q. Adams	Opp.	1			Richard Stockton		8
					Daniel Rodney		4
					Robert G. Harper		1
					Richard Rush		1
					Votes not cast		3
John Q. Adams	Opp.	84	105,321	1824	John C. Calhoun	Rep.	182
Andrew Jackson	Rep.	99	155,872		Nathan Sanford		30
Henry Clay	Rep.	37	46,587		Nathan Macon		24
Wm. H. Crawford	Rep.	41	44,282		Andrew Jackson	Rep.	13
					M. Van Buren	Rep.	9
					Henry Clay	Rep.	2
Andrew Jackson	Dem.	178	647,231	1828	John C. Calhoun	Dem.	171
John Q. Adams	Nat'l R.	83	509,097		Richard Rush	N. R.	83
					William Smith	Dem.	7
Andrew Jackson	Dem.	219	687,503	1832	M. Van Buren	Dem.	189
Henry Clay	Nat'l R.	49	530,189		John Sargeant	N. R.	49
John Floyd	Ind.	11	33,108		Henry Lee	Ind.	11
William Wirt	Anti M.	7			Amos Ellmaker	Anti-M.	7
					Wm. Wilkins	Dem.	30
Martin Van Buren	Dem.	170	761,549	1836	R. M. Johnson	Dem.	147
Wm. Henry Harrison	Whig.	73			Francis Granger	Whig.	77
Hugh L. White	Whig.	26	736,656		John Tyler	Whig.	47
Daniel Webster	Whig.	14			Wm. Smith	Dem.	23
Willie P. Mangum	Whig.	11					
Wm. Henry Harrison	Whig.	234	1,275,017	1840	John Tyler	Whig.	234
Martin Van Buren	Dem.	60	1,128,702		R. M. Johnson	Dem.	48
James G. Birney	Lib.		7,059		L. W. Tazewell	Dem.	11
					James K. Polk	Dem.	1
James K. Polk	Dem.	170	1,337,243	1844	Geo. M. Dallas	Dem.	170
Henry Clay	Whig.	105	1,299,068		T. Frelinghuysen	Whig.	105
James G. Birney	Lib.		62,300		Thomas Morris	Lib.	
Zachary Taylor	Whig.	163	1,360,101	1848	Millard Fillmore	Whig.	163
Lewis Cass	Dem.	127	1,220,544		Wm. O. Butler	Dem.	127
Martin Van Buren	F. Soil.		291,263		Charles F. Adams	F. Soil.	
Franklin Pierce	Dem.	254	1,601,474	1852	William R. King	Dem.	254
Winfield Scott	Whig.	42	1,380,578		William A. Graham	Whig.	42
John P. Hale	F. Dem.		156,149		George W. Julian	F. Dem.	
James Buchanan	Dem.	174	1,838,169	1856	John C. Breckinridge	Dem.	174

For President.	Party.	Electoral Vote.	Popular Vote.	Year.	For Vice-President.	Party.	Electoral Vote.
John C. Fremont	Rep.	114	1,341,264	1856	Wm. L. Dayton	Rep.	114
Millard Fillmore	Amer.	8	873,538		A. J. Donelson	Amer.	8
Abraham Lincoln	Rep.	180	1,866,352	1860	Hannibal Hamlin	Rep.	180
Stephen A. Douglas	Dem.	12	1,375,157		Joseph Lane	Dem.	12
J. C. Breckinridge	Dem.	72	845,763		Edward Everett	Dem.	72
John Bell	Union.	39	589,581		H. V. Johnson	Union.	39
Abraham Lincoln	Rep.	212	2,216,067	1864	Andrew Johnson	Rep.	212
Geo. B. McClellan	Dem.	21	1,808,725		Geo. H. Pendleton	Dem.	21
Ulysses S. Grant	Rep.	214	3,015,071	1868	Schuyler Colfax	Rep.	214
Horatio Seymour	Dem.	80	2,709,615		F. P. Blair, Jr	Dem.	80
Ulysses S. Grant	Rep.	286	3,597,070	1872	Henry Wilson	Rep.	286
Horace Greeley	D. & L.		2,834,079		B. Gratz-Brown	D. & L.	
Charles O'Conor	Dem.		29,408		John Q. Adams	Dem.	
James Black	Temp.		5,608		John Russell	Temp.	
Thomas A. Hendricks	Dem.	42			Geo. W. Julian	Lib.	5
B. Gratz-Brown	Dem.	18			A. H. Colquit	Dem.	5
Charles J. Jenkins	Dem.	2			John M. Palmer	Dem.	3
David Davis	Ind.				T. E. Bramlette	Dem.	3
					W. S. Groesbeck	Dem.	1
					Willis B. Machen	Dem.	1
					N. P. Banks	Lib.	1
Rutherford B. Hayes	Rep.	185	4,034,950	1876	William A. Wheeler	Rep.	185
Samuel J. Tilden	Dem.	184	4,284,885		Thomas A. Hendricks	Dem.	184
Peter Cooper	Greenb.		81,740		Samuel F. Cary	Gr.	
Green C. Smith	Pro.		9,522		Gideon T. Stewart	Pro.	
James B. Walker	Amer.		2,636		D. Kirkpatrick	Amer.	
James A. Garfield	Rep.	214	4,449,053	1880	Chester A. Arthur	Rep.	214
W. S. Hancock	Dem.	155	4,442,035		Wm. H. English	Dem.	155
James B. Weaver	Gr.		307,306		B. J. Chambers	Gr.	
Neal Dow	Pro.		10,305		H. A. Thompson	Pro.	
John W. Phelps	Amer.		707		S. C. Pomeroy	Amer.	
Grover Cleveland	Dem.	219	4,911,017	1884	T. A. Hendricks	Dem.	219
James G. Blaine	Rep.	182	4,848,335		John A. Logan	Rep.	182
John P. St. John	Pro.		151,809		William Daniel	Pro.	
Benjamin F. Butler	Peop.		133,825		A. M. West	Peop.	
P. D. Wigginton	Amer.						
Benjamin Harrison	Rep.	233	5,440,216	1888	Levi P. Morton	Rep.	233
Grover Cleveland	Dem.	168	5,538,233		Allen G. Thurman	Dem.	168
Clinton B. Fisk	Pro.		249,907		John A. Brooks	Pro.	
Alson J. Streeter	Un L.		148,105		C. E. Cunningham	Un L.	
R. H. Cowdry	U'd L.		2,808		W. H. T. Wakefield	U'd L.	
James L. Curtis	Amer.		1,591		James B. Greer	Amer.	
Mrs. Belva Lockwood	E. Right.				Chas. S. Weller	E. R.	
A. E. Redstone	I. R.				John Calvin	I. R.	
Grover Cleveland	Dem.	277	5,556,918	1892	Adlai E. Stevenson	Dem.	277

PRESIDENTIAL CANDIDATES AND ELECTORAL AND POPULAR VOTES—Continued.

FOR PRESIDENT.	Party.	Electoral Vote.	Popular Vote.	Year.	FOR VICE-PRESIDENT.	Party.	Electoral Vote.
Benjamin Harrison	Rep.	145	5,176,108	1892	Whitelaw Reid	Rep.	145
James B. Weaver	Peop.	22	1,041,028		James G. Field	Peop.	22
John P. Bidwell	Pro.		264,133		J. B. Cranfill	Pro.	
Simon Wing	Soc. L.		21,164		Charles H. Machett	Soc. L.	
Joshua Levering	Pro.			1896	Hale Johnson	Pro.	
Charles E. Bently	Nat'l.				James H. Southgate	Nat'l.	
William McKinley	Rep.				Garret A. Hobart	Rep.	
Charles H. Machett	Soc. L.				Matthew Maguire	Soc. L.	
William J. Bryan	Dem.				Arthur Sewall	Dem.	
William J. Bryan	Silver				Arthur Sewall	Silver.	
William J. Bryan	Peop.				Thomas E. Watson	Peop.	
John M. Palmer	Nat'l D.				Simon B. Buckner	Nat'l D.	

NOTES—The name of the successful candidate for President is placed first in each campaign list, except in that of 1896. In this list the names of the candidates are arranged in the order of their nomination.

Prior to 1804, electors cast their votes for two candidates for President ; the one receiving the highest number of votes was declared elected President, and the one next highest Vice-President.

In 1800 there was a tie between Jefferson and Burr, and the choice devolved upon the House of Representatives, which elected the former President and the latter Vice-President.

Beginning with 1804, the Constitution of the United States having been amended, electors voted for candidates for President and Vice-President separately.

The record of the popular vote prior to 1824 is very meagre.

In 1824, no candidate for President having a majority of the electoral vote, the House of Representatives elected John Quincy Adams.

In 1836 the electoral vote for Vice-President was so divided that no candidate had a majority, and the Senate of the United States chose R. M. Johnson.

In 1864, eleven States being in Confederate territory, did not vote.

In 1868, three Southern States were disfranchised.

Horace Greeley died after the election of 1872 and electors chosen for him scattered their vote.

The election of 1876 was decided by an electoral commission of fifteen, seven Democrats and eight Republicans.

In 1892 the Democrats endorsed the People's party national ticket in Colorado, Idaho, Kansas, North Dakota and Wyoming ; and the Republicans of Louisiana endorsed the same ticket.

TABLE OF CONTENTS.

ʊʊʊʊʊʊ